# WARFARE IN THE WESTERN WORLD, 1882–1975

# *Warfare in the Western World,* 1882–1975

Jeremy Black

Indiana University Press
Bloomington & Indianapolis

This book is a publication of

Indiana University Press
601 North Morton Street
Bloomington, IN 4704-3793 USA

http://iupress.indiana.edu

*Telephone orders*   800-842-6796
*Fax orders*   812-855-7931
*Orders by e-mail*   iuporder@indiana.edu

Published simultaneously outside North America by Acumen Publishing Limited

**Library of Congress Cataloging-in-Publication Data**

Black, Jeremy.
  Warfare in the Western world, 1882–1975 / Jeremy Black.
    p. cm.
  Includes bibliographical references (p. ) and index.
  ISBN 0-253-34050-0 (alk. paper) — ISBN 0-253-21509-9 (pbk. : alk. paper)
    1. Military art and science—History—20th century. 2. Military art and
  science—History—19th century. 3. Military history, Modern—20th century. 4. Military
  history, Modern—19th century. I. Title.

  U42 .B53 2002
  355'.009'04—dc21

                                                                    2001039628


1   2   3   4   5   07   06   05   04   03   02

Designed and typeset by Kate Williams, Abergavenny.
Printed and bound by Biddles Ltd., Guildford and King's Lynn.

For Peter Spear

# Contents

# *Preface*

This short book is an attempt to take forward my *European Warfare 1660–1815* (UCL Press 1994) and my *Western Warfare 1775–1882* (Acumen 2001). It reflects the features of the earlier books, specifically the focus on the global dimension and the importance of locating military capability and conflict within their political and social contexts. In addition, war is treated not only as a feature of international relations, but also with due weight devoted to civil conflict.

In this study, Western warfare is seen not only in terms of conflict between Western powers, but also in conflicts between them and others. This helps to set the parameters of the book. It begins in 1882, the year of the British defeat of Egypt, which is seen as a major date in Western military history, the subjugation of a leading non-Western state, and, also, as indicative of the pace and process of Western imperialism in the late nineteenth century. Conversely, 1975 marks the end of the last of the transoceanic European empires, that of Portugal. Furthermore, the fall of South Vietnam and its American-trained and supplied military in 1975 was a major blow to confidence in Western military methods. In addition, after 1975 there has been no intervention by a non-Communist power elsewhere in the world to match that of the Americans in Vietnam. The Vietnam War also permits discussion of the limitations of Western military technique, doctrine and technology, without moving on to discuss the problems of conflicts that are still current. More generally, the global perspective records the impact of Western military power and also offers a way to approach the issue of military capability.

A closely related viewpoint promoted throughout the book is caution against unitary models of military modernity, indeed a questioning of the idea of modernity itself. In addition, there are warnings against the technological determinism and linear conceptions of developments in military science that still characterize so much of military history, at least as written in the West.

Separate chapters for sea and air warfare ensure that, to avoid duplication, some of the discussion of the two World Wars and the inter-war period will be found there. Due to space constraints, quotations, references and bibliography have been kept to a minimum, and, in light of the likely readership, material not written in English has been omitted. Unless otherwise stated, the place of publication is London.

This book reflects the fruits of over two decades teaching military history. I am fortunate that successive generations of students have let me try out ideas on them. In addition, I benefited, while writing this book, from being invited to give papers at Rutgers and Sam Houston State Universities, Blinn and Christ Church Colleges, the Foreign Policy Research Institute in Philadelphia, and the Plymouth branch of the Historical Association. I would like to thank Steven Gerrard for commissioning the book and proving a supportive editor, two anonymous readers for their comments on an earlier draft, Michael Alpert, John Buckley, Christopher Duffy, Stewart Lone, Bill Purdue, Roger Reese, Larry Sondhaus and Spencer Tucker for their advice on particular chapters, Peter Davidson and Ann Jones for taking me to see an exhibition on the New Holland Waterline, Kate Williams for exemplary copy-editing, and Rick McLane for help with the index. None of them is responsible for any errors in the text. Each is thanked for encouragement and assistance.

# Introduction

Among the wealth of first-rate works on this period, it is difficult to offer a distinctive voice. Readers, nevertheless, are entitled to a preliminary attempt to locate the work. In style, I am seeking to offer an analytical narrative, but both elements are constrained by issues of space. In content, I am trying to follow on from the two previous volumes in the trilogy with their engagement with the global context, consideration of naval as well as land warfare, and their concern about political and social contexts. I am also concerned to query the standard "meta-narrative" of war, with its stress on the material culture of war and its focus on the impact of technological change, and, in particular, for this period, the modernizing, if not revolutionary, characteristics of the machinization of war.

Modernity, change and revolution are all important issues and analytical devices in military history. The analysis of change is intertwined with the issue of military capability, for change is seen as providing an account and an explanation of shifts in capability. Thus, the relationship between change and non-change is used to explain success and failure. A prime example is the argument that Westernization in military practice was the key to capability over the past half-millennium and that those states that failed to Westernize were likely to fail. Military capability, more than many other organized human activities, can, indeed, be a life and death issue for a state, so gaining a military edge over, or at least keeping up with, rivals (i.e. changing), can be seen as absolutely critical. Military capability covers arms, training, size of forces, logistical infrastructure, tactical doctrine, leadership, morale, and so on. However, there is also economic potential (and realization), geographical advantages, administrative efficiency and integrity, quality of government and the measure of support it has in the country, and so on. War tests the resilience and cohesion of entire societies, but relative, as much as absolute, capability is the key factor in conflict, and this was set by the tasks demanded of the military. Thus, for example, in the late nineteenth century the British army was largely designed to hold down an overseas empire, while the Germans confined themselves to the prospect of war in Europe.

A narrative of change dominates military history, particularly as the present day is approached. This is due both to a perception that the tempo and impact of military change have increased, and to the weight of scholarly attention. This ensures that, within a general narrative of change, there is debate about which particular changes were most important, about why they were crucial and about their interrelationship. However, it is also necessary to note that there was no simple dichotomy of change and continuity, and no inevitable relationship between a failure to adopt particular changes and defeat. Both of these points emerge more clearly if a global dimension is adopted.

Such an approach by an individual scholar faces many difficulties, not least problems of linguistic limitations, but rather than, therefore, assuming that a book on Western warfare can assert the superiority of this warfare and neglect the rest of the world, this study is, in part, based on the idea that an assessment of capability requires the wider context. This is doubly so because much of the importance of Western warfare in world history rests on its role in facilitating and maintaining Western imperialism.

The notion of modernity is possibly ambiguous. It can entail the judgement of which was the most up-to-date state, or leader of change as believed at the time (for example the Germans in 1866–1914), or, as in this book, can focus on considering aspects of warfare and armed forces in the past that can be proposed as marking the path to the modern world.

Defining any period of study invites an accusation of artificiality. Yet there is a coherence in *this* period. It centres on the highpoint of Western territorial control over the rest of the world, and begins shortly after a Russian advance to within six miles of Constantinople in 1878 that altered power relations in the Balkans, and after the British had defeated both the Zulus (1879) and Egypt (1882), two of the dynamic non-Western forces of the century. Mention of these conflicts is deliberately stressed in order to emphasize the variety of Western warfare and the danger of assuming that any one model prevailed, or would serve. The Russians in Asia, the British in India and the French in Africa all demonstrated great flexibility in successfully adapting to campaign in very difficult terrain and climate against opponents with very different military traditions from those found in Europe.

This study throws doubt on the notion of a linear continuum of "progress" towards warfare in the modern world. Instead, a more complex dynamic is proposed. If it encourages readers to read on in the wealth of first-rate literature and to think about the impact of war in the making of the modern world, it will have worked.

CHAPTER ONE

# From Egypt to Ethiopia: Western Expansionism, 1882–1936

The fact cannot be too plainly stated that throughout Egypt and the Soudan, and throughout the great Protectorates of Uganda and British East Africa, our whole position depends entirely on prestige. We are governing with a mere handful of white officials vast populations alien to us in race, language and religion, and for the most part but little superior in civilization to savages. Except for the small, and from a military point of view inadequate, British force in Egypt, the authority of these officials is supported only by troops recruited from the subject races, whose obedience to their officers rests on no other basis than a belief in the invincibility of the British government and confidence in its promises. If that belief and confidence be once shaken, the foundations of all British authority between Cairo and Mombasa will be undermined, and at any moment a storm of mutiny and insurrection will sweep us into the sea.               (British Director of Military Operations, Military Situation in Somaliland, March 1904)[1]

## Introduction

The prime global context of this book is that of the rise of the West to a situation in which Western economic and financial power and Western norms and values had an impact throughout the world. That is not the same as Western territorial power, which indeed receded in this period. The latter, however, is the main focus of the global dimension of the military history of the period, as force was involved in making and retaining conquests and,

1

frequently, in the loss of territorial possessions. For ease, this global section has been divided into two chapters. This chapter deals with the high point of Western imperialism, from the British defeat of Egypt in 1882 to the Italian conquest of Ethiopia in 1936. The second (Chapter 8) focuses on subsequent decline.

The principal value of such a coverage in this book is twofold. First, although security within Europe was the foremost concern of the grand strategy of European powers, and the pull of European concerns on imperial policy grew stronger in the 1900s, nevertheless, individually and collectively, conflicts outside the West were of enormous importance to the history of the world. Control over large tracts of the globe, and over a significant portion of its population, changed hands. Furthermore, areas that did not experience such a change in control, most obviously Japan, were, nevertheless, affected by processes of modernization that hinged on the need to respond to the challenge of Western imperialism. Secondly, the range and variety of these conflicts underlines the hazard of thinking of Western warfare largely in terms of a paradigm, or key pattern or example – most prominently, for the first three decades of the period, the German army. Instead, it is possible to stress a multiplicity of challenges facing Western armies, and the need to be flexible in response.

Two other general points should be made at the outset. First, the choice of dates for this chapter represents a deliberate attempt to look for continuity through World War One. The operations of Western militaries in the 1920s and 1930s, such as in Morocco and Ethiopia and on the North-West Frontier of India, need to be assessed in the perspective of campaigns prior to 1914. Secondly, military achievements have to be set in a wider context. This is not easy in a book devoted to military history, for there is neither the space nor the intention to write a history of everything else. Nevertheless, Western expansion was about more than the military progress of the West against much of the rest of the world. Military success was an enabler of Western expansion but by no means the sole one. Demographic, economic, cultural-ideological and political factors were also all very important. The first was particularly so where the indigenous population was sparse. Western demographic growth in this period was rapid and this led to significant levels of emigration. Successful imperial expansion provided both opportunity and encouragement for migration. Thus, Russians went to Kazakhstan, the French to Algeria, and the British to Australasia and Canada, while, although imperial links were not involved, many different kinds of Europeans went to the USA. Migration to all of these areas had begun prior to 1882, but continued thereafter, helping to consolidate Western control. Migration within large states that had internal "frontiers" of control, where the effective power of the state ceased, such as Argentina, Brazil, Chile and the USA, was also very important.

The supposed economic value of colonies expanded as states looked for sources of raw materials and for markets, and as steamships and railways

2

aided continental and global economic integration; as they also did migration. Furthermore, economic growth within the West greatly increased the available investment capital for the world outside.[2] However, some areas did not yield the anticipated economic return until after the colonial period.

Cultural-ideological factors focused on the romantic attraction of empire. Imperialism became normative in Western political culture. This drew on a sense of mission, as well as on triumphalism, racialism and cultural arrogance, all supporting a belief that the West was unbeatable and was bringing civilization to a benighted world. The net result was a commitment that encouraged persistence in the face of adversity. Imperialism, a compound of force and a self-righteous commitment to betterment on European terms, led to a determination to win over local support, but also to destroy native culture if necessary, which was described by Sir Ralph Moore, British High Commissioner, speaking at the recently devastated town of Iboum in south-eastern Nigeria in January 1902:

> There was a big palaver of chiefs and himself [Moore] . . . He told them that we had come to help them in order that they might learn how to help themselves – we came for the good of the black man but that they would be subjects of the Great White King – not his slaves. While war lasts they must obey the order of any white man in the country. When war is over equal justice to all. The one thing to end the war was absolute submission, the handing over of all juh-juh priests and guns. He also compared a threepenny bit which he held up in his hand to the size of a native "rod" of same value. He held out two pounds ten shillings – the value of 200 rods – and showed the ease with which large amounts could be carried whereas £2 10s worth of brass currency is an impossible medium of exchange.[3]

Despite some defeats and failures, Western expansionism maintained a pace unprecedented in the seventeenth and eighteenth centuries. Furthermore, this was true in a variety of military environments. As victory and conquest became easier, so expansionism and a sense of superiority were encouraged. However, because it was not necessary to transform Western armies (or navies) to achieve these goals, this expansionism did not have an impact on Western military thought or practice comparable to that of conflict within the West.

## 1880–1900

The last two decades of the nineteenth century saw the rapid allocation among the European and American powers of a sizeable amount of the world's surface; European expansion was especially rapid in Africa. In part, this was achieved at the expense of developed states with armed forces using firearms, such as Madagascar, which the French conquered in 1895 and annexed in 1896.[4] At another scale of conflict, a war between France and China in 1883–85, that arose as a result of French expansion into Indo-China, was a victory for the French and was followed by the annexation of Tonkin.

Peoples who lacked such armed forces also suffered; for example in New Guinea, which was divided between Britain, Germany and the Netherlands. The same process can be seen in the New World. Native American resistance was crushed, the Sioux being defeated in 1890 at Wounded Knee, the last major clash in more than 350 years of conflict. This was less a battle than a policing operation gone amiss: the clash arose from a scuffle during an attempt to disarm the Miniconjou Sioux. Outnumbered, they lost most of their men, in part to shells from the four Hotchkiss guns deployed by the American Seventh Cavalry.[5] Historic centres of resistance to Western power also fell: Oman became a British protectorate in 1891, while the Dutch overcame guerrilla resistance in the hinterland of Aceh in Sumatra, forcing their leading opponents to surrender in 1903.[6]

Western expansion, however, was not achieved without considerable difficulty, including some significant reverses. These included French defeats in Indo-China, such as at Lang Son (1885), a Chinese victory that destroyed the political career of Jules Ferry, Italian defeats by the Ethiopians at Dogali (1887) and, even more seriously, Adowa (1896), and the French loss to a surprise night attack of a force near Timbuktu in 1894. Some of these defeats were small in scale, although they could still be important given the modest size of colonial armies. The French lost only 82 men near Timbuktu in 1894, which was the largest French loss on a single day in the conquest of the western Sudan,[7] but the Italians lost 430 at Dogali, north of Asmara, when the Ethiopian use of enveloping tactics destroyed an Italian column. At Adowa, the outnumbered and badly led Italians lost 10,000 men.[8]

Menelik II, the victor at Adowa, serves as a reminder that it was not only Western states that were expanding, although it was they who did so most successfully. The Ethiopians had developed a successful army, 150,000 strong by 1896, with nearly half armed with modern weapons. French and Russian advisers improved the Ethiopian artillery in the 1890s, and this helped at Adowa. Hotchkiss machine guns were used there, but victory over the far smaller Italian army owed more to poor Italian tactics, not least the failure to coordinate operations. After the Italian threat had been disposed of, Menelik made a major push to the south. Although Adowa earned Ethiopia a reputation as a leader of the liberation struggle in Africa, the neighbouring Somalis saw it differently. Ethiopia joined Italy, Britain and France in dividing up Somaliland, gaining the Ogaden region, which was later to poison relations after decolonization.

No other African state was as successful as Ethiopia, although a number of powerful, but short-lived, polities developed. In the 1870s and 1880s, Toure

Samory, leader of the Mandinke people, the "Napoleon of the Sudan" according to the French, who thus acquired greater glory by fighting him, established a state on the upper Niger. He relied on the *sofa*, professional troops, trained along Western lines and equipped with modern firearms, who were supported by a larger militia. The firearms were bought in part from British traders, but also manufactured in Samory's own workshops: he had placed agents in the French arsenal in Senegal to learn how to make rifles and cannon. Samory's forces fought a mobile and, frequently, guerrilla war that delayed the French conquest of the western Sudan.

Another dynamic African polity, the Hova Kingdom of Merina in central Madagascar, conquered most of the island by 1880. The potential of African forces with a different force structure to that of Westerners was shown in the Sudan, much of which was taken over from 1881 by Muhammad Ahmad-Mahdi. He destroyed a demoralized Egyptian army under the command of William Hicks, formerly an officer in the British Indian army, at the battle of Shaykan on 5 November 1883. He then captured Khartoum by assault on 26 January 1885, pre-empting the arrival of a British relief force. The Mahdists saw spearmen as crucial, although they also had an infantry force armed with Western rifles, the *jihadiyya*, which played a crucial role at Shaykan.

It was not only in Africa that successful non-Western forces could be found. In the Far East, Japan heavily defeated China on land and sea in the Sino-Japanese war of 1894–95, acquiring Formosa (Taiwan), which they had unsuccessfully attacked in 1874, and the neighbouring Pescadores islands as a consequence. In the war, the Japanese were victorious on land and sea. Despite problems with logistics and transport, Japanese forces advanced through Korea into Manchuria, and captured the major bases of Port Arthur and Weihaiwei, while their fleet beat the less speedy and manoeuvrable Chinese at the Yalu River (1894). But the West could still dominate the situation if it chose; Japan was obliged in the peace settlement to limit its territorial gains from China due to pressure from Russia, Germany and France.[9]

On the world scale, therefore, it was not a case of Western powers expanding into a passive void of decrepit states and undeveloped societies, but rather of the Westerners as an increasingly dominant element in the dynamic non-European world. The West eventually prevailed in most places due to superior military force, improved disease control and enhanced communications. Precisely because non-Western societies were not decrepit, primitive, undeveloped or weak, the Western success in conquering large areas was a formidable military achievement. By 1900, the British had an empire covering a fifth of the world's land surface and including 400 million people; France had one of six million square miles and 52 million people. Belgium, Germany, Italy, Portugal and Spain each also had African colonies, and the Dutch ruled an empire in the East Indies.

In this, better weaponry played a major role. Hilaire Belloc observed, "Whatever happens we have got | The Maxim Gun; and they have not" (*The*

*Modern Traveller*, 1898). Indeed the Maxim (machine) gun, introduced in 1883, was important, although, across much of Africa, it would have been more appropriate for Belloc to mention the breech-loading rifle, because it was better suited for the dispersed fighting that was more characteristic of colonial warfare. The French did not use machine guns in Africa: they could jam, and early types, such as the Mitrailleuse, were heavy, which was a major problem in an area where mobility was crucial. The Germans were slow to use machine guns. Single-shot breech-loaders, such as the British Martini-Henry and the French Gras, were replaced by more effective magazine rifles, such as the Lee-Metford, the Kropatschek, and the model 1886 Lebel.

Artillery was also important. In 1885, General Roberts stressed the unsuitability of light guns:

> [P]ower is of even more importance than mobility. In Afghanistan, from the absence of roads, it is seldom that artillery can move faster than infantry, and no field gun that we now possess can make any impression on the thick mud walls of which all forts and houses in that country are built.[10]

In Senegal and Algeria, the French used artillery to breach the gates of positions, and then stormed them. Artillery, especially 95 mm siege guns using powerful explosives, played a crucial role in the conquest of the Tukulor forts by the French in 1890–91, and the walls of Kano in Nigeria were breached within an hour by British cannon in 1903.

Artillery also played a role in the field, although in the mountainous terrain of the North-West Frontier of India, the British found it difficult to use artillery effectively. However, as was characteristic of European military activity, there was a process of challenge and response, and a practical engineered solution was devised. Mobile screw-guns were found best. These guns were light, and were carried in sections and then screwed together for firing.

In Africa, in the 1890s, the Belgians used Krupp 75 mm cannon and machine guns to help overcome opposition in the Congo, while, further east, the Germans used their Krupps against the Unyamwezi people: the latter's rifles were simply outgunned. In the Sudan, at Atbara, on 8 April 1898, advancing British troops also outgunned the Mahdists, who had no artillery, and successfully stormed their camp. The Anglo-Egyptian forces lost 81 killed and 487 wounded, and their opponents 3,000 and 4,000. At Omdurman, on 1 September 1898, British rifles, machine guns and artillery, including high-angle howitzers, devastated the attacking Mahdists. Winston Churchill, who was present, wrote of Omdurman, "It was a matter of machinery". The Anglo-Egyptian forces lost 49 killed and 382 wounded, and their opponents about 11,000 and 16,000.

Far more than "machinery" was involved in European expansion, including in the battles and other engagements. Bayonets, rather than cannon, were crucial to the French conquest of most of West Africa, and at Tel el Kebir in Egypt, in 1882, the British attacked the Egyptian earthworks with bayonets, without any preliminary bombardment. The British commander, Wolseley, preferred to gain the advantage of surprise. Logistics were also very significant in the war theatre, for example in the Sudan campaign.[11] In the wider field of grand strategy, mobility, as well as force, was important. Steamships, railways and telegraph lines combined to facilitate transfer and return, permitting a greater integration of the European and transoceanic military structures of individual states. This process became more diverse after 1945, as air power came to play an increasingly important role in the movement of troops and supplies, but its origins and effects can be traced to the nineteenth century. Having said that, mixed railway gauges, insufficient rolling stock and poor organization could lessen the advantage the Europeans had in this respect.

Railways were both important in deploying troops towards areas of operation, and, more generally, played a major role in structuring and linking imperial space. In 1896, the British army invading the Sudan built a railway straight across the desert from Waida Halfa to Abu Hamed. It was pushed on to Atbara in 1898, and was vital in the supply of the British forces. In 1897, the British in India moved troops by train against the Waziris on the North-West Frontier. In Latin America, three years later, the building of a railway across the rebel area in 1900 helped to end long-standing Mayan resistance to the Mexicans, although the impact of cholera, smallpox and whooping cough in weakening the defenders was also important. The role of rail helped to ensure that track and trains became strategic targets. In China, in 1900, the Boxer destruction of part of the track between Tientsin (Tianjin) and Beijing forced the abandonment of the initial attempt to relieve the foreign legations in the capital. Significantly, no railways were built in Afghanistan, a country that was not brought under Western control.

Railways were seen as a way to spread Western political and economic power. In 1896, the Russians obliged China to grant a concession for a railway to Vladivostok across Manchuria, and the Chinese Eastern Railway was accordingly constructed in 1897–1904. The French embarked on extensive railway construction projects in Africa and Indo-China from 1898; the German Berlin–Baghdad railway project was designed to create a new geopolitical axis in Eurasia; while, by 1900, the British had constructed 20,000 miles of railway in India.[12]

This was all part of a more general process of building the infrastructure of empire, an infrastructure that greatly focused on military capability. In Eritrea, which the Italians occupied in 1885, they used telegraph lines, steamships, barbed wire, electric mines and bridge, road, fortress and rail construction to anchor their presence.[13] The Russians developed a naval presence in Manchuria, building ports at Dairen and Port Arthur on the Liaodong peninsula, which was leased to them by the Chinese. Telegraph systems facilitated the more rapid transmission of messages, and were developed to bind empires together. The British, with the most far-flung system, preferred transoceanic links in order to limit the possible interference of foreigners in their imperial communications.[14] The construction of an infrastructure of sanitation, offering pure water, effective sewage systems and sanatoria, greatly increased the survival rates of Western troops.[15]

The political context, in areas of expansion as well as within Western states and in the Western states system, was also important. The Westerners were able to use large numbers of indigenous mercenary soldiers to aid their imperial advance. For example, the Afghans were defeated at Penjdeh in 1885 by a Russian force largely composed of Central Asian troops armed with breech-loading rifles. In West Africa, the French were supported by well-equipped and trained African light infantry, especially the Tirailleurs Sénégalais.[16] The King of the Belgians' Congo Free State was conquered for Leopold I by the Force Publique – Belgian-officered Hausa mercenaries from West Africa. The British successfully invaded Hunza on the North-West Frontier in 1891, with 1,000 Gurkha and Kashmiri troops under 16 British officers. In Nigeria, the British benefited from the West African Frontier Force. The Italians used Eritrean *askaris* (auxiliaries) when they invaded Ethiopia in 1895; while the Dutch employed Ambonese and Moluccan troops. At Omdurman, the Sudanese brigade in Kitchener's force played a crucial role, while in Somaliland, the British used native levies and Indian and African troops, as well as British forces.

The ability to win local support was in part a product of local rivalries, which greatly helped the Westerners in many cases. Thus, the Portuguese were able to defeat the Kingdom of Gaza in southern Mozambique in 1895 in large part because of rebellions against the kingdom by its subject peoples. In battle, Portuguese squares used their Kropatschek magazine rifles to defeat Gaza charges. In addition, the British and French came to the task of fighting in Africa with considerable experience of treating with non-Western peoples and of fighting outside Europe. This experience encompassed the recruitment, training and use of local levies and allied forces, the development of logistical capability, and combined operations using coastal and river vessels.

Politics within Western states were also important. In contrast to earlier periods of transoceanic expansion in Asia and Africa (although not America), there was now a greater emphasis on territorial control. Sovereignty became more crucial than informal influence.

In addition, the profit motive was subordinated to geopolitics. Much imperial expansion from 1880 arose directly from the response to the real or apparent plans of other Western powers, although the search for markets was also important. Imperialists such as Cecil Rhodes and Frederick Lugard, who developed British power in Southern Africa and Nigeria respectively, were proponents of both business and great power rivalry.

From within the West, there was both impetus and opportunity to seek colonial expansion, and increasing military professionalism and capability interacted with a growing sense of an imperialist military mission. The military came to be a bigger element in, and often came to play a greater role in, national and international politics. This can be seen in improved public images of the army in late Victorian Britain.

The major powers competed in part outside Europe, a sphere where rivalries could be pursued with a measure of safety and without too substantial a deployment of resources. Indeed, relatively few troops were sent, ensuring that there was a heavy reliance on locally raised troops. The Spanish–American War of 1898 was unusual in that the ambitions of major Western powers were generally pursued without direct conflict with each other. Like Japan in the Russo-Japanese War of 1904–1905, the Americans were unconstrained by European power politics and alliances, and convinced, instead, that force was necessary to achieve a position in a world where their territorial options were limited by their late entry into international military competition and territorial expansion. Nevertheless, the Americans were in general not disposed to confront militarily the European powers; despite tension over a number of issues, war with Britain was avoided, as was, indeed, war between all the great powers except Russia and Japan.

Instead of open conflict between themselves, European powers tried to pre-empt their rivals by grabbing territory. The doctrine of "effective occupation", developed at the Berlin Congress of colonial powers in 1884–85, encouraged a speeding up of the process of annexation. For example, concern about French ambitions led to the British capture of Mandalay in 1885 and the annexation of Upper Burma the following year, although much of it was only brought under limited control and the British had to face a serious insurrection for several years. Similarly, French and German expansion in Africa led Britain to take counter-measures, although economic factors, such as the search for markets and the wish to secure raw materials, for example palm oil, also played an important role. Having abandoned the Sudan in 1885, the British invaded it in 1896 in order to pre-empt the French. German moves in East Africa led Britain to establish its power in Uganda in the 1890s. British expansion in Somaliland was, in part, a consequence of concern about French schemes in the region.

The combined effect of the drive from the centre and local initiatives from the imperial periphery was a major increase in Western territorial power in the 1880s and 1890s, although it is also worth noting some governmental and political concern about these rising commitments.[17] In West Africa, the British occupied the interior of the Gambia in 1887–88; campaigned successfully against the Asante in 1895–96 and annexed Asante in 1901 after a rebellion had been crushed; captured Benin; defeated the Yorubas in Nigeria; and established the Protectorates of northern and southern Nigeria in 1900. The French conquered Dahomey in 1892–94 and captured Samory in 1898. Timbuktu had been occupied in 1893. In the Sudan, the Mahdi's successor, the Khalifa Abdullahi, was defeated and killed by a British cavalry force at

Umm Diwaykarat in November 1899. In southern Africa, the British overran what they renamed Rhodesia, and suppressed a rebellion by the Ndebele and Shona in 1896, while the Portuguese overran much of modern Angola and Mozambique.

Elsewhere in Africa, Germany claimed protectorates over Togo, the Cameroons, and South West Africa in 1884 and in Tanganyika in 1885, while Leopold I of Belgium's forces successfully invaded the Katanga in 1891. Further afield, the French conquered Indo-China. Annam became a French protectorate in 1883, Laos a decade later. The islands of the Pacific were divided up by the imperial powers.

## 1900–1914

This process of scrambling for possessions continued without slackening in the early years of the twentieth century. The aggressive nature of the Western military pressure and the stress on mobile operations were captured in a British memorandum of 1904 on the military situation in Somaliland, where the British were at war with Mullah Sayyid Muhammed: "in so much as passive defence, unless combined with active offence, is a costly policy, rarely leading to decisive issues, active operations outside the actual sphere of the Protectorate were deemed essential to ultimate success".[18]

Areas where the Westerners had not hitherto sent troops were made fully aware of the potential of Western power. In 1900, the French seized the Touat oasis in the Sahara, the first loss of territory by Morocco for over a century. This campaign, which cost nearly 20 million francs and for which 35,000 camels were requisitioned in Algeria, indicated the ability and willingness of the colonial powers to spend in order to achieve results. The French went on to make significant local gains and by 1912 had established a Protectorate over most of Morocco,[19] the remainder becoming a Spanish Protectorate; the Spaniards had begun to play a major role in the interior in 1909, but most of their Protectorate was not really under Spanish control.

The French also advanced south from Algeria into the Sahara. In 1900, the fall of In Rhar, after French artillery had breached its walls, broke the resistance of the Tidelkt. Columns crossed the Sahara from both north and south, the latter advancing from Timbuktu and Gao on the Niger and St Louis on the Senegal. The submission of the Ahaggar Tuareq in 1905 ended effective resistance to the French in the Sahara,[20] but the further extension of French authority still involved military action. In 1909, Abéché, capital of Wadai in eastern Chad, was occupied. The following year, a column of 300 riflemen captured Drijdjeli, capital of Massalit, beating off local resistance.

In 1904, a British force had advanced to Lhasa, the capital of Tibet, in order to dictate terms. *En route*, at Guru, it opened fire on Tibetans who were unwilling to disarm. Due in large part to their two Maxim guns, four cannon and effective rifles, the British killed nearly 700 Tibetans without any losses of their own. Thanks to the resources of the British empire, this advance had been supported by 10,000 coolies (human porters), 7,000 mules, 5,000 bullocks and over 4,000 yaks.

Meanwhile, the Dutch seized and enforced control of more of the East Indies. In 1904, they and the Portuguese agreed to divide the island of Timor. This was followed in 1912 by the Portuguese suppression of the independent Timorese nobles, while the Dutch imposed control on their side of the border. In 1905–1906, the resistance of the Bugis, Makasarese and Toraja of Sulawesi was broken: Dutch power was effective both against developed states (the first two), and against the head-hunting Toraja. In 1906, the last resistance to Dutch rule in Banjarmasin in Borneo ended, while the Dutch intervened in South Bali. At Den Pasar and later at Pamescutan, the two *raja* families ritually purified themselves for death and fought their final battle (*puputan*): armed only with daggers and lances, they were all slaughtered as they advanced in the face of Dutch firepower, killing their own wounded as they did so. On Sumatra, Jambi was brought under control in 1907, while, in 1908, the Dewa Agung of Klungkung staged his own *puputan* when the Dutch attacked.[21]

In 1911, another area not hitherto conquered by Europeans in part succumbed, when an Italian expeditionary force of 34,000 men landed in Turkish-ruled Tripolitania and Cyrenaica, and called their conquest Libya. The Italian force was larger, more modern and better trained than their Turkish opponents. This was the first war in which armoured cars and aeroplanes were used: grenades were dropped from the air on a Turkish army camp on 23 October 1911. Giulio Douhet (1869–1930), the commander of the Italian aerial bombardment unit, was to be a major theorist of aerial warfare. Further east, in 1911–12, the Russians established a protectorate in Outer Mongolia, replacing Chinese influence.

The frequently brutal and devastating character of Western imperialism was captured in the letters and diaries of Donald Alexander MacAlister who served as a transport officer with the British field force sent against the Aros of south-eastern Nigeria in 1901–1902:

We have to trek through the jungle in single file. In order to prevent flank attacks flankers are sent out who cut paths through the jungle parallel . . . We are 1,500 men against 80,000. However the blacks do not combine so that all the column do is to attack village after village.
(22 November 1901)

The burning of the town was very exciting and Stewart and myself were the first to apply matches but we had to go through to see if the road was freed of enemy. Our carriers and bushmen have cleared the bush all round and everywhere trees are being felled and the ruins of the huts pulled down . . . We had the Maxim pouring into the bush this morning. There must be a great deal of dead . . . I have seen no skulls of humans . . . As I write the millemeter gun is pouring case shot into the bush. It is a glorious day.           (25 December 1901)

The Colonel has given us all a little lecture on biffing natives. He said we must *not* biff them. A case was brought to his notice where Fox . . . had so mashed one man that his eye had to be removed and other things. I am glad to say I have not found it necessary to do much biffing but a native sergeant who was very impudent on the matter of keeping silence the other evening when I told him to stop his clatter got a hard one in the ribs and laid himself up for 2 days . . . This morning I went on a small punitive column. The enemy who had surrendered refused to make roads. We marched on Okerojee farm and took all livestock and captured everybody and looted the place. One of the enemy killed.           (2/4 January 1902)

The size of Iboum is much reduced. It is now a small fortified place with everything outside the walls levelled to the ground . . . The natives have been crowding in with guns of all kinds and some of these guns are very fine specimens of Sneider. The bulk of those brought in lately could if properly handled have done us a good deal of damage. They have all been broken up and burned.
           (12 January 1902)

If a native breaks our laws his house is burnt down – very simple.
           (2 February 1902)[22]

A similar process occurred on the other side of the world, as, in 1900–1902, Filipino nationalists mounted a guerrilla war to resist American annexation of the Philippines from Spain, leading the Americans to add counter-insurgency methods to their ideology of racialism and divine purpose. Prisoners were killed and prison camps were created in which 11,000 people died. The Americans lost 4,200 troops. Although, in 1902, they claimed that resistance had been crushed, it continued. There was a fresh revolt on Samar and Leyte – the Pulahan revolt – in 1904–1907.[23]

At the same time as the geographical range of conquest expanded, there was also an increase in rebellion against European rule. This was not new: there had been a major uprising in north India in 1857–59: the Indian Mutiny. Nevertheless, the extent of rebellion in the 1900s was noteworthy. Already, the range of anti-European rebellion had been seen in the late nineteenth century with, for example, the nationalist revolt of Arabi Pasha in Egypt and in 1893 the Tetela rebellion in the Congo. An anti-French revolt broke out in Madagascar in 1898.

In the 1900s, the extent of rebellion broadened, in large part as a response to the implementation of control in newly annexed territories. In 1905, the rebellion by the Nama and the Hereros of South-West Africa, which had begun in 1904, was finally crushed with great brutality. The war required the deployment of a very large German force, 70,000 strong. The Germans practised extermination against their opponents, killing them in large numbers, driving the Hereros into a waterless desert, and treating the prisoners sent to labour camp with great cruelty, such that over half of the population died there.[24] In 1905, the Germans suppressed the Maji Maji uprising in German East Africa (Tanganyika), using a scorched earth policy against guerrilla warfare: about 250,000 Africans died of famine.

Elsewhere, Acehnese resistance to the Dutch in Sumatra was largely quelled by 1903, although fighting continued, and the revolt in Madagascar was suppressed in 1904, as was an anti-British Zulu revolt in Natal in 1906 and the revolt of the Beni Snassen in north-east Morocco in 1907. The Boxer movement in China was anti-Western and has recently been labelled the China War of 1900.[25]

The difficulties facing the Italians in newly seized Libya indicated the problems facing Western conquerors. Although the Turks, denied reinforcements by Italian naval superiority, eventually accepted defeat, determined resistance by Senussi tribesmen in the interior made it difficult to consolidate and expand Italian coastal positions, a situation that repeated much of the history of European military expansion, including the earlier Italian experience in the Horn of Africa. The Libyans first used traditional cavalry charges, but they were defeated by European firepower, as at Asaba in 1913. The Libyans then switched to guerrilla tactics with some success. The Italians were untrained for such a conflict. In 1915, an Italian force of 4,000 troops was largely destroyed after its Libyan auxiliaries turned against it, and the Italians were driven back to the coast.[26]

## 1914-18

Italian pressure in Libya was dramatically reduced from 1915 when Italy entered World War One, although fears of Turkish and German support for the Senussi proved exaggerated.[27] By then, the Western imperial powers had annexed most of the territories they sought in the world and had defined spheres of influence in most of the countries in the Old World still outside Western imperial control, for example China and Persia (Iran). Thus, World War One did not cut into a process of territorial expansion, as it might have done had it broken out in the 1880s or 1890s.

Nor did it have a disruptive impact on the Western empires outside Europe akin to that of World War Two. There was a major defeat for the British in

Mesopotamia (modern Iraq) at the hands of the Turks at Kut in 1915, and the attempt that year in the Gallipoli campaign to force the Dardanelles failed, but these did not have an impact on the prestige of the British empire comparable to the fall of Singapore to the Japanese in 1942. There were indeed rebellions against European empires – against the French in Tunisia in 1915–16 and against the Russians in Central Asia in 1916 – but none was successful or posed a more major threat to these empires. The widespread Muslim revolt in Central Asia against the Russian introduction of conscription was defeated, with great brutality and heavy casualties. French concern that Allied failure against the Turks in 1915 might lead to serious trouble in Algiers, for which they had no spare troops due to the fighting on the Western Front, proved misplaced.[28]

Instead, the successful articulation of imperial systems on a global scale was readily apparent. Both Britain and France benefited from the support of their empires. The French deployed about 140,000 West African troops on the Western Front,[29] and more than 800,000 Indian soldiers fought for the British in the war, so that, far from the British having to garrison South Asia, it was a crucial source of manpower. The British used large numbers of Indians on the Western Front at first, as well as a substantial Canadian force. Indian troops captured Basra in 1914, protecting British oil interests in southwest Persia, and advanced into Mesopotamia the following year.[30] The impact of raising troops in the Punjab was such that it became a virtual "home-front" for the British war effort.[31] Australian and New Zealand troops played the major role in the unsuccessful attempt to force the Dardanelles in 1915, and were also sent to the Western Front, while South African troops captured South-West Africa from the Germans in 1915.

The importance of imperial manpower resources was demonstrated from the start when late in 1914 Gurkha and Indian units, supported by British and French warships, defeated Turkish attacks on the Suez Canal. Without the empire, the British would have been unable to mount offensive operations in the Middle East, would have been largely reduced to the use of the navy against German colonies, and would have been forced to introduce conscription earlier than 1916. The use of imperial forces was helped by the absence of an enemy in East Asia, with the exception of the German base at Tsingtao in China in 1914, which was captured by Britain's ally Japan. The situation was to be very different in World War Two when Japan allied with Germany.

In some respects, World War One, for a while, led to an intensification of European military control in the colonies. This was particularly so in and near areas of conflict, as imperial forces manoeuvred in the interior. Forces were also available to enforce imperial authority, as with the British expedition of 1918 against the Turkana of Kenya.

## 1918–36

World War One was followed not by a retreat of European empire, but by its advance. The imperial ethos remained strong, and the British in particular saw the events of the war outside Europe as reflecting the value and appeal of empire. The defeat of Germany and its allies ensured that Western control over the world's surface reached its maximum extent. Although the redistribution of Germany's colonies resulted in gains for Japan in the western Pacific, the partitioning of the Ottoman Empire led, in 1920, to British rule over Palestine, Transjordan and Iraq, and French rule over Syria and Lebanon, all under League of Nations mandates. Arthur Balfour, then British Foreign Secretary, had already proposed indirect control in May 1918:

> [T]hough the establishment of an Arab kingdom in the Hejaz [part of Saudi Arabia], of an autonomous Arab protected state in Mesopotamia and of an internalised Jewish "home" in Palestine will not increase the territories under the British flag, they will certainly give increased protection to British interests, both in Egypt and in India . . . "buffer states", of all the greater value to us because they have been created not for our security but for the advantage of their inhabitants.[32]

Whether direct or not, the intention was to add to imperial security. There was also an advance in Russian, now Soviet, power. In 1920, the autonomous Islamic states of Bukhara and Khiva, which had been Tsarist protectorates, were subjugated by the Red Army, the army of the new Communist state, although, the following year, the Afghans hoped to gain both and more if the Russian Civil War led to a break-up of Russia.[33] In 1921, first White (anti-Communist) and then Communist forces subjugated Outer Mongolia, hitherto largely autonomous, and a pro-Soviet government was established. This achievement was in part due to technological factors, in particular the gap in firepower between the Mongolians and their invaders, but other factors also played a role, including the low density of the local population.

Throughout the colonial world, there was a deepening of imperial control as areas that had been often only nominally annexed were brought under at least some colonial government. Thus, in southern Sudan posts were established by Arab troops under British officers and military patrols were launched. Their effectiveness, however, was limited and the patrols were gradually abandoned.[34] In the more favourable terrain of northern Sudan, where the forests of the south were absent, the armoured cars of the machine-gun batteries in the Sudan Defence Force were found effective as a means of maintaining control.[35] Roadbuilding improved the British position on the North-West Frontier of India.[36]

However, the European imperial powers, exhausted by World War One, began to sense that they had overreached themselves, particularly in the

Islamic world. Revolts in Egypt (1919) and Iraq (1920–21) led to Britain granting their independence in 1922 and 1924 respectively, although Egypt remained under *de facto* British military control. British influence collapsed in Persia (1921), and the confrontation with Turkey in the Chanak Crisis (1922) caused a political crisis in London that led to the abandonment of the confrontation. Prefiguring modern concerns, General Rawlinson, the Commander-in-Chief India, argued in 1922 that war with Turkey would lead to trouble in India and the Middle East: "To undertake offensive action against the Turk is merely to consolidate a Pan-Islamic Movement".[37]

Other European powers faced growing similar problems. The French and Spaniards encountered opposition in Morocco, while the Druze rebelled against the French in Syria in 1925–27 in reaction to attempts by the governor to introduce what he considered to be modernizing reforms in the Jebel Druze area. This alienated the notables, the crucial intermediaries in successful imperialism. In Spanish Morocco, the weak state of the colonial administration and military did not dissuade the Spaniards from attempting to expand their control from 1919 when the Tangier peninsula was brought under their control. In 1920, the offensive broadened, but insufficient effort was made to win local support: political advance was not combined with military gains. In 1921, the Spaniards moved deeper into the interior, but the opposition, under Muhammed Abd-el-Krim, became better organized, and it moved on to the attack in July. The unprepared and outmanoeuvred Spaniards, poorly led by the feckless and vainglorious Manuel Fernández Silvestre, were unable to hold their ground, a situation exacerbated by the collapse of morale among the conscripts and by growing dissension among the Moorish auxiliaries. As they fell back the Spaniards lost cohesion, while their opponents gained fresh support. In the battle, or rather rout, of Annual, at least 12,000 Spanish troops were killed, and Abd-el-Krim captured large numbers of rifles and pieces of artillery, a crucial addition of strength. Success encouraged more tribes to rally to Abd-el-Krim.

A renewed Spanish offensive was blocked at Tizi Azza in November 1922, and, in 1923, the Moors resumed the attack. A Spanish attempt to win peace in 1924 by offering autonomy was rejected and the Spaniards had to evacuate much of what they still held in the interior. The mobile Moors, armed with modern firearms, including machine guns and mountain howitzers, were not dependent on the cumbersome supply routes of their opponents. Suffering food shortages, Abd-el-Krim looked towards French Morocco, and in April 1925 attacked, making rapid gains: a number of posts fell after artillery bombardment.[38] The Dutch came under attack in the Far East, from the PKI (Indonesian Communist Party) in Java (1926) and Sumatra (1927).

The net effect of these uprisings might suggest a reduction in Western military superiority. This was perhaps further illustrated by the failure of Western powers to enforce their post-World War One settlement on Turkey. In particular, the Turks defeated Greek attempts to subordinate them; a Greek

16

advance on Ankara was blocked by Kemal Atatürk at the battle of the Sakkaria (24 August–16 September 1921) and the Greeks were driven right out of Anatolia by the Turks in 1922: Smyrna fell to Atatürk on 9–13 September.

Nevertheless, an impression of Western failure would be misplaced. The colonial powers still had sufficient military superiority to reimpose control in most cases. By attacking the French, Abd-el-Krim greatly weakened his position, not least because the French and Spaniards agreed to coordinate operations. Furthermore, Spanish forces were better armed and trained than hitherto: tanks, artillery and planes bought from the French were delivered in 1922, although the use of light tanks at Ambar in March 1922, their first deployment in Africa, was unsuccessful: unable to keep up, the infantry could not prevent the tanks from being disabled by stone-wielders, while many of the tanks' machine guns jammed due to faulty ammunition.[39]

In 1925, while the French attacked in the south, the Spaniards, with French naval support, launched a successful amphibious assault in the Bay of Alhucemas in September, supported by air attack and naval gunnery. The Moors were defeated in pitched battle, and their capital Ajdir fell on 2 October.[40] More generally, the Moors had constructed fortifications that were vulnerable to Franco-Spanish artillery, and their opponents were present in overwhelming force and able to mount simultaneous attacks. This was a campaign more similar to those in Algeria the previous century than to others in West Africa because it was an imperial victory obtained not by small, lightly armed, mobile units, but rather by a substantial force. The rebellion was finally crushed in 1926. In this conflict a certain Spanish officer, Francisco Franco, made his name as commander of the Spanish Foreign Legion.

The French regained control in Syria and the Dutch in Indonesia in 1926–27. The French had used heavy artillery bombardments to thwart Druze progress in Damascus in 1926. The Dutch benefited from a lack of coordination among the PKI and from the disruption of its leadership caused by earlier police action, including many arrests. The uprisings were rapidly suppressed.

Earlier, in 1920, the British had succeeded in suppressing opposition in Somaliland: earlier hostilities had ended in 1904 but resumed in 1913. There had been an important shift in native tactics there, reflecting the extent to which throughout the world these were not fixed. A British intelligence report of 1919 noted that "Dervish rushing tactics", as with the attack on a British square at Dul Madoba in August 1913, had been superseded by a stress on the defence:

[T]he large increase in the number of rifles in the Mullah's possession and the consequent discard of the spear ... We may expect the Dervishes to take up defensive positions which they will defend stubbornly behind cover without exposing themselves. We must be ready to carry out attacks against most difficult positions and up

narrow and steep-sided valleys, to employ covering fire and frequently to capture the heights or the key to the position before it will be
possible to make any headway. It will also be necessary to employ
artillery, firing high explosive-shell, if the various Dervish strong-
holds are to be captured without very heavy casualties. In short,
whereas in the past the training of troops in Somaliland could, in the
main, be carried out with a view to meeting one form of savage
warfare, namely, the Dervish rush in bush country, troops must now
be trained to readily adapt themselves to a more varied form of
fighting which will in some degree, resemble hill warfare in India.[41]

After World War One, a combination of the Somaliland Camel Corps and the
British Royal Air Force's (RAF's) Z Force brought the necessary combination
of force and mobility.[42]

The Italians had recognized Libyan self-government in 1919, but Benito
Mussolini, who gained power in 1922, was not prepared to accept this.
Employing great brutality against civilians, of whom over 50,000 were
probably killed, the Italians under Field Marshal Pietro Badoglio, Governor
of Libya 1928–34, who had already served there in 1911–12, subdued the
colony in 1928–32. Their tactics included the use of columns of armoured
cars and motorized infantry, the dropping of gas bombs, and the employment
of Eritreans rather than Libyans as auxiliaries. These tactics were
accompanied by a ruthless suppression of the population – wells were blocked
and flocks slaughtered, both effective forms of economic warfare – and the
Libyan population was disarmed and resettled in camps in which 20,000
died. A largely pastoral society, much of which was nomadic, was brought
under control, three decades after the French had subjugated the Algerian
Sahara. The Bedouin population of Libya was halved.[43]

In the post-war world, although they were very different as states, it is also
possible to see both the Soviet Union and, albeit to a lesser extent, the USA as
empires. Having gained control in Russia in the Russian Civil War, the
Communists ensured that Tsarist gains in the Caucasus and Central Asia were
retained. Soviet forces occupied Armenia in 1920 and overran Georgia in
1921. A major uprising in Georgia in 1924 was suppressed. The Basmachi
uprising, a Muslim attempt in the early 1920s to organize a government in
Turkestan, was crushed by the local Russians, who had more modern
weapons, as well as the benefit of control over the major towns and railways.
Overwhelming force, the use of artillery against mountain villages, and the
ability to call on some local support, enabled the Soviets to crush an Islamic
uprising in Daghestan and Chechnya in 1920–21, and also subsequent
uprisings in 1924, 1928, 1929, 1936 and 1940.[44]

Although not a major colonial power (Alaska, Hawaii, Puerto Rico, Guam,
American Samoa and the Philippines can all be regarded as colonies), the
Americans enjoyed a quasi-imperial position, supported by extensive and

growing trade and investment in the Caribbean and Mexico. In both, they intervened to protect their interests, but they encountered nationalist resistance in Mexico and in parts of the Caribbean, especially Haiti. Popular guerrilla movements in Haiti and the Dominican Republic in the 1920s proved able to limit the degree of control enjoyed by occupying American marine forces who found that rebel ambushes restricted their freedom of manoeuvre. American bombing was no substitute, particularly in face of guerrilla dominance of rural areas at night. However, the Americans were not defeated in pitched battles, and in 1922 the guerrillas in the Dominican Republic conditionally surrendered. Nevertheless, American troops sent to Nicaragua in 1927 failed to defeat a rebel peasant army under Augusto Sandino; their occupation ended in 1932. Despite these checks, the Americans dominated the region militarily, not least due to their naval power and to the operational effectiveness of the Marine Corps.[45]

Opposition to, and uprisings against, imperial powers testified to the more general problems created by the steady growth of anti-imperial feeling and sometimes by the more positive emergence of national identity. The global diffusion of Western notions of community, identity and political action, and of practices of politicization, challenged imperial structures, although it is important not to underrate indigenous notions of identity and practices of resistance, many of them central to a peasant culture of non-compliance. In 1885, the Indian National Congress was founded, followed, in 1897, by the Egyptian National Party. In 1920, the Soviet Union hosted a Congress of Peoples of the East at Baku, although initial attempts by Communists to exploit anti-imperialism, as in Indonesia, were of limited success. The National Congress of British West Africa was established in 1920, the Young Kikuyu Association in Kenya in 1921, and the African National Congress in South Africa in 1923. Within French Africa, there was the Etoile Nord-Africaine in Algeria and the Destour in Tunisia.

The practice and range of "informal empire" (areas not under direct colonial control) were also under pressure. In China, the British abandoned their concessions in Hankou and Jiujiang on the Yangtze, in 1927, after the local British military presence was overawed by massive public protests. A Chinese trade unionist was killed in each city by British troops, but, whereas, in 1925, the position in Hankou had been underpinned by local warlords, in 1927 there was no such backing.[46] Western military methods, however, continued to enjoy a degree of prestige and influence in China. In 1934-35, Hans von Seeckt, Commander-in-Chief of the German army in 1920-26, played an important role in increasing the effectiveness of the Chinese army.

Military opposition to the imperial powers continued in the 1930s. The French crushed an uprising at Yen Bay in Vietnam in 1930 and had pacified the tribes of the Moroccan Atlas by 1933. An anti-Soviet rebellion in Mongolia was defeated in 1932, but the American withdrawal from Haiti in 1934 owed much to a sense of the intractability of the conflict; the Americans were unwilling to devote resources comparable to those of the French in Syria and lacked the same sense of mission.

The most far-flung empire, that of Britain, faced the most widespread opposition. Aside from hostility from the Nationalist Party in Malta, and Greek Cypriot nationalist riots in 1931, there was serious Arab violence in Palestine in 1936–39.[47] In India, the growing strength of the non-violent Indian National Party created a serious political problem. There were also problems in specific parts of India. In the 1920s, a permanent garrison of 15,000 men, supported by 10,000 Pathan militia, had been assigned to Waziristan on the mountainous North-West Frontier after the suppression of the 1919 rebellion there; the area, between the Kurram Valley and Baluchistan, had been annexed in 1893. The effective locally produced rifles used by the tribes had led to heavy British casualties in the winter of 1919–20. In 1936, rebellion broke out again under the Faqir of Ipi and, the following year, the British deployed over 60,000 men to crush it. The Faqir's peak strength was only 4,000 men, and, although his men had good rifles – an example of the shrinking arms gap in hand-held weapons between Western forces and their opponents – they lacked artillery and machine guns. Nevertheless, the British were able to subdue the region as much because of tribal rivalries and financial inducements as superior numbers and firepower. The British deployed about 50–60 armoured cars, which were used mainly to escort road convoys, and proved quite effective in that limited role. A handful of light tanks also went for an occasional trundle on open ground, but could get nowhere near the kind of mountainous terrain on which the principal engagements took place. The campaign also revealed the limitations of Western communications. The tribesmen cut telegraph lines. As wireless was still in its infancy in the British forces, most signalling below brigade level was carried out using old-fashioned coloured flags, the heliograph and despatch riders. Only the largest bases and headquarters had reliable wireless communications. British success was consolidated by new roads, but guerrilla opposition in Waziristan continued until 1943.[48]

Thus, in some cases, large numbers of troops had to be deployed to maintain the imperial position. In 1938, the British used 50,000 troops to suppress the Arab rising in Palestine. There were also attempts to employ new technology; the RAF bombed Jalalabad and Kabul during the Third Afghan War in 1919, tribesmen in Central Iraq in 1920, and Wahabi tribesmen who threatened Iraq and Kuwait in 1928. British air power also played a role in ending long-standing resistance in British Somaliland in 1921, and was successfully used against Yemen in 1927–34. The British also used aeroplanes in Waziristan, but their effectiveness was probably exaggerated as their novelty wore off and tribesmen learned how to evade their attacks.[49]

If some rebellions could be suppressed by small forces supported by air power, the overall burden of imperial security remained high. Nevertheless, real costs were lessened by the use of non-Western troops, both local forces and those from elsewhere in the empire. Regions that had been conquered in the late nineteenth century provided many soldiers for the colonial powers, and both they and troops from areas that had been ruled for longer were trained in Western methods of warfare and organized accordingly. Hitherto independent armies of local allies were similarly organized or were integrated into imperial forces. The result was a high level of military resource. For example, in response to the Arab rising in Iraq in 1920, four divisions were sent from India.

Locally raised troops helped the French suppress the Druze rebellion. French military control of Syria and Lebanon substantially rested on the Armée du Levant, which, 70,000 strong in 1921, was a force largely composed of colonial troops from Africa, and on local military and police forces: the Troupes Spéciales du Levant, 14,000 strong in 1935, and the Gendarmerie. Both had a strong element of local minority groups, such as Christians, that could be relied on in the event of clashes with the rest of the population. Divide, recruit and rule were the crucial objects and processes of imperialist control. Just as well for, due to concern about Germany, the French could not concentrate military resources on extra-European commitments and their navy, yet their empire was still militarily effective. Moroccan troops and the Spanish Foreign Legion were used to suppress the Asturias miners in 1934 and in the Spanish Civil War.[50]

Two very different images of empire can be offered, reflecting the different and contradictory policies of repression and conciliation followed by the British after World War One. The Amritsar massacre in April 1919, when General Dyer ordered troops to fire on a demonstrating crowd, causing nearly 400 fatalities, dented British authority in India by suggesting that it had an inherently repressive nature.[51] But, that same year, a Government of India Act established the principle of dyarchy: responsible self-government in certain areas. This reflected British Liberal aspirations, which were not shared by all Conservatives. Views of the military situation were coloured by racism. In 1922, Rawlinson wrote to a fellow general,

> You are wrong to draw a parallel between Ireland and India. The two problems are entirely different: (1) one is a black country and the other is a white, (2) no black man, as you well know, would ever have the pluck to do what the Sinn Feiners have done, (3) so long as we have the Army as it is at present, there can be no real danger in the situation.[52]

The Government of India Act of 1935 moved India towards self-government, although it was also designed to ensure British retention of the substance of power. However, the provincial elections of 1937 were a success for the Indian National Congress. A section of the Conservative Party, led by Churchill, bitterly opposed the 1935 Act. They saw it as a move towards the abandonment of empire. For Churchill, the new policy was more than a, perhaps misguided, tactical step and he offered an apocalyptic vision of its consequences that appeared out of place to many. The Viceroy of India described Churchill in 1929 as an "Imperialist in the 1890–1900 sense of the word", but that word now appeared less relevant.

The bitterness of the parliamentary rebellion against the 1935 Act was a testimony to the pull of empire in Britain, the leading imperial power, and the Conservative rebels' fear of its demise, but also to their failure. After 1918, there was a more general sense that empire had to change, and that reform of the government of India was, alongside Imperial Trade Preference and more equal relations with the Dominions, the best means to give the British empire a future. It was to that end, that Leo Amery, an ardent imperialist, supported the legislation in 1935, while Lord Irwin, the Viceroy of India, backed eventual Dominion status for India. The process of adaptation from empire to commonwealth was enshrined in the Statute of Westminster of 1931: Britain, Australia, New Zealand, Canada and South Africa enjoyed an autonomous and equal relationship, and were "freely associated as members of the British Commonwealth of Nations".

A very different image of empire was offered by the successful Italian invasion of Ethiopia in 1935–36. This was a brutal conquest in which advanced weaponry was used alongside native auxiliaries: Eritreans bore much of the fighting. The new military technology was employed with harsh effectiveness. Motorized columns were supported by aeroplanes, and large quantities of mustard gas were also used. The new technology compensated for Ethiopian bravery, for the ineffectiveness of much Italian generalship and for the logistical problems of campaigning in the difficult mountainous terrain; the last forced the Italians to devote much energy to roadbuilding. They invaded from Eritrea in the north on 3 October 1935 and from Italian Somaliland in the south-east early in 1936. Fortunately for the Italians, the Ethiopians chose to engage them in battle, rather than to avoid engagements and rely on guerrilla tactics. Thus, mistaken native strategy as well as superior Italian weaponry played a role in Italian success, which was easier than British and French military commanders had anticipated.[53] The force from Eritrea fought its way through Tigre and in March and April 1936 delivered powerful blows against the main Ethiopian defence. The Ethiopians were defeated at the battle of Mount Aradam, and the Ethiopian capital, Addis Ababa, was captured on 5 May. Mussolini annexed Ethiopia on 9 May and officially declared the establishment of the new Italian empire.

As in Morocco in the 1920s, numbers were also important. The Italians deployed nearly 600,000 men, of whom 1,537 died. The ignominy of Italian defeat at Adowa in 1896 was wiped out. Badoglio, who commanded the invasion, had survived Adowa. The Italians were greatly helped by the failure of other Western powers to act on the League of Nations' condemnation of the Italian invasion. The support of the French and the British Foreign

Secretary, Sir Samuel Hoare, for a settlement of the dispute at the expense of Ethiopia, was seen as appeasement and led to Hoare's enforced resignation. Hoare, however, had been authorized by the Cabinet to accept Italian conquests. The British government then considered oil sanctions against Italy and closing the Suez Canal to Italian resupply ships, but France was only willing to cooperate if Britain undertook to guarantee the demilitarization of the Rhineland, which it refused to do. The British government wanted to keep Italy true to the Stresa Front against Germany, feared provoking Italian attacks on British shipping and bases in the Mediterranean, and did not wish to antagonize the Americans by stopping their tankers. Fear of inter-European conflict prevented any move against imperial gains, as it had also done prior to 1914.

Once established, Italian rule proved harsh and this led to a guerrilla campaign from 1937, which had some effect. The response was savage, and Emperor Haile Selassie did not regain Ethiopia until British and Commonwealth forces defeated the Italians there in 1941.[54]

Thus very different images of Western imperial strength and military capability can be discerned in the late 1930s. As with much else, it is unclear what would have happened had World War Two not broken out. Its consequences for relations between the Western powers and the rest of the world are considered in Chapter 8.

# CHAPTER TWO

# The West, 1882–1913

Fire is now, or should be, the all-important factor in a battle.
(Report on the Campaign in Manchuria in 1904 by Colonel
W. H. W. Waters, British Military Mission with the Russian army)[1]

The military historiography of this period is understandably dominated by knowledge on the part of historians writing after 1914 of the forthcoming world war. This approach is not without its uses, for it serves as a reminder of what was to be the product of the military developments of these years, but it is also misleading. First, while planners and generals prepared for war, they did not foresee its precise nature. Secondly, there was much military activity that cannot be fitted into an account focused on preparations for a major war.

Planning and preparations, nevertheless, were at the heart of modern armed forces. As Western militaries became more institutionalized and professional, so planning came to play an ever greater role. Planners looked ahead, but were also greatly influenced by the recent past. This led to a much more intense observation and analysis of contemporary forces and conflicts. For example, the Prussian General Staff system was given much of the credit for the victories over Austria in 1866 and France in 1870–71, which had led to the creation of the German empire. Training of staff officers had certainly given the Prussian army a coherence its opponents lacked and ensured that its large numbers and reserves could be mobilized successfully.

In response, other states sought to emulate Prussia, although the nature of this emulation varied. The purchase of German military equipment and the use of German advisers was important in some countries, such as Chile.[2] German military advisers were used from the 1880s by Japan and Turkey, the two leading non-Western military powers. Elsewhere, the impact was less direct. General staffs were created, for example in Italy in 1882, the USA in 1903, and Britain in 1904, although none had the efficiency or autonomy of the German model. Hugh Arnold-Forster, who was to be the British Secretary of State for War, referred to "the perfect organization of the German army under the direction of the German General Staff".[3]

Military education was also emphasized. The École Supérieure de la Guerre was founded in 1878 in order to provide France with a staff college. The General Service and Staff College was created at Fort Leavenworth, Kansas in 1902.[4] Like staff officers elsewhere, the graduates of Leavenworth learned how to coordinate and sustain large bodies of men on active duty. More generally, the prestige of German war-making rose. Hitherto relatively obscure, Clausewitz's *On War* (1832) became an internationally known work, used, for example, at the École Supérieure de la Guerre.[5] The Prussian campaigns were studied in American staff colleges.

Contingency planning developed and interacted with arms races. Military plans, such as the German Schlieffen Plan of 1905, drove policy.[6] Historical campaigns were analysed at length in military institutions and publications in order to prepare better for the future.

There was an emphasis on the offensive. Throughout Europe, planners drafted blueprints for offensive operations, which were seen as the sole way to secure success. This arose from the dissection of the conflict of 1870–71, for lessons, by the generation of officers ultimately to hold high command positions in World War One, such as Franz Conrad von Hötzendorf, Chief of the Austrian General Staff from 1906 until 1916, and his French and Russian counterparts.

The Schlieffen Plan called for an offensive envelopment of the French army, before advancing further into the interior; this was to be followed by the use of the same strategy against France's ally, Russia. As far as France was concerned, the plan stressed the strength of the advancing German right wing, which was designed to outmanoeuvre the French. The violation of Belgian neutrality was to provide the space for this plan. Its author, Field-Marshal Alfred von Schlieffen, a veteran of the Austro-Prussian and Franco-Prussian wars, was Chief of the General Staff in 1891–1906:[7] he had to plan for a much greater problem than had faced Prussia in 1866 and 1870–71, namely war on two fronts. The prestige of the German army and the consequent Austrian determination to emulate German strategy were to lead to disastrous Austrian offensives against Russia and Serbia in 1914.[8]

The offensive also held sway in Germany's likely opponent, France. Mistaken analysis of the failure of 1870, by officers such as Colonel François-Jules-Louis Loyzeau de Grandmaison, Director of Military Operations 1908–11, led to a doctrine of *offensive à l'outrance*, the offensive at all costs, which was seen as the best way to express and sustain the nation's martial fervour, a concept that was important in the culture of the period.[9] Furthermore, attacking appeared to be the best way to encourage and hold the enthusiasm of the troops, and thus to ensure superior morale to that of the defenders. This was an important element in thought about war in the period. Better morale appeared valuable tactically, as a means to offset the killing character of defensive firepower, but also operationally, providing a crucial capability gap between similarly armed forces. The emphasis on morale is an instructive reminder of the danger of considering military developments largely in terms of improved technology. Tactically, the stress on the offensive was linked not only to the *élan* and morale of the attacker but also to a belief in the value of the bayonet. There was also a belief strong in French colonial military thought wherein native resistance was to be destroyed by French bravado.

For the French, the "spirit of the offensive" was seen as a necessary counter to German numerical superiority. It also seemed the only way to regain Alsace-Lorraine, which had been ceded to Germany in 1871, and the loss of which was keenly felt. Thus, political objectives played a major role in framing strategy and tactics. They were to lead to heavy losses and failure in 1914.[10] At the same time, taking the offensive seemed the only way to deny the Germans the initiative. War Plan XVII, which was followed by the French when World War One broke out, was a plan for attack.

It would be mistaken to ignore the wider cultural context that affected both military planning and the willingness of the average male citizen to acquiesce in the burdens of military spending and, in Continental Europe, of peacetime conscription. The Social Darwinism of the late nineteenth century, with its emphasis on natural competitiveness, encouraged interest in aggressive military planning, and this was supported, both with resources and psychologically, by the tremendous demographic expansion of the period and by the major increase in industrial capacity.

Academics, scientists, artists, clerics and intellectuals also played a major role in formulating rationales and objectives for expansion and conflict. War was seen as a glorious means to renew a people's energies and escape cultural and moral decadence. Most intellectuals were convinced nationalists: internationalism was of only limited appeal. A concept of triumphant will linked the Romanticism that was culturally important to international relations. Millenarian theology and providentialism also both contributed to a sense of the rightness of conflict. Educated elites came to believe in the moral value of war. This was a "rationality" centred on themes of sacrifice and ideas of vitalism. Contributing to the same end, industrialists pressed the economic and social utility of weapons programmes. Such ideas proved more influential than those that contributed to the attempt to decree accepted laws of war, although the latter led to a series of international congresses.

The absence of major wars contributed to the popularity of the idea of war, and the acceptability of military service: it was a non-risk rite of passage, at a time when other male rites of passage had been discredited. Bright uniforms symbolized the appeal of military service.

With the offensive in vogue, Clausewitz's chapter on defensive warfare (the longest in *On War*) was largely ignored; some translations omitted it altogether. To sustain the offensive and achieve victory in the face of ever more lethal technology on the battlefield, strategists and tacticians called for ever larger armies and emphasized the value of conscription and the substantial reserve forces that universal military training permitted: having fulfilled their allocated period of permanent military service, conscripts moved into the reserves, where their military effectiveness was maintained by annual manoeuvres.

Pressure for larger armies led to a concern about population size and birth rates, especially in France, where they were lower in the late nineteenth century than in Germany. An alliance with the vast Russian army, over a million strong in 1900, excluding reservists, came to appear crucial to French politicians; the two powers were allied from 1894. The Russian army was far larger than that of Germany, and, once the Russians started investing in enhanced effectiveness, it became a more serious threat. The net effect of conscription was the availability of millions of men trained for war. The British tradition of volunteer service ensured that their military thinkers faced the dilemma of how to fight a future mass-army war with a small professional army and without conscription.

At the same time, there was a major increase in the battlefield and general capability of Western militaries. This owed much to the size and flexibility of the industrial base of the major powers, although industrialization itself accentuated stresses in society, creating a situation in which war appeared to governments as a viable solution to domestic crisis. Thanks to the nature of industrial culture, and the availability of organizational expertise, investment capital and trained labour, it was possible to translate novel concepts rapidly into new or improved weapons. Due to mass production, it was also possible to provide such weapons in large quantities. Germany was thus able to double the complement of field guns to 144 per corps between 1866 and 1905. The British War Office report on developments in 1910 noted: "The general tendency is still to increase the artillery and new guns are being acquired in almost every country".[11] They benefited from better sights, new propellants and fuses, steel-coated projectiles, high-explosive fillers, and new recoil systems whereby the gun tube recoiled in a slide against springs that returned it to its original position.

Probably the best of these was the French 75 mm rapid-firing field gun that was introduced by the firm Schneider-Creusot in 1893. Although light, the gun was stable as a result of compressed air counteracting energy. This ensured accuracy as well as rapid deployment, and the combination helped to make the open battleground dangerous for opposing infantry. The impact of this gun was increased by foreign sales. It could fire 20 shells a minute up to six miles and was highly mobile.

More generally, guns became more powerful. They were necessary to silence opposing artillery and to kill opposing infantry, and gave rise to the World War One maxim "artillery conquers, infantry occupies". The logistical strain created by such artillery was immense, especially in offensive operations.

Aside from moving the guns themselves, it was also necessary to provide very large quantities of ammunition to feed the favoured prolonged barrages before a big attack. As guns and ammunition were heavy and could best be moved in the campaign zone on paved roads, logistical problems increased, as did the need to match plans to existing means of communication. Advance by paved road became an adjunct to mobilizing by railway.

Russia was determined to build up its artillery. In 1901 British Intelligence reported "Russia has lost no time in realising that infantry is unlikely to be employed in the future without its own proportion of guns always with it". The Russians obtained guns both from foreign suppliers and from domestic production. Indeed, in 1900, the Russians ordered 1,000 quick-firing field guns from the Putilov iron works, which was producing artillery as good as that from elsewhere in Europe.[12] Resources for such expenditure came from economic growth and French loans. They permitted very high rates of peacetime expenditure on military preparations. In 1907–13, Russia spent heavily on both army and navy, defence spending increasing from 608.1 million roubles in 1908 to 959.6 million in 1913, a rise well above inflation. The percentage of Russian government expenditure on defence rose from 23.2 per cent in 1907 to 28.3 per cent in 1913.[13]

Growing Russian strength led to pressure in Germany for a pre-emptive war. Heavy Russian spending on the military, combined with the development of its strategic railroad network, was one reason why the young Count Helmuth von Moltke, Chief of the General Staff in 1906–14, pressed for war in 1913–14; he feared that Germany might not be able to win a war with Russia later.[14] More generally, budgetary competition between states played a major role in military expenditure,[15] as states scrutinized the spending plans of rivals.

The availability of improved weaponry owed much to better steel production methods, particularly the Bessemer steel converter and the Gilchrist–Thomas basic steel process, thanks to which steel output rose dramatically from the 1870s. Earlier methods of casting guns became obsolete, as they could not ensure uniformly cast guns. Alfred Krupp of Essen had developed an important expertise in producing breech-loading steel guns.[16]

There were also continued design improvements in infantry firepower, including, in the 1880s, the adoption of smokeless powder, which burned more efficiently and permitted an increase in the range and muzzle velocity of bullets. There was also the development of an efficient system of magazine feed, permitting reliable repeating rifles, such as the French Lebel (1886) and the German Mauser (1889), which used a spring action to feed cartridges into the breech at a rapid rate. Smokeless powder also ensured that the field of vision was not blocked and that it was harder for opponents to discern the source of fire. After the Boer War, there was also renewed interest in camouflage. The development of the spitzer, or boat-tail bullet, provided a smaller, more aerodynamically stable, and longer-range bullet.

The machine gun, an automatic repeating weapon, was a metaphor of the application of industry to war. The most famous, the Maxim gun, patented by Hiram Maxim in 1883, used recoil energy, and was both reliable and readily transportable. It was water cooled and fully automatic. Early models of the gun readily broke and tended to be fouled by the black powder used as a propellant, so Maxim patented an improved gunpowder.[17] Refinements in the manufacture of cartridges meanwhile reduced jamming. The Vickers–Maxim machine gun, adopted by the British army in 1912, fired 250 rounds per minute: the combined fire of many riflemen. Although it was to be famous in World War One as a defensive weapon, the machine gun was seen before the war as a useful tool for attack, especially by clearing ground of defenders (for this, the development of the sub-machine gun was vital). The rate of fire of this and other weapons, however, ensured that supply needs for ammunition rose, and this in turn led to financial and logistical pressure for a rapid victory.

Enhanced firepower was an obvious threat to cavalry, and already in 1866 and 1870, attacks by Austrian and French heavy cavalry had been bloodily repelled by Prussian infantry and cannon. Thereafter, cavalry came to play a smaller role in armies and military planning, but there was much resistance to this process. This reflected the continued role of traditional notions about military activity, the ongoing part played by cavalry in colonial wars, and the legitimate search for strategic mobility in the event of a European conflict.

Improved firepower was also a threat to fortifications. There had been much investment on defensive positions in the middle decades of the nineteenth century. In the 1850s, the British had constructed forts along the Channel coast, especially near Portsmouth, for protection in the event of French invasion. After 1871, the French created an extensive defensive belt to prevent further German advances from the east in the event of another war: the French had less space to trade than hitherto. Military bases, such as Belfort and Verdun, were surrounded with fortified positions. Russia spent heavily on fortresses and fortress artillery, too heavily, as the field army was short of artillery as a result. The Dutch built forts along the New Holland Waterline, a system of inundations designed to limit the impact of any German invasion.

However, the effectiveness of traditional fortifications was affected by advances in artillery, especially the development of rifled steel breech-loaders, of improved pneumatic recoil mechanisms that obviated the need for re-siting, and of delayed action fuses.[18] As so often in military history, an enhanced capacity for the offensive led to improvements in the defensive, in this case changes in fortification design and construction techniques, including lower profiles for the batteries and the use of steel and reinforced concrete. Much was spent on fortifications in the years before World War One, including by Belgium, France, Germany, Austria and Russia. They were designed both to resist offensives, and to support them, by securing supplies and communications and by freeing troops for operations. In some respects this looked forward to the use of trenches in World War One; they were defensive systems that fused the characteristics of fortifications and field entrenchments.

Initially, only a small number of European thinkers anticipated the horrific casualties that developments in military methods and the expansion of army size were likely to produce in any future major war. The Marxist Friedrich Engels argued that the American Civil War (1861–65) indicated the likely destructiveness of future intra-European conflict, and he thought that this would undermine existing state and class hegemonies and make revolution possible. In his *War of the Future in its Technical, Economic and Political Aspects* (1897), part of which was published in English as *Is War Now Impossible?* (1899), the Polish financier Ivan (or Jean de) Bloch suggested that the combination of modern military technology and industrial strength had made great power European warfare too destructive to be feasible, and that, if it occurred, it would resemble a giant siege, and would be won when one of the combatants succumbed to famine and revolution. Bloch argued that the stalemate on the battlefield that came from defensive firepower would translate into collapse on the home front. The elder Moltke himself had become increasingly sceptical about the potential of the strategic offensive after 1871, and, presciently, was fearful that any major war would be a long one.[19]

However, fears about the consequent impact on casualty figures and military morale, and emphasis on the dangers of battlefield stalemate and of breakdown on the home front only encouraged an emphasis on preventing the stalemate by winning the initial offensive. The short war in 1914 "was a necessity".[20]

Military commentators could search for clues on the future of war both in recent and in current conflicts. The American Civil War had provided indications of the potency of defensive firepower, but the broader relevance of trench warfare at Petersburg in Virginia in the winter of 1864–65 became apparent only 50 years later. The impact of the American Civil War on European military thought was negligible on the Continent, where the leaders of professional armies and the officer corps saw no lessons in a war fought by mass militia armies.

Furthermore, despite the experience of the Civil War, the American army itself continued to emphasize the offensive. Field service against Native Americans provided education neither in the manner in which firearms became more deadly in the last third of the century, nor in the problems of handling large numbers of troops. Instead, there was in American military thought an emphasis on morale and spiritual qualities, rather than on massive firepower support or the indirect approach, as the means to get across the killing zone created by opposing firepower.

Nevertheless, it would be misleading to suggest that all commentators came to this view. Colonel Waters, a British observer at the Russo-Japanese War, wrote, judging by what I have seen of the German army in peace and of the Russian army in war time, neither the one nor the other puts into practice the true theory underlying magazine rifles, namely, that their power of fire, both in attack and defence, enables fewer men to do greater execution than a large number can do with the single-loader, and tactics can be affected in consequence.[21]

Actually, the Germans were aware of the challenge of defensive firepower. This led them to emphasize infantry–artillery coordination and advancing in dispersed formations that coalesced for a final assault. As a consequence, when the autumn manoeuvres of the Saxon army were reviewed in 1909, the thickness of the firing lines was severely criticized.[22] Furthermore, it was observed that defensive firepower could be challenged by field artillery operating in support of the attacking force. A British observer at the German manoeuvres in September 1897 was impressed by the methodical character of German operational art, and by the high morale of the troops, but was less certain about the likely impact of German tactics:

[T]he complete system of organization which exists throughout the German army . . . Drenched to the skin with rain, deep in mud as were the infantry, no sign of discomfort was noticed, nor word of grumbling heard. All ranks seemed to take the heavy rain and hard work as a matter of course, and as a natural consequence of the day's proceedings . . . on many occasions it was observed that companies were kept in company columns at effective artillery and even at decisive infantry ranges. The idea is consistently observed that everything should be sacrificed, even human life, to a steady cohesive discipline upon the field of battle.

The most extensive latitude is left to individual commanders as to when or how the final rush, or the prepared assault, for the enemy's position, is to take place . . . The only solution of the problem of attack, which appears to be permissible is "success" . . . Each man seemed to know his place and what was expected of him . . . The firing was entirely "independent" and hardly a volley was heard . . . The steady, almost machine-like discipline insisted upon with the reserve was perhaps the most striking feature. No effort is spared by means of mechanical drill and precision to prevent confusion, to minimize skulking, and to make the timid firm in the critical moments of an assault. The individual initiative of all, including company commanders, is evidently fostered and encouraged, with the result that an attacking line when opposed resolves itself, as a rule, into a succession of minor tentative assaults, rarely barely a brigade . . . more often by a battalion, and still more often by a company. The actual formation adopted is left to the idea and caprice of the individual commanders, and the actual assault is carried out as circumstances seem to indicate. It is open to question whether such a system of individual, spasmodic, and unsupported effort is sound against anything but a weak and indifferently disciplined enemy . . . the frequent weak attacks in close formations gave the impression that a terrible loss of life must be entailed . . . the reserves were brought up, and there was something peculiarly impressive in the slow, methodical, onward movement of a mass of men thus formed, resistless as a rising tide! It was, doubtless, very effective in appearance, and against irresolute, half-trained troops should prove very demoralizing, but against steady infantry in line, it seemed a question if such a series of spasmodic efforts in attack could possibly succeed.[23]

As militaries grew in size and soldiers were drawn, as in Germany, from industrializing societies undergoing rapid change, there was a heavy emphasis on discipline within armies. A stress on planning encouraged this emphasis. Captain Holland, a British observer at the German manoeuvres of 1898, commented on "a system by which losses of smaller units are ignored, provided the main object is gained, the great aim being to train the soldier to carry out his orders regardless of consequences". Two years earlier, Captain Birkbeck had commented: "It is impossible not to be deeply impressed by the smoothness and ease with which the German military machine works . . . a well-trained and thoroughly practical staff . . . The German army corps is no collection of units hurriedly collected for a time".[24]

Far from being inflexible, these disciplined military systems were responsive to the pace of technological advance, and it was relatively easy to introduce innovations. In 1900, foreign military observers noted that volley firing was being abandoned in favour of individual fire. In addition, Belgian manoeuvres displayed the defensive strength of trenches and the lessons being learned from the Boer War then being waged.[25] The state of discipline was seen as a measure of morale, and the two combined were presented as crucial to effectiveness. Thus, weaponry alone did not suffice, and, indeed, morale was seen as more important. Contemporary attitudes were captured in a disparaging British report on Italian army manoeuvres in 1894: "the evil traits of character generated by despotism and superstition. There is no wholesome spirit of patriotism and religious morality in the country – no sense of duty – nor any adequate infusion of the military virtues which are indispensable to form a solid army".[26] Such stereotyping was important in the perception of military capability.

The major wars of the years 1882–1913 fought between "Western" armies, at least in the sense of forces armed with modern weaponry, were not waged in Europe itself, with the exception of the peripheral Balkans. As later with the Cold War, there was no clash between the major powers. Furthermore, unlike during the Cold War, wars were not closely linked to great power rivalry.

Nevertheless, they were followed carefully by observers from these powers keen to establish if these conflicts offered any relevant lessons. The four major wars were all international conflicts; there was no major civil war, either social or secessionist in character. They were the Spanish–American War of 1898, the Second Boer War of 1899–1902, the Russo-Japanese War of 1904–1905, and the Balkan wars of 1912–13.

## The Spanish–American War, 1898

This was a consequence of the rise of American assertiveness and economic and naval power. In 1898, the concept of an American "manifest destiny" and bellicose political pressures within the USA helped lead to a war with Spain. Neither the Spanish fleet nor the army was in good shape. The army had been intensely politicized for decades, and this affected both the quality and the quantity of command: there were far too many officers. The financial implications, combined with the limited extent of Spanish industrial development and the determination to restrict expenditure, ensured that the Spanish army lacked training. It was also inexperienced. Aside from the absence of a European war involving Spain to reveal deficiencies, there had also been a lack of foreign conflict.

Nevertheless, the Americans also lacked appropriate experience. Although their navy was ready for war, with new ships and well-trained crews, the army was small and untrained for such operations. Furthermore, the climate and terrain of Cuba created problems for the Americans. Fortunately for them, the Spaniards fought badly at the operational level, despite a major man-power advantage. They failed to dispute the American landing in late June, retired into a poor defensive perimeter round Santiago and did not attack American communications. The Spaniards were more successful tactically than operationally, and did not collapse when Santiago was attacked. However, crucial positions were lost to frontal attack on 1 July and Santiago surrendered on 17 July.

The fighting indicated the importance of entrenchments and the firepower provided by magazine rifles firing steel-jacket, high-velocity, smokeless bullets. The German Mauser rifle used by the Spaniards proved particularly effective, and their artillery was also superior as a result of the use of smokeless powder, which kept their position secret. The American regulars had the Krag–Jorgensen rifle, but the volunteers were armed with the old, black-powder, traditional Springfield. The war was a more obvious triumph for the newly developed and powerful American fleet than for the army.

This war did not encourage foreign respect for the American army, which had been victorious but had not fought particularly well. Despite their victory, the Americans were not prepared for a major war.[27] The impact of their army

33

over the following century was not anticipated by them or by the rest of the world. Equally, the lessons of the possible importance of guerrilla warfare were not heeded. The Cuban insurgents resisting Spain from 1895 had decided that it was best to harass Spanish forces through guerrilla attacks, and to avoid holding territory that would expose them to conventional attack. They had shaken Spanish rule, and forced an offer of full autonomy. Earlier, the deficiencies of the Spanish military had been exacerbated by disease, hostile weather, and rainy seasons.[28] In 1900–1902, the Americans in turn met grave difficulties in a guerrilla war mounted by Filipino nationalists.

## The Second Boer War, 1899–1902

This took place in a greater blaze of foreign attention, in large part because of interest in the capability of the leading world empire against a Western-style opponent. Nationalism had developed in the Afrikaner republics of Transvaal and Orange Free State, leading them to oppose Britain's attempts to dominate both them and southern Africa. In 1899, the two republics declared war on Britain. The war is often seen as a classic example of capitalist-driven empire-building. However, many capitalists with interests in the region concerned themselves with politics and war only when aggressive business methods did not meet all their needs. British ministers were greatly influenced by the fear that gold and diamond discoveries would enhance Boer power and ensure that the Boers would work with Britain's imperial rivals, especially the Germans in South-West Africa, and threaten its strategic interests at the Cape. Although the Boer War might never have happened had it not been for the gold and diamonds upsetting the economic balance of power, it is necessary to be cautious before ascribing too much to the capitalists: those in business were less important than government figures concerned about power and prestige rather than profits. Alfred Milner, the aggressive Governor of Cape Colony from 1897 to 1901, was essentially driven by political considerations and his own ambition. Ministers in London thought the Boers were bluffing and would not put up much of a fight if war followed; while the failure of the British to send significant reinforcements persuaded the Boers to think it was the British who were bluffing.

The British had already experienced the skill of defensive Boer firepower at the battle of Majuba Hill of 1881 in the First Boer War, which had led them to acknowledge Boer independence. The second war proved more difficult than had been anticipated because the Boers took the initiative and were also more tactically adept. Superior Boer marksmanship combined with smoke-less, long-range Mauser magazine rifles, and the effective use of the strategic offensive with the successful employment of the tactical defensive, inflicted heavy casualties. In December 1899, the British were defeated at Stormberg,

Magersfontein and Colenso, and their positions at Kimberley, Ladysmith and Mafeking were besieged, although these sieges led to a loss of Boer momentum that threw away the initiative gained by beginning the conflict; the following month, the British were defeated at Spion Kop. British fighting methods proved inadequate. For example, artillery was still sited in the open, as it was thought this was the best way to get range. Such a deployment ignored the vastly improved rifles available to the Boer infantry, and the gunners were shot down. Furthermore, the Boer use of trenches, as at Magersfontein, limited the impact of artillery.

Boer firepower forced a rethink in tactics, prefiguring the process that was to occur during World War One, although then the situation was complicated by the need to train vastly larger numbers of new recruits. In 1900–1902, the British developed an appropriate use of cover, creeping barrages of continuous artillery fire, and infantry advances in rushes, coordinated with the artillery.

More effective generalship under Lord Roberts and his Chief of Staff, and later successor, Horatio Kitchener, changed the situation in 1900, and the British were able to seize and maintain the initiative. The Boer field army proved less effective than their commandos, and Piet Cronje was trapped and forced to surrender at Paardenberg on 27 February 1900. Roberts pushed on to capture Bloemfontein (13 March), Johannesburg (31 May), and Pretoria (5 June), and to overrun the Transvaal, an illustration of the possibility of a rapid advance in the colonial campaigning of the period. Roberts's victories hit Boer morale and exacerbated divisions within the Boer camp. Aside from tensions between the Orange Free State and Transvaal, there were political, social and religious rifts. These were more important than is suggested in the usual military narrative of the conflict.

The British were also helped by their readiness to allocate about £200 million to the war and to deploy 400,000 troops, which was a testimony to the strength of their economic and imperial systems, although the dispatch of so much of the regular army left it below normal strength in the British Isles. This gave rise to concern and to pressure for the introduction of conscription. Britain's dominions, especially Australia, Canada and New Zealand, also sent troops.

Britain's unchallenged control of the South African ports also allowed it to bring its strength to bear and ensured that foreign intervention was not possible; the Boers lacked the coastline and naval power that made the USA and Japan such formidable opponents respectively to Spain and Russia. The navy also provided more direct support in the shape of naval artillery mounted on wheels and used to help the British army. In addition, the railways that ran inland from the ports facilitated the easy deployment of the military resources brought into southern Africa, an obvious contrast with British campaigning in North America during the War of American Independence. However, it proved necessary to supplement the railways with less cumbersome wagon trains.

Once the Transvaal had been overrun in the summer of 1900, Boer forces concentrated on dispersed operations in which their mounted infantry challenged British control. In response, the now vastly more numerous British adopted counter-insurgency practices used later in the century in Malaya and Vietnam. They relied on composite columns and on an extensive system of fortifications: a blockhouse system of barbed-wire fences and small positions. In addition, they employed scorched earth policies and reprisals. Thus, in April 1901, Malcolm Riall recorded, "H Company go off to burn and destroy a farm close by as a carabinier has been shot by a Boer sniping from there".[29] To deprive the guerrillas of civilian support, the British ravaged their farms and moved their families into what the British termed concentration camps: the Spaniards had used the same tactics in Cuba. These brutal policies had a certain impact, and, after a final and decisive drive against the Boers in the Western Transvaal in April 1902, led them to capitulate by the Treaty of Vereeniging – a bitter surrender.

All the Continental armies sent observers but, afterwards, there was considerable disagreement over whether to consider it just another colonial war (therefore, in contemporary eyes, not relevant to possible war in Europe), or as a war between two opponents of European stock, and thus with lessons to teach. German and Austrian commentators used the Darwinian language in vogue in reference to the "racial characteristics" of the Boers, praising them as warriors while at the same time underscoring their uniqueness as opponents. Most Continental military experts saw little in the conflict that was relevant to European warfare. Many analysts correctly observed that factors such as the long-range marksmanship of the Boers and their tenacious guerrilla warfare of 1900–1902 were not likely to be duplicated in clashes between mass armies on the Continent. The war played an important role in the debate over the respective merits of cavalry and mounted infantry, but its lessons were highly ambiguous in this as in other respects.

Nevertheless, the war had important implications for World War One, including the use of indirect artillery fire, smokeless powder, long-range rifle fire and camouflage. However, due to their notorious unreliability at the time, machine guns did not dominate the Boer War battlefield.[30] More generally, there was a technological leap forwards between the Boer War and World War One, like that from the early string-tied aeroplanes of the 1900s, to the nippy, useful planes of 1914–18.

## The Russo-Japanese War, 1904–1905

A far larger conflict broke out in 1904. Competing Russian and Japanese interests in the Far East interacted with domestic pressures, including the view in some Russian governmental circles that victory would enhance the internal strength of the government, and a foolish unwillingness to accept Japanese strength, interests and determination. The Russian government did not seem to have been looking for a war, but it failed to see that serious dialogue with Japan was necessary if it was to be avoided. The Tsar and his advisers did not think the "yellow devils" would dare to fight, and assumed that if there was a war, then Russia would begin it. In fact, a pre-emptive strike was necessary if Japan was to secure the crucial naval advantage.

Russian behaviour and arrogance did much to create ultimate unity in Tokyo in 1904. The "moderates" agreed that Japan had to fight while it enjoyed a temporary advantage over the potentially stronger Russians; and this was to be repeated (against the USA) in 1941 in the preparations for Pearl Harbor. The Russians paid the price for treating the Japanese as a lesser people. The Japanese, however, had gained great confidence in their military system as a result of their victory over China in 1894–95.

In one respect, the war was a triumph for Europeanization in the form of Western military organization. The Japanese won by employing European military systems and technology more effectively than the Russians; their army was modelled on the German, their navy on the British. Yet the Japanese victory also came as a shock, in part because of Western racialist assumptions.

The fighting featured many elements that were also to be seen in World War One, including trench warfare with barbed wire and machine guns, indirect artillery fire, artillery firing from concealed positions, a conflict that did not cease at nightfall and a war waged with continuous front lines. Advocates of the offensive argued that the Russians stood on the defensive and lost, while the Japanese took the initiative, launched frontal assaults on entrenched forces strengthened by machine guns and quick-firing artillery, as at Port Arthur and Mukden in 1905, and prevailed, despite horrific casualties. Observers came away noting that frontal assaults were still feasible, and the bayonet still relevant, the latest technology notwithstanding.

As was often the case, the situation was more complex. For example, in the battle of Liaoyang (25 August–3 September 1904), the Russians were attacked by a larger force on three occasions and repulsed them on each, but the commander, Aleksei Kuropatkin, believed himself defeated and retreated. He came closer to success than is sometimes appreciated, not least at Sandepu (26–7 January 1905). Moreover, if he had been able to fight as he had wanted, luring the Japanese deeper into Manchuria, while bringing to bear the overwhelming Russian superiority in numbers, they would have been defeated. The Japanese had the advantage of fighting close to home.

Colonel Waters, a member of the British Military Mission with the Russian army in Manchuria, thought the Russian reliance on close-order formations and shock attack foolish, and noted that firepower could beat off the bayonet, but he also commented that the manpower available affected tactical best practice:

Frontal attacks were a very conspicuous feature of both sides during the late campaign in Manchuria. In some instances they could have been advantageously omitted, and flank attacks made in their stead, but when armies, each numbering say a couple of hundred thousand combatants, cover the whole of the ground available for a battlefield, as on the Shaho, frontal attacks cannot be avoided.[31]

## Drawing conclusions

Most commentators overlooked the extent to which land battles had not been decisive, but had, instead, only caused the Russians to fall back, and ignored the extent to which the conflict so strained Japan that it could not afford, economically or militarily, to pursue the Russians deeper into Manchuria.[32] The Russian retreat into Manchuria (and their army's escape from Japanese encirclement at Mukden) strained Japanese supply lines and forced them to the peace table. Japanese victory owed much to political weakness in St Petersburg. The government had a revolution to confront in 1905, a revolution in part fostered by Japanese military intelligence. The distance of Manchuria from the centres of Russian power also did not help. Japanese success ensured that the tactical superiority of the defence revealed in the American Civil War was not seen as the problem the First World War was to show it to be. Given contemporary racist attitudes, European experts concluded that the infantry of the superior races of Europe would be capable of at least similar deeds, albeit at heavy cost.

From 1905, army leaders fully expected to suffer one-third casualties in a European war.[33] This expectation dramatically altered thinking on manpower needs and provided the impetus for programmes to expand army size. In the event of war between Britain and Russia, Waters was

> certain that we should only defeat Russia by means of a vigorous offensive, *entailing heavy casualties*, when once the opposing forces are within reach of each other, and since battles will probably last for days, both quality and numbers must be readily available, in order that Russia may acknowledge defeat, and cease to organise her enormous potential resources.[34]

The need for greater manpower troubled informed British commentators. In 1905, H. A. Gwynne of the *Evening Standard* was also fearful of war with Russia over the Indian frontier: "in six months of a war we should exhaust the regular army, and we should be absolutely obligated to fall back on the people". In order to be able to do so, Gwynne felt that it was necessary to train volunteers and that the way to do so was to talk of the threat of invasion.[35] Pressure for more men across Europe interacted with an increase in armaments[36] to produce a growth in military preparedness. In Russia, defeat at the hands of Japan was followed by a period of reform, including the establishment of a Council for State Defence in 1905, a major increase in military expenditure, and the introduction of very modern artillery.

However, the large numbers of troops (and officers) in European armies created problems of effective management and use. This was true of soldiers and also of officers. Enhanced preparedness was a matter not only of more men and material, but also of improved organizational means and systems that permitted their integration and increased their effectiveness. These included railways, steamships, lorries, telegraph lines, telephones and, eventually, radio. They were incorporated into war plans and military manoeuvres. However, the machinization of the European military should not be exaggerated. The lack of motor transport greatly limited mobility once troops had detrained behind the front. When World War One broke out, there was an average of only one machine gun per thousand troops. In part, this reflected the assumption that a future conflict would be mobile and that heavy machine guns would be an encumbrance as their value was in the defence, not the offence. Despite heavy expenditure, there were important equipment deficiencies in the Russian army, in part, it has been argued, because a successful combination of government and industry to foster effective rearmament had not been achieved. The Serbs in part relied for their communications on 192 homing pigeons.[37]

## The Balkan Wars, 1912–13

Immediately before World War One, European observers had an opportunity to observe a conflict nearer home. The First Balkan War (1912–13) arose from the ethnic and territorial rivalries of a Balkan world where violence was the principal method of pursuing disputes. The long-standing drive to partition Turkish possessions in the Balkans led Bulgaria, Greece, Montenegro and Serbia to attack. The Turks were beaten, being especially heavily defeated by the Bulgarians at Kirkkilese/Lozengrad (22–4 October 1912) and Lyule Burgas (29 October–2 November). In these battles, the Bulgarians benefited from taking the initiative and from maintaining tactical fluidity. This was seen in particular in successful flanking operations. The Bulgarians also benefited from good leadership, disciplined infantry with strong morale, who attacked boldly, making skilled use of bayonets, and effective artillery that inflicted heavy losses. These were the most intense battles of the two Balkan wars, and they showed how heavy fighting could lead to a decisive result.

Victory in battle gave the Bulgarians control of most of Thrace, although they, in turn, were to be hit by logistical problems and cholera. Furthermore, they failed to exploit their successes rapidly, and, by the time the Bulgarians had advanced towards Constantinople, the Turks had improved a line of fortifications and natural features at Chataldzha. These were assaulted on 17 November 1912, but the Bulgarian artillery had failed to destroy its Turkish counterpart, and the latter blunted the Bulgarian infantry assault. The power of entrenched positions supported by artillery when neither had been suppressed by superior offensive gunfire had been abundantly shown, well before it was to be displayed on an even greater scale on the Western Front in 1915, and by the Turks that year at Gallipoli. Defeat at Chataldzha persuaded the Bulgarian General Staff not to launch an assault on Adrianople.

Further west, against far weaker resistance, the Greeks (who had been defeated by the Turks in 1897) had gained entry to Macedonia by successfully storming Turkish positions in frontal attacks at the Sarantaporos Pass on 22 October 1912. At Kumanovo, on 23–4 October, superior artillery helped give victory to the Serb frontal attacks and the latter were also effective at Prilep on 5 November and Bitola on 16–18 November. Under the Treaty of London of 30 May 1913, the Turks lost most of their European empire.

The victors fell out, and, in the Second Balkan War (1913), Bulgaria fought the others, as well as Romania and a revived Turkey. The Bulgarians achieved defensive victories against the Greeks and the Serbs, but a Romanian crossing of the Danube on the night of 14–15 July, advance to near Sofia, and link-up with the Serbs on 25 July, led Bulgaria to settle. Bulgaria lost important recent gains, including Adrianople/Edirne, which had been regained by the Turks in July.

In some respects, these conflicts were the first blows of World War One, at least in the Balkans. Important signs of what was to come included the unsuccessful Bulgarian attacks on the entrenched Turkish positions at Chataldzha, in which Turkish artillery and infantry inflicted considerable casualties. In addition, aeroplanes were used by all participants, except for Montenegro, mainly for reconnaissance, although cities were also bombed.

Nevertheless, the Balkans wars did not challenge contemporary military assumptions. Due to difficulties in obtaining reliable information, to a stress on strategy rather than tactics, and to a focus on success rather than casualties, observers saw the wars as confirming their faith in the offensive, more specifically in massed infantry assaults. This lesson was in particular taken from the Bulgarian victories of 1912, which appeared to show the effectiveness of high morale and of infantry charging in to the attack. There was a general failure to note the degree to which the effectiveness of rapid-firing artillery and machine guns might blunt infantry attacks.[38] It is too easy to close with the observation that observers were rapidly to be proved wrong. Instead, it is necessary to turn to the problems of waging successful war between great powers.

CHAPTER THREE

# *World War One, 1914–18*

The popular image of World War One – of total futility and mindless slaughter – is so powerful and yet so limited that it can claim to be the most misunderstood major conflict in history. This image is important to subsequent Western military history, as it reflects a powerful disenchantment with war understood both as a pursuit of state interest and as fighting.[1] However, there is a need to distinguish between the horrors of suffering and loss, and the degree to which the conflict was not a mindless slaughter.

The origins of the war have inspired a vast historiography. For our purposes, it is important to note that war was seen by contemporaries as a way to achieve goals, but that anxiety as much as opportunity conditioned these goals. This was true of the Germans, who were concerned about growing Russian military preparedness, especially the connection of a strategic railroad network. The policy of a watchful prudence, resting on support for an international order based on a mutual acceptance of great power interests that the German Chancellor Bismarck had managed in 1871–90 had been replaced under Wilhelm II, from the 1890s, by a more volatile search for German advantage. The Germans were also affected by a belief in the inevitability of war, which encouraged a desire to begin it at the most opportune moment for themselves. Furthermore, Germans could look back with pride and confidence to successful recent wars.

Germany's main ally, Austria-Hungary (Austria for the sake of simplicity), was equally concerned about its apparently worsening strategic and political situation, specifically Russian-supported Serbian assertiveness, and its challenge to the stability of Austria's Balkan possessions, and even the dual monarchy itself. There was growing frustration among the Austrian leaders at not being able to shape their own destiny in external affairs, and Serbia had a great deal to do with that feeling. The same sense of being powerless was also strong in respect to politics within the Austrian empire, not least as a result of the demands of ethnic groups, and war with Serbia seemed the answer to this problem.

The Russians, in contrast, were encouraged by Serb success and ready to see Serbia as a crucial protégé. As recently as the autumn of 1912, international tension over the position of Serbia had led Austria and Russia to deploy troops in mutually threatening positions, but the forces had withdrawn in the spring of 1913.[2]

The Austrian heir, Archduke Franz Ferdinand, and his wife Sophia, were assassinated in Sarajevo on 28 June 1914 by Gavrilo Princip, a Bosnian Serb. The terrorist group was under the control of the Black Hand, a secret Serbian nationalist organization pledged to the overthrow of Habsburg control in South Slav territories. When the news reached Vienna, there was shock and the customary response to an unexpected and dramatic event: a sense that a display of action was needed. This interacted with an already powerful view that war with Serbia was necessary. It provided the excuse to take care of Serbia. A promise of German support reflected the sense that a forceful response was necessary, appropriate and likely to profit Austrian and German interests. As a consequence, Germany found itself in a crisis in which it controlled neither the parameters nor the timetable.

Austrian threats to Serbia in the aftermath of the assassinations posed a challenge to Russian interests and the Russian perception of international relations in eastern Europe. Confident that German backing would deter Russia, the Austrians sought a limited war with Serbia, not agreement with the Serbs, who were willing to make important concessions and prepared for binding arbitration on the points to which they objected. The Serb response to an Austrian ultimatum of 23 July was deemed inadequate, and on 28 July the Austrians began hostilities. The Russians had responded to the ultimatum by beginning military preparations on 26 July. They were confident of French support and believed it necessary to act firmly in order to protect Serbia.

Efforts to contain the crisis, and localize the conflict, were pre-empted by its rapid escalation. On 30 July, rather than abandon Serbia, Russia ordered a general mobilization against both Austria and Germany. This put pressure on Germany, whose war plans called for action against France before Russia could act. The refusal of both Russia and France to halt their preparations led the German government – unwilling to back down and as if trapped by its strategic concepts – to attack. In addition, German leaders opportunistically sought to use the Balkan crisis to change the balance of power in their favour. They were willing to risk a war because no other crisis was as likely to produce a constellation of circumstances guaranteeing them the commitment of their main ally, Austria, and the support of the German public. General mobilization was implemented on 1 August. Despite the international recognition of Belgium's perpetual neutrality in 1839, on 2 August the Germans issued an ultimatum to Brussels demanding acceptance of the passage of their troops. When Belgium refused on 3 August, Germany declared war, in order to permit an advance on Paris from the north-east. This led Britain, one of the guarantors of Belgian neutrality, to enter the war on 4 August, although her major reason was to defend France as a great power and a vital element in the balance of power.[3]

Military considerations, and the army leaderships themselves, played a major role in pushing governments to act; this was because mobilizations were seen as the crucial indicators of intentions and mobilizing faster than one's adversary bestowed a major advantage. The military were especially important in Austria, Germany and Russia. Military pressure in power politics rested on the argument of necessity. War was not seen as an easy challenge but as a danger in which it was vital to act first. It has been argued by some scholars that the European war plans of 1914, with their dynamic interaction of mobilization and deployment, made war "by timetable" difficult to stop once a crisis occurred. This was clearly the case with the German war plan, which required that hostilities rapidly follow mobilization.[4]

It has also been claimed by other scholars that politicians were not trapped, and that their own roles and preferences were important. An awareness of precarious domestic and international situations did not inevitably have to lead to war.[5] Furthermore, alliance did not dictate participation: despite being their ally, Italy did not join Germany and Austria. An awareness of likely risks had helped prevent former crises from leading to war. In 1914, the situation was different because Austria chose to fight, Germany to support her, and Russia to respond.

The political ambitions of the war helped to drive the offensive strategy of the participants. The Austrians sought to capture Belgrade, the capital of Serbia, and the Germans Paris, while the French advanced to regain Alsace-Lorraine, and the Russians advanced to reduce pressure on their allies and to overrun much of Austria and march on Berlin. The Russians made a major mistake in dividing their resources between offensives against Austria and Germany. The goals of the powers altered during the war, but substantially continued to rest on gaining or regaining territory. This helped to sustain the central role of the offensive, both strategically and tactically.

At the outset, everyone failed. The Germans tried to repeat Moltke's strategy of envelopment, and to achieve victory more rapidly than in 1870–71, when they had had no other opponents. Relying on rail transport and forced marches, the Germans advanced on an open front through Belgium into northern France, in a modification of the Schlieffen Plan. This permitted them to avoid the heavily fortified French frontier that bordered Germany, a strategy that had been predicted by commentators.[6]

Belgian fortifications did not stop the German advance, in large part because the Belgians were not supported by a powerful field army. The extensive fortress complexes, offering defence in depth, circling Antwerp, Liège and Namur, that had been designed by Henry Brialmont, the "Belgian Vauban" (1821–1903), all fell after bombardment by 305 mm and 420 mm heavy howitzers. Nevertheless, Liège took far longer to fall than the Germans anticipated – ten days instead of two – and this delayed the provision of an adequate supply system to support the advance. Thereafter, the Belgians were not able to offer adequate resistance; they were greatly outnumbered by the Germans, who had sent 16 corps into Belgium. The Germans dealt with sporadic resistance by harsh reprisals; they shot civilians and burned towns, especially Louvain, with its priceless library, on 26 August, thus demonstrating that they were determined to let nothing prevent a rapid victory.[7] In this, they were helped by the positioning of most of France's army south of Verdun, and by Joffre's decision to counter the invasion of Belgium by an advance into Lorraine; this was designed both to regain territory and to force the Germans to respond.

The advancing French forces were stopped by heavy defensive fire, while other French armies that attacked the Germans in the Ardennes were also beaten off. The German right wing continued its advance, pushing the French back at the Sambre on 21 August and forcing the British Expeditionary Force, which had been added to the French left, to fall back. However, the Germans were slowed down by the need to transport food and ammunition for their formidable numbers. This gave the French an opportunity to regroup, counter-attack in the Battle of the Marne in September, and wreck the German plan. In doing so, they were aided by the opportunities that interior lines and railways provided for moving troops between fronts. The Germans had also weakened their forces on the Western Front by sending two corps to East Prussia to counter the Russian advance; and had mishandled their advance near Paris, leading to a deployment that was vulnerable to counter-attack.

The French seized the opportunity in the Battle of the Marne, but their execution did not match the plan. The Germans were not defeated, but the high command suffered a failure of nerve and the Germans withdrew from the Marne. Both sides then unsuccessfully sought to outflank the other to the north-west in order to avoid the high casualties of frontal attacks. By October 1914, there was a stalemate with the front line stretching to the North Sea.

The manoeuvre stage of the war in the west, with its emphasis on a strategy of envelopment in order to secure total victory, and on a battle of annihilation, was now over. Generals were to try repeatedly to recreate this flexibility, and, in particular, to reopen a war of movement by breaking through their opponents' front line, but this goal was to prove elusive and risked losing large numbers without causing comparable casualties to the enemy. The alternative was a strategy of attrition, which focused primarily on killing large numbers of opponents.

The absence of a speedy military victory and France's membership of a powerful coalition ensured that the Germans could not repeat their rapid triumphs of 1866 and 1870–71. Instead, in contrast to these earlier wars, a front line, the Western Front, soon crystallized, with its stability expressed in trench systems. In the west, this was the basic strategic fact of the war: Germany had seized much of Belgium and part of France and, without any plan to supersede that of Schlieffen, had dug in to protect its gains. This put the Western Allies, principally Britain and France, under the necessity to mount offensives; another was provided by the wish to reduce German pressure on Russia and to prevent it from being knocked out of the war. Furthermore, there was a conviction that only through mounting an offensive would it be possible for the Allies to gain the initiative and, conversely, deny it to the Germans, and that both gaining the initiative and mounting an offensive were prerequisites for victory.

More specifically, in early 1915 it was widely believed that the stalemate of the winter reflected the exhaustion of men and supplies in the previous autumn's campaigning, and that it would be possible, with fresh men and munitions, to restart a war of manoeuvre. It was not generally appreciated by the Allies, nor among all German generals, that stalemate and trench warfare reflected the nature of war once both sides had committed large numbers and lacked the ability to accomplish a breakthrough. The Allies did not understand the strength of the German defensive positions, and Joffre, the French commander, continued to seek a strategic breakthrough. German lines were carefully sited on favourable terrain, while Allied lines were sited on the Germans. This gravely hampered Allied offensives.

The general course of the war in the West was characterized by offensives, such as those of the British at Neuve-Chapelle and Loos in 1915, the Somme in 1916, and Arras and Passchendaele in 1917, and the French in Artois and Champagne in 1915, and on the Chemin des Dames in the poorly handled Nivelle offensive of 1917. Such a bald list, however, risks the misleading suggestion that offensives were much the same. While there were, indeed, important similarities at the tactical level, there were also differences at this same level; more generally, it should not be assumed that comparable tactical details ensured a similarity in operational and strategic circumstances, planning and political contexts. The contrary was the case. For example, the somewhat *ad hoc* French and British attempts in 1915 to ensure a strategic breakthrough on the Western Front by frontal attacks were followed by a more coherent and ambitious grand plan for a series of concerted assaults by the British, Italians and Russians on all major German fronts in 1916. This was designed to inflict sufficient all-round damage on the German army to permit follow-up attacks by the French, with the goal of achieving the long-awaited breakthrough. This strategy was derailed by the pre-emptive German assault on Verdun in February 1916, while the eventual Anglo-French attack on the Western Front at the Somme in July 1916 was poorly prepared, both in the sense of inadequate supporting firepower and in the definition of attainable objectives.

In 1917, the French tried, not the methodical, heavily prepared offensive underpinned by effective firepower that was to bring the Allies success in 1918, but, instead, another breakthrough approach. This was designed to rest on a sudden assault, initially intended for a weak sector. Ultimately, however, it was launched against well-prepared defences that were forewarned and prepared. The failure of the Nivelle offensive and the mutiny that followed in the French army were succeeded by a more cautious holding strategy, designed to reduce the increasingly controversial casualty level until the Americans arrived.

There were also major German attacks, most particularly at Verdun in 1916, where the aim was focused attrition, and at a number of places along the front in 1918, hoping for breakthroughs before American power kicked in. But they were fewer, however, in part because the Germans in 1915 and 1917 concentrated on offensives against Russia in an attempt to force it out of the war and to reduce their commitment to one front, thus facilitating a killer punch in the west. As a consequence, while the Germans seemed more successful on the Western Front in both 1915 and 1917, that defensive success was only of wider strategic value if it could help them achieve a breakthrough on the Eastern Front; this was because the continuation of the war of attrition, especially thanks to the British blockade, was more debilitating to the Germans than to the Allies.

Aside from their own major offensives, the Germans mounted counter-attacks against Allied advances, designed to win back territory, which cost them dearly, especially on the Somme. Their response to the losses on the Somme was to sack their Commander-in-Chief, Falkenhayn; Ludendorff, his effective successor, built massive defences, the Hindenburg Line, further back on the Somme, behind which the army retired early in 1917.[8]

None of the major attacks on the Western Front, prior to the final Allies' advance in late 1918, achieved their goal. Instead, each led to heavy casualties. This was not only true of forces from the major powers. At Passchendaele, on 12 October 1917, New Zealand suffered the heaviest casualties of any one day in its military history. Although the losses were more spread out, the New Zealanders at Gallipoli in 1915 had more than one in five fatalities, while, at the Somme in 1916, they suffered 40 per cent dead or wounded in 23 days' operations.

General problems dominated offensives on the Western Front. The concentration of large forces in a relatively small area ensured that any defender was able to call on plenty of reserve troops to stem an infantry advance. The effects were exacerbated by the intrinsic defensive strength of trench positions. Trenches protected troops from artillery, enhanced defensive capability and freed troops for offensives elsewhere. The strength of trench positions also owed much to the weaponry available, especially quick-firing artillery and machine guns with their range and rapidity of fire. Barbed wire and concrete fortifications also enhanced defensive positions, while German reserves provided defence in depth.

Furthermore, even if such positions were breached, it was very difficult for an attacker to make substantial gains. Local superiority in numbers could not be translated into decisive success. Although it was possible to break through at least some of the opponents' trench lines, it was difficult to exploit such successes, in part because the attacking army had exhausted itself in the first stage. As yet, aeroplanes and motor vehicles had not been effectively harnessed to help the offensive and exploit a breakthrough.

Cavalry was the only arm of exploitation available, and its potential was limited by the terrain and because of firepower; although Haig, the British commander, was reluctant to accept this and planned for cavalry break-throughs on the Somme and at Passchendaele. Even so, the British cavalry came to place a greater emphasis on firepower.[9] Moreover, once troops had advanced, it was difficult to recognize, reinforce and exploit success: until wireless communications improved in late 1917, communications remained primitive, which stultified control of forward operations. This was part of a more widespread limitation in command structures, specifically poor communication and, often, cohesion between front-line troops and more senior command levels. In addition, the devastating impact of shell fire so damaged the terrain that it was difficult to bring up supporting artillery behind any advance. The impetus of the initial attack could not be sustained unless the enemy had already been substantially weakened, as happened to the Germans in August 1918. Prior to that, at the tactical level, one of the German traditions that paid off in this war was to delegate authority for initiatives and seizing opportunities right down to tactical units.

Although much of the discussion of firepower focuses on machine guns, artillery was the great killer of the war; estimates claim that artillery fire caused up to 70 per cent of battlefield deaths. The relative stability of the trench systems made it worthwhile deploying heavy artillery to bombard them. The guns could be brought up and supplied before the situation changed, as it did in manoeuvre warfare. It was also necessary to provide artillery support in order to batter an enemy's defensive systems. The trenches themselves provided plentiful targets for attritional warfare. The tactical reasons for a stress on artillery were matched by operational factors. Artillery came to be seen as the method to unlock the static front, as a substitute for, or complement to, the offensive spirit of the infantry emphasized in the opening stage of the conflict.

As an example of the weight of firepower available, the Italians, not the strongest or most industrialized of powers, deployed 1,200 guns for their attack on the Austrians in the Third Battle of the Isonzo in October 1915. The British used 2,879 guns – one for every nine yards of front – for their attack near Arras in April 1917. This was far more than those used on the Somme on 1 July 1916, and there the guns were spread too widely to be effective. During the war, the number, strength and precision of artillery improved vastly. The French used successively more heavy guns (and troops) in their three major offensives on the Western Front in 1915, all of which were unsuccessful. On 18 July 1918, the French counter-offensive on the Marne was supported by a creeping barrage, with one heavy shell per 1.27 yards of ground and three field artillery shells per yard.[10] Such a weight of metal was effective: enemy batteries could be destroyed, trench systems heavily battered, and enemy firepower repressed. This was a marked contrast to offensives earlier in the war, as on the first day of the Somme. Artillery was designed to cut casualties among the attacking infantry, although it may, instead, simply have fulfilled its role of increasing casualties among the defenders.

Artillery bombardments inflicted devastating losses, especially at the outset of offensives, before shell fire produced the cover of shell-holes, as when the Germans attacked Verdun, deploying the largest number of guns hitherto used. Maurice Hankey, Secretary to the British Committee of Imperial Defence, suggested, in 1914, that "one of the lessons of the present war appears to be that the German infantry are not very formidable unless supported by their highly efficient artillery".[11] Even day-by-day routine strafing of enemy trenches and behind the lines inflicted a steady flow of casualties. In the British army, 58 per cent of battlefield deaths were from artillery and mortar shells, and slightly less than 39 per cent from machine-gun and rifle bullets. Although the French, who had not envisaged trench warfare, lacked heavy artillery at the outset of the war, their 75 mm field gun could fire over 15 rounds a minute and had a range of 9,000 yards, while German 150 mm field howitzers could fire only five rounds per minute. However, the 75 mm gun was designed for the open field, and its flat trajectory and light calibre were unsuited for the conditions of trench warfare, where heavier high-trajectory pieces were more effective. The lack of heavy artillery greatly hindered the French attacks in 1915, but by 1916 they had rectified the situation. Air-burst shrapnel shells increased the deadly nature of artillery fire, and the spread of steel helmets offered only partial protection. In contrast, in Spain, which did not take part in the war, steel helmets were not issued until 1935, and it was only then that the Spanish army was provided with any significant number of medium and heavy guns.

Artillery was devastating in support of both the attack and the defence, and machine guns devastating in support of the defence. German machine guns, which were concentrated by deployment in companies, rather than dispersed among the infantry, were especially destructive to the French in 1914 and against British troops advancing slowly and in close order on the Somme in 1916. The number of machine guns per unit increased during the war.

In western Europe, where the ratio of troops and firepower to space was high, frontal attacks were costly. This was true from the outset of the war. On 8 September 1914, Hankey wrote about "the absolute disregard of human life by the Germans in the recent fighting. Time after time prepared positions have been captured on land in frontal attacks by sheer weight of numbers notwithstanding terrible losses".[12] These losses in the early stages of the war, like those in the closing campaign, reflected the large number of troops involved, and the advance across the killing zone along an extended front. In intervening campaigns, the front of attack was more compressed, and, as a consequence, total casualties were lower, but not the ratio of casualties to men engaged. For example, the British lost fewer men at Passchendaele than in their more successful 1918 offensive. Casualty rates also owed much to the length of time of battles. "The Somme" and "Verdun", for example, were campaigns rather than battles; otherwise, Verdun has to be seen as the longest field battle in history.

The Americans, who entered the war on the Allied side in 1917, were to discover the cost of frontal attacks when they launched human-wave assaults on the Western Front. The belief of their commander, Pershing, in "open warfare" itself fell victim to German firepower; and by the armistice the Americans had suffered 120,000 casualties.[13] In addition, the Americans initially made slow progress in 1918, and this led Georges Clemenceau, the French premier and war minister, to call for Pershing's dismissal. Nevertheless, especially if supported by adequate artillery, such mass frontal attacks could prove successful. The British gained some initial successes in the 1915 battles, but then lost them as the high command dithered and failed to exploit or at least consolidate them; the same was true at Cambrai in 1917.

More generally, the nature of most contemporary generalship, British, French, German, Austrian, Russian and Italian, with its preconceived ideas, and tactics of slogging forward, did not help. Some generals were slow to adopt different approaches, but, at the same time, it would be wrong to assume that generals and politicians were unable to appreciate their dilemma or unwilling to think about new approaches. In January 1915, Arthur Balfour, a member of the British Committee for Imperial Defence, wrote,

> I agree, and I fear that everybody must agree, that the notion of driving the Germans back from the West of Belgium to the Rhine by successfully assaulting one line of trenches after another seems a very hopeless affair, and unless some means can be found for breaking their line at some critical point, and threatening their communications, I am unable to see how the deadlock in the West is to be brought to any rapid or satisfactory conclusion.[14]

This breakthrough strategy was tried, unsuccessfully, leading to an emphasis on attrition, either in one major struggle, as at Verdun, or, by a number of smaller attacks. The latter was supported by Kitchener in 1916, "not because their [the German] front will have been broken by assault, but because the increasing shortage of men will make it impossible for them to keep up a sufficient reserve to hold their present defensive positions".[15] This was the grand strategy agreed in December 1915, which got derailed when the Germans got their blow in first at Verdun. Both sides believed that attritional conflict would be more successful if they could take the initiative, and thus choose both the terrain and a battlefield where they had amassed artillery.

The German attack on Verdun in 1916 was designed to do little more than inflict heavy casualties on the French and to create what was termed a "blood mill". This reflected the view of Erich von Falkenhayn, Moltke's successor as Chief of the General Staff, who felt that a breakthrough attack was not possible given the nature of warfare on the Western Front and the constraints of troop numbers. Falkenhayn planned to gain the advantages of the strategic offensive and the tactical defensive. He aimed to do this by advancing rapidly on the front of his choice to capture territory, which the French would then suffer heavy losses seeking to regain. He regarded France as weaker than Britain, and hoped the offensive would knock her out of the war.

However, Falkenhayn attacked at Verdun on 21 February on too narrow a front (and initially with too few troops). He also exposed the German troops to artillery fire from the other bank of the Meuse. As the offensive developed, it served no strategic purpose, and cost the Germans heavily: 336,000 compared with 378,000 French casualties. The French were greatly helped by an effective use of artillery, including the creeping barrage employed to support the counter-offensive in October 1916, as well as by an impressive logistical effort, such as the use of motorized supply columns.[16]

The Germans also suffered very heavy casualties on the Somme: about 400,000 men. As a consequence, they did not mount a major attack on the Western Front in 1917, while their 1918 offensives were dependent on troops transferred from Russia. The shortage of men on both sides due to heavy casualties made American entry into the war particularly important. It also led the British government to introduce a Conscription Bill for Ireland in 1918; this only helped alienate Irish opinion.

The British (and, later, the Americans) had a greater problem than the French, Germans or Russians in that they had to transform a small regular army essentially designed for colonial wars into a massive force operating on the Continent.[17] Their commanders lacked the relevant operational experience. At the same time, it would be misleading to exaggerate the effectiveness of the pre-war Continental armies. The German army has recently been harshly dissected:

> Depending on and diluted by reservist officers and enlisted men, it demonstrated neither the tactical finesse nor the operational virtuosity required to diminish at least the objective imbalances among firepower, mobility, and shock that shaped the Great War . . . the emptiness of the army's operational and tactical notebooks as well as its strategic one.[18]

And, of course, unlike the British and French armies, it had had virtually no combat experience since 1871.

The major operations in 1916, Verdun and the Somme, were larger in scale than earlier battles on the Western Front. This reflected the success of the combatants in raising more troops and concentrating resources, especially their ability to sustain large numbers of men in the same area for long periods, a formidable administrative achievement, as well as the pressure on commanders to break through. The resulting combats and combat zones were horrifying. A British Quarter Master Sergeant in the Somme offensive noted in his diary,

> the whole place smells stale with the slaughter which has been going on for the past fourteen days – the smell of the dead and lachrymatory gas. The place is a very Hell with the whistling and crashing of shells, bursting shrapnel and the rattle of machine-guns. The woods we had taken had not yet been cleared and there were pockets of Germans with machine-guns still holding out and doing some damage. A sergeant sinks to the ground beside me with a bullet wound neatly drilled through his shoulder. Lucky man. It is not likely to prove fatal. It is too clean and it means a few months in Blighty for him.[19]

On the first day of the offensive, the 120,000-strong attackers had suffered 20,000 dead.[20] In citing contemporary comments, it is worth noting the variety of responses. For example, Captain P. L. Wright and Private J. T. Darbyshire of the First Buckinghamshire Battalion of the Oxfordshire and Buckinghamshire Light Infantry left very different accounts in both tone and content. As an example,

> the condition on the ground was such as to render the chances of a successful attack exceedingly small, if not impossible, but the progress made actually was considerably greater than expected, though casualties were high. (Wright)

> At 4am Oct 9 we were relieved by the Woster Regt who went "over the lid" we raced like hares along the duck board to try to get away before the barrage opened, but we were caught in it and several of the fellows who had been in England training with me met their end "God rest their souls in Peace" left in the land of desolation (Darbyshire)[21]

Nevertheless, allowing for differences in perception, there was still much about trench life and warfare that was ghastly, and this despite the ability of armies to improve the circumstances of their troops once they were in fixed entrenchments. The circumstances of trench life varied, in particular with surface geology and weather: in some soils, it was easy to dig deep in order to gain cover, and in others, for example the stony soils of Champagne, it was not; some soils and terrains were free-draining, others were not. Wet weather increased exposure to vermin and to trench conditions such as trench foot and frostbite. In conflict, trenches were vulnerable to plunging shell fire, while the men who moved above ground were vulnerable to both machine guns and artillery.

At the same time, units were rotated out of the front line, while in the latter there were long periods without attacks. These could still be hazardous as a result of shell fire, sniping, and raids, especially night raids, but the frequency of these should not be exaggerated.[22] In addition, the need to conserve shells for major offensives ensured that fire between these was restricted. There were also differences for the better between this war and earlier conflicts, not least in the area of medical care. The military infrastructure also ensured plentiful rations. Both medical care and food supplies were better than those that many of the soldiers had experienced in civilian life, although this was far less true of the "housing" offered in trench systems. German trench facilities tended to be superior to those of the Allies. In eastern Europe, where the front was more fluid, and the Russians and Austrians lacked the resources of Britain and France, supplies were less plentiful and disease was more of a problem.

The horror of what appeared to be military futility in World War One has distracted attention from the effectiveness of the European military system. Despite the nature of the conflict on the Western Front in 1915–17, World War One was not an impasse created by similarities in weapons systems. In eastern Europe, the force-to-space ratio was lower, and it was easier to break through opposing lines and advance rapidly, as the Germans demonstrated at Russian expense in 1915. Having smashed a poorly commanded and inadequately coordinated Russian invasion of East Prussia at the battles of Tannenberg and the Masurian Lakes in 1914,[23] and having helped check Russian offensives against the Austrians, the Germans again defeated the Russians at Garlice-Tarnow the following May, and seized large portions of Russian territory. Warsaw, then, like much of modern Poland, part of the Russian empire, fell on 5 August 1915.

In 1916, however, the Russians attacked again as part of the scheme for concerted pressure on the Central Powers. The greatest success was won by Brusilov against the weaker Austrians, who were affected by poor morale, by the movement of troops to the Italian front, and by the effectiveness of Brusilov's methods. In June, Brusilov made major advances and captured a third of a million prisoners. However, an attack further north towards Vilnius/Vilna against the Germans, mounted in July, failed, and German reinforcements for the Austrians drove Brusilov back, causing him to forfeit all his gains.

German successes played a major role both in the collapse of Tsarist power within Russia in 1917, and in the subsequent weakness of the Kerensky regime; this provided the Bolsheviks with an opportunity to seize power in November. Indeed, the fall of the Kerensky regime owed much to its failure on the battlefield in 1917 (or, alternatively, to pull out of the war altogether).

In July, the Russians, under Brusilov, had successfully attacked into eastern Galicia, winning success at the expense of the Austrians, but a German counter-attack led to Russian defeat and retreat and to the collapse of the Russian army.[24]

The Bolshevik triumph in Russia appeared to signify a likely German victory. Indeed Balfour, then British Foreign Secretary, suggested in January 1918 that the Allies help anti-Bolshevik movements in Russia that

> might do something to prevent Russia from falling immediately and completely under the control of Germany ... While the war continues a Germanized Russia would provide a source of supply which would go far to neutralize the effects of the Allied Blockade. When the war is over, a Germanized Russia would be a peril to the world.[25]

The Bolsheviks were certainly willing to negotiate separately. A Russo-German armistice in December 1917 was followed by negotiations. Lenin had hoped that the spread of revolution to Germany would make these unnecessary, but, instead, the Germans drove the pace of negotiation. When the Bolsheviks refused to accept the terms offered, the Germans rejected their policy of "neither peace nor war" and, on 18 February, 1918, resumed the offensive. Their rapid success forced the Bolsheviks to accept even harsher terms in the Treaty of Brest-Litovsk, ratified on 16 March. In this, the Bolsheviks ceded sovereignty over Poland, Lithuania, Ukraine, Courland (modern western Latvia) and Finland. This did not stem the German advance, and in April they overthrew the democratic government that had gained power in the Ukraine. In its place, they installed a puppet regime. On 27 August, Lenin agreed trade terms providing grain and other economic concessions. The Bolsheviks additionally abandoned sovereignty over Estonia, Livonia and Georgia.

In addition, Serbia was overrun in 1915 and Romania in 1916: these were alliance operations with Austria, Bulgaria and Germany providing the troops and with the Bulgarians the largest contingent in 1915. Both conquests demonstrated the ability of contemporary armies to achieve decisive victories in certain circumstances: large forces were ably deployed and coordinated over difficult terrain. Serbia was attacked on 6 October 1915 from the north by Austrian and German forces and from the east by Bulgarians. By 9 October, Belgrade had fallen and the Bulgarians moved on to overrun southern Serbia and Macedonia. The Serbs had to retreat across Albania. The following autumn, a Bulgarian army under a German Field Marshal, August von Mackensen, invaded south-eastern Romania, while a German and Austrian army invaded from Transylvania. Romanian forces were quickly defeated and on 6 December both attacking armies entered Bucharest.[26] Once Russia had been knocked out of the war, Romania accepted first an armistice (December

1917) and then peace: under the Treaty of Bucharest of May 1918 it agreed to accept both occupation and German control of its oil and wheat.

Outside Europe, the Allies also demonstrated the potential effectiveness of their military systems. They rapidly overran all the German colonies, bar German East Africa, but the Turks were a more formidable foe, not least because their forces were neither small nor cut off by Allied sea power (as was the case of those of Germany outside Europe). The initial Allied advance into Mesopotamia was unsuccessful, although Turkish resistance was overcome in 1918.[27] In 1917-18, the British drove the Turks from Palestine. They used both tanks and aeroplanes to do so, while cavalry played a major role in the breakthrough. However, the Allied achievement there rested primarily on effective artillery–infantry coordination and a skilful British strategy, which kept the Turks guessing.[28]

The Allies were less successful in trying to create a new centre of offensive operations on the southern flank of the Central Powers. In 1915, the Turks defeated a British attempt to force open the Dardanelles. After a naval attack had fallen victim in March to Turkish mines and to a lack of bold leadership, the Allies landed troops on the Gallipoli peninsula in April. However, the Turks had strengthened local defences under German direction. The Allies failed to push initial advantages, and their advances were contained. The following winter, they withdrew; this retreat was one of the few well-managed aspects of the operation, although amphibious operations were notoriously difficult to mount.

In May 1915, Italy joined the Allies in order to gain territory from Austria, but successive Italian attacks on the Austrians on the Isonzo front were unsuccessful: on a concentrated front, Austrian defensive firepower prevailed and the Italians suffered heavy casualties with very few gains. The Italians were poorly trained, equipped, supplied and led. The Allies landed an expeditionary force at Salonica in Greece in October 1915, with a view to moving north into Serbia. However, they were blocked by Bulgarian forces, creating a new set of trench lines. Political factors played a major role in such operations. In November 1915, Kitchener found the French leadership unwilling to withdraw troops from Salonica: "They simply sweep all military dangers and difficulties aside and go on political lines such as saving a remnant of Serbs, bringing Greece in and inducing Roumania to join".[29] In fact, the Serbs were not saved by this intervention. The entire history of Balkan operations in World War One indicated the strategic limitation of amphibious forces at that juncture.

It would be unwise to present an inability to end the war rapidly as a consequence of tactical stasis. Instead, both sides learned from initial experiences and developed more flexible attack and defence doctrines; there was an important degree of flexibility, not least in response to the introduction of what has been termed "machine warfare", which the British have been seen to had developed in the Somme offensive. What were later called blitzkrieg tactics actually began in 1916. The so-called (although not by the Germans) Hutier tactics built on a captured French manual and on the Russian General Brusilov's successful, surprise June 1916 offensive against the Austrians. Captain Reginald Benson, a British liaison officer with the French, wrote a memorandum in July 1917 about German attacks in the Chemin des Dames: "surprise attacks usually at day-break or dusk: assaulting infantry keep well up with the [creeping barrage] . . . Stosstrupps . . . They consist of bombers, pioneers carrying flame-projectors, wire-cutters, and artillery liaison officers." Benson reported that such units had been used ably since the beginning of the year, but that they drained the best men from the infantry.[30]

The tactics were used by the Germans on a large scale and in a major offensive on the Eastern Front at Riga in September 1917; and then, that October and November, by the Austrians and Germans on the Italian Front at Caporetto. The emphasis was on surprise and speed, not attrition. The Austrians and Germans advanced rapidly with machine guns and light artillery on lorries, avoiding Italian strong-points as they advanced, and destroyed the coherence and communications of the Italian defence. The Italian collapse indicated the potential effectiveness of the offensive using the new tactical approach. Italy was nearly knocked out of the war: its forces were pushed back 80 miles and lost possibly as many as 700,000 men, especially if deserters are included, as well as nearly 5,000 pieces of artillery.[31]

Thereafter, the Italian Front was shored up with major Allied contingents, despite the opposition of generals on the Western Front, most notably Haig. Drawing on their experience, the British helped improve the effectiveness of the Italians in trench warfare, and played a significant role in the successful Italian Vittorio Veneto offensive in October 1918.[32]

The Germans first employed the tactics used at Caporetto on the Western Front on a large scale in November 1917. This allowed them to regain most of the ground near Cambrai that the British had recently gained thanks to their first use of massed tanks. This new tactical approach was adopted more generally in 1918 and, at the tactical level, transformed the stalemate that had characterized the Western Front since 1914. German "storm troopers" advanced in dispersed units under cover of artillery barrages and broke into Allied trenches, bypassing strong-points. Their firepower was increased by their carrying lightweight arms, including sub-machine guns, flame-throwers, trench mortars, hand grenades and machine pistols.[33] Instead of lengthy preliminary bombardments, that gave ample warning of attack, there were short bombardments, with a pre-registration of the artillery and the use of a mixture of shells. Troops were extensively trained on mock-ups of opposing trench positions and then moved forward in preparation for the attack.

Alongside an emphasis on these innovations, it is worth noting the salutary comments of one recent scholar, Paddy Griffith:

British tactics on the Somme were already in essence the same as those used by both sides in their decisive manoeuvres of 1918. The exclusive charmed circle which is conventionally drawn around the Great War's "tactical innovators" – whether Germans, ANZACs or tankies – turns out to be quite illusory, since tactical innovation was a game that almost everyone was playing, even including the woolly old cavalry generals themselves . . . By the beginning of 1917 the whole shape of modern infantry tactics had been settled.[34]

The broadening out of the process of innovation, noted by Griffith and other recent commentators on World War One tactics, has a wider applicability. A central theme of this book is that innovation was not a process restricted to a few individuals and groups able to conceive and achieve paradigm shifts, but, instead, a characteristic integral to modern war, as the process of adapting peacetime forces and doctrines to the exigencies of combat and victory drove change forwards. Innovation, both in general and during World War One, was not restricted to tactics: "The Somme marked the beginning of a learning curve, in command and control . . . Mission command was extended further down the command chain, giving the brigade commanders and even more junior leaders considerable discretion in their conduct of the battle".[35]

The Western Front was not merely a site of stasis. It was also the stage for the decisive actions of the war. The blocking of German offensives in 1914, 1916 and 1918 was the essential precondition of Allied victory, and in 1918 the Germans were dramatically driven back in the theatre of operations where their strength was concentrated. Using 62 divisions from the Eastern Front, freed by the Russian collapse in 1917 (although more could have been transferred), the Germans gained great swathes of territory in their 1918 offensive, but failed to destroy their opponents' fighting ability or break their line. Furthermore, the Germans outran their supplies and were eventually stopped by Allied reinforcements. The German offensive emphasized surprise, tempo and tactical flexibility, with, for example, only a short preparatory artillery bombardment and a non-linear infantry advance. The Germans aimed for breakthrough, not as an end result of heavy fighting, as in offensives on the Western Front in 1915–17, but as the immediate goal.[36]

This proved successful on the battlefield, but the British were able to deploy sufficient reserves to stop the German tactical success being translated into strategic victory. In addition, the Germans failed to sustain their offensive in a particular area, instead launching successive attacks in different directions. Indeed, the greater tactical effectiveness shown by the Germans in their spring offensive was not matched operationally; advancing troops suffered from logistical problems and from the failure of artillery and machine guns to maintain the same rate of advance. Even more seriously, German strategy was poor. Instead of maintaining their initial advantage by keeping their opponents off-balance, the successive German attacks were disjointed. Erich Ludendorff, the powerful German Deputy Chief of Staff, altered his plans in the midst of the offensive. The Germans also failed to achieve their original goals: separating the British and French forces, pushing the former back to the Channel, and driving on Paris.

Instead of German success, the war ended on the Western Front with a campaign leading to a decisive Allied victory, not an impasse as in earlier Allied offensives. Subsequently, German nationalists might claim that their army had been stabbed in the back by a rebellious public; in fact, they were defeated at the front, and dramatically driven back in the very theatre of operations where their strength was concentrated. The British recovered swiftly from the German advances in March–April 1918, and in July–November they, the Canadians and Australians, and, to a lesser extent, the French and Americans, launched a series of attacks in which they outfought the Germans, overrunning their major defensive system in September 1918.[37] What had begun as limited assaults became a general advance. This was the unexpected result of initial successes, among which the Franco-American counter-offensive of 18 July and the British combined arms attack on 8 August near Amiens were particularly important.

In the Allied triumph, tanks played a role, although this should not be exaggerated. They were more important than when they had been first used by the British at the Somme on 15 September 1916, and by the French the following April. The British use of them *en masse* at Cambrai in November 1917 was certainly a shock to the Germans. On 8 August 1918, no fewer than 430 tanks broke through the German lines near Amiens. That November, the French planned to deploy 600 tanks to support an advance into Lorraine, and by 1918 they had 3,000 tanks. Tanks could be hit by rifle bullets and machine guns without suffering damage. They could also smash through barbed wire and cross trenches. The Germans deployed tanks in 1918, but did so in far smaller numbers and to less effect than the British: these tanks, some captured from the British, did not influence the outcome of the spring battles. German industry was unable to manufacture them in sufficient quantities.

The use of tanks had been considered from the start of the conflict. In December 1914, Hankey wrote a memorandum noting that "such deadlocks are not a feature peculiar to the present war . . . Either a special material has been provided . . . or an attack has been delivered elsewhere . . . can modern science do nothing more?" He suggested,

> Numbers of large heavy rollers, themselves bullet proof, propelled from behind by motor engines, geared very low, the driving wheels fitted with "caterpillar" driving gear to grip the ground, the driver's seat armoured, and with a Maxim gun fitted. The object of this device would be to roll down the barbed wire by sheer weight, to give some cover to men creeping up behind, and to support the advance with machine gun fire.[38]

The tank seemed a fitting symbol of the overcoming of the impasse of trench warfare. However, it had its disadvantages. Many tanks broke down even before reaching the assault point, and, in battle, tanks rapidly became unfit for service, understandably so given their technical problems. For these reasons, there was a reaction in British circles against the use of armour after August 1918. Tanks were appropriate for infantry support, but were not yet a fast-moving mechanized force. The British also suffered from a failure to produce sufficient spare parts. The French tanks contributed little to the unsuccessful Nivelle offensive of 1917.[39]

Other factors have to be stressed. Thanks to Allied improvements, the Germans had lost their superiority in weapons systems. On the Allied side, in place of generalized firepower, there was systematic coordination, reflecting precise control of both infantry and massive artillery support, and improved communications.[40] The British army had 440 heavy artillery batteries in November 1918, compared to six in 1914. British gunnery inflicted considerable damage on German defences. Counter-battery doctrine, science and tactics had developed appreciably, as had the creeping barrage. Both were used effectively by the French in late 1916 in regaining territory near Verdun. The absence of comparable coordination hit the Americans hard when they attacked towards Soissons in 1918.[41] Aside from artillery–infantry coordination, the British had successfully developed planned indirect (three-dimensional) firepower. The 1918 Allied campaign can be described as attritional at a strategic level (with rolling attacks along the front from the north to Verdun), but it also shows that such campaigning had the capacity to deliver a decisive result.

Towards the end of the war, British commanders, at both senior and junior levels, obviously had greater relevant operational experience than in 1916.[42] This was important, as the nature of the conflict was such that officers on or close to the battlefield had to be able to take effective command decisions in order to sustain the tempo of effective attack. Due to the complexity of operations and to problems with communications, supreme commanders and their staffs were simply not well placed to provide these decisions. In one respect, this represented the primacy of the tactical over the operational dimension of conflict.

Clearly, other factors were also important. On the Western Front, the adoption of unity of command under Foch in April 1918 greatly helped the Allies. His methodical qualities were also important.

Germany was also affected by the collapse first of Bulgaria and then of its major ally, Austria,[43] and by the degree to which the exacerbation that year of its military, economic and domestic problems destroyed its will to fight. There were serious food shortages. More specifically, manpower shortages hit not only the army but also the economy. Thus, coal production declined in 1917, and both this and the shortage of manpower hit the rail system. The cumulative impact of such shortages was a run-down in the economy and its growing atomization, which hindered attempts to coordinate and direct production. Germany had no equivalent to the support provided to Britain and France by the Americans, nor to the prospect of future help that it offered. Pressing the domestic population harder only helped to undermine public support for the war.[44]

The strain that the attempt to mobilize the resources for total war imposed on German society was heightened by the failure of the 1918 spring offensive. This led to the loss of many of the best German troops and, more generally, to the exhaustion of the army. Army morale collapsed after the offensive did not bring the victory promised by Ludendorff. Large numbers of troops surrendered, and German officers no longer felt they could rely on their units.[45] For the first time in the war, large numbers of German troops deserted. The army was also badly hit by the epidemic of Spanish influenza then sweeping the world.

These factors helped ensure that the Allied expectation that the war would continue until 1919 was not fulfilled. Instead, an armistice came into force on 11 November. Allied leaders and generals initially thought the conditions offered to Germany would be judged unacceptable, and that they would have to use tanks and the Americans to win victory in 1919. The strains of war, however, had gathered to a point of political crisis. Wilhelm II was forced to abdicate in the face of incipient revolution, and the new government was eager to end the conflict.[46] In a sense, Russia in 1917–18 became Germany in 1918, although there was no comparable social collapse.

Deficiencies in German strategy were seen in the last year of the conflict, as in the first. The Germans failed in the west in 1914 and did so as the result of a plan that brought Britain into the war. This was not their sole questionable judgement on the Western Front. The Verdun offensive of 1916 seems surprising given that there was a better prospect of knocking Russia out of the war, and because the pursuit of a policy of attrition when Germany had fewer troops can appear maladroit.

These problems suggest a need for caution before accepting the customary arguments about the superiority of German strategic insight and staff methods. More generally, the benefit the Germans had gained from being able to launch the war in the west in 1914 (and against vulnerable Belgium), and from the weakness of Russia, could not counteract the deficiencies in their military system and international position. Looked at from a different angle, the Allied victory was not simply a matter of solving the tactical problems of trench warfare.

The way in which the resource situation was altered by political contingencies, namely American intervention on the Allied side from 1917, was also important. Thanks in part to Germany's crass wartime diplomacy, including military policies pursued without regard to the consequences, the USA had become persuaded of the dangerous consequences of German strength and ambitions. In 1914, there had been active hostility to the idea of participation in the European war; it was seen as alien to American interests and antipathetic to its ideology. However, over the next three years, German actions, especially the unrestricted submarine warfare that led to the sinking of American ships, and the apparent German willingness to support Mexican revanchism against the USA, led to a shift in attitudes.

The American military machine had moved on from the unpreparedness and administrative shortcomings revealed by the Spanish–American War of 1898. This was partly because the Americans had had several years to prepare for conflict and their industry was already geared up to supplying the Western Allies. Once America entered the war, President Wilson agreed to the French request to provide one million troops by July 1918. That July, he agreed to another request for 100 divisions by July 1919. In April–October 1918, over 1,600,000 American troops crossed the Atlantic, transforming a German superiority on the Western Front of 300,000 in March 1918 to an Allied superiority of 200,000 men four months later. This was the largest movement to date of troops across an ocean.

The Americans were fresh troops and, had the war continued, they would have been decisive, although a lack of training combined with command faults helped to ensure heavy casualties in early operations. Pershing, the commander, was convinced that American methods were superior to those of the European powers, and he took time to understand the characteristics of trench warfare. Furthermore, the Americans were heavily dependent on the French for artillery and machine guns.[47] As with the movement of German troops from the Eastern Front, the arrival of Americans was important because of the state of the forces on the Western Front. The French, in particular, had lost much of their available manpower, their effective strength had fallen, and, in late 1917, Pétain focused on limited attacks – at Verdun in August and the Malmaison in October – rather than on the quest for the strategic breakthrough. The Americans also made a significant contribution to the war in the air and at sea.

Important as American troops were on the Western Front, in both defensive and offensive operations in 1918, American financial resources and industrial capacity were even more crucial. The role of all three looked towards the decisive part played by the USA in World War Two and subsequently. As World War One ended before American forces could play the role envisaged for the 1919 campaign, their potential was not yet clear to all contemporaries, although the German Supreme Army Command was well aware of the issue. Having failed to win a quick victory by unrestricted submarine warfare or by attacking in the West in spring 1918, Germany had lost. The example and its implications had not been adequately digested by Hitler and his circle when they declared war on the USA in December 1941.

In World War One, America's industrial resources and technology were available to the Allies from the outset. They were crucial, because, in 1914, neither Britain nor France had an industrial system to match that of Germany.

For machine tools, mass-production plant and much else, including the parts of shells, the Allies were dependent on the USA. Thus, in 1915–16, shells from the USA and Canada were necessary for the British on the Western Front, while French munitions production, which was more effective than that of Britain, depended, in part, on American steel.[48] For the transportation of shells and steel, as for other reasons, routes across the Atlantic were fundamental to the Allied war effort. However, by 1917, the British production of munitions had greatly increased, and a war economy had been developed. Nevertheless, inter-Allied economic assistance continued to be essential. For example, American and British technicians and locomotives helped to sustain the French rail network.

German industrial capacity was in turn crucial to the Central Powers. The Turks, for example, relied on German ammunition. Part of the reason for overrunning Serbia in 1915 was to improve supply links within the Central Powers' bloc.

New technology played a role in the war. Submarines and aeroplanes are discussed in Chapters 6 and 7, and tanks have already been mentioned. Gas, first used by the Germans in 1915 (on both the Eastern and the Western Fronts), and by the British later that year, was deadly at times, but had less effect than submarine warfare, although its psychological effect was considerable. Gas could be blown back by the wind, as happened to the British at Loos in 1915. Mustard gas, which harmed by contact, as well as by the ingestion that had brought death with the earlier chlorine and phosgene gas attacks, was first used in 1917, by the Germans at Passchendaele. Mustard gas was primarily an incapacitant, burning and blistering its victims, and so compounding the problems of medical and support services. Gas added considerably to the horror of fighting. It also forced the pace of equipment and tactics, as effective ways of employing gas and also anti-gas defences were adopted. The role of gas in the defeat of the Germans in 1918 is a matter of some controversy. It has recently been argued that the British artillery made effective use of gas shells in order to silence German guns. This has been seen as an instance of the success of the British in responding to possibilities and problems.[49]

Less spectacular developments were also important. The flame-thrower was first used in 1914 by the Germans, who then introduced the weapon to their Austrian allies. It was used in significant numbers at Verdun in 1916. New British weapons included the Stokes mortar, which was effective against machine guns and pillboxes. Grenades and shells became more effective, with, for example, better time and impact fuzes for the latter. The rapid infantry advance tactics that both the British and the Germans employed in the latter stages of the war owed something to the development of more portable weapons, which could be carried forwards by the infantry while still providing considerable firepower. Grenades, both thrown by hand and fired from rifles, were important, as were lightweight machine guns and mortars, and light artillery pieces.

Aside from new and improved weaponry, there were also important developments in other aspects of technology. The use of motor vehicles enhanced logistical flexibility. By 1918, the French army was using nearly 90,000 motor vehicles, although the Germans had only 40,000.[50] Radios and telephones enhanced communications, helping to improve artillery coordination. Technological advances were widely diffused and copied.

There was a major effort to mobilize scientific expertise and resources.[51] In 1915, Balfour wrote about

> the matter of the Cambridge Laboratory . . . There is one problem which, I think, is deserving of immediate consideration, namely the explosion of hydrogen in zeppelins [airships]. There is no doubt that the result of the recent air-fight between the zeppelin and our air-craft was very disappointing. The incendiary bullets were fired through and through but with no effect; and I gather our authorities are puzzled.[52]

## Conclusions

Casualty figures for the war were extreme: 9.45 million men died, and millions more were badly injured. Individual countries lost particularly heavily: about two million Germans died, as did about 1.81 million Russians, and 1.4 million French, and 750,000 British troops (confirmed British and British empire military dead came to just below one million). Direct expenditure on the war totalled $208 billion. These figures reflected not so much the futility of war, or of this war, but, rather, the determination of the world's leading industrial powers to continue hostilities almost at any cost. More specifically, casualties were high because of the strength of counter-strategy and tactics, or, phrased differently, the advantage weapons technology gave the defence and the value of defence in moderate depth, given the contemporary constraints on offensive warfare, and the numbers of troops available for the defence.

The contrast between operations on the Western and Eastern Fronts highlighted the importance of the number of troops. Although more than density of defending troops was involved in this contrast, it was a key factor: as trench lines were longer on the Eastern Front, there were fewer defenders per mile. In addition, the greater length of trenches helped ensure that they were less well prepared than on the Western Front. Indeed, it is worth considering how far our image of World War One would be different if the Eastern Front received equivalent scholarly attention to the Western, or if the ratio of past and current scholarship on the two had been reversed. The stress might be much more on the possibility, despite the deployment of vast forces, of achieving a decisive result, and of the ability of armies to achieve operational freedom (although the Germans won eventually principally because of internal Russian collapse). In short, tactical problems did not preclude operational and strategic mobility. Furthermore, the key problems in eastern Europe were strategic (rather than tactical), specifically the decision where to mount offensives and how best to distribute forces between widely separate areas of the front. The ability to sustain an advance was a key operational issue. In eastern Europe, cavalry played a greater role than on the Western Front, although this increased the logistical problem of providing sufficient fodder.

The question of the extent to which impressions are created in large part by the focus of public interest and scholarly attention is not restricted to World War One. It is also an issue for all aspects of the subject of this book. Thus, for example, a different impression of conflict prior to 1914 can be created if the emphasis is on the Boer War or the Balkan Wars. As far as the question of eastern and western Europe is concerned, there is an interesting parallel in the early eighteenth century. The inability of powers in western Europe to deliver a "knockout blow" in the Wars of the Spanish (1701–14) and Polish (1733–35) Succession is frequently cited in order to demonstrate the indecisiveness of warfare in western Europe, more specifically the tactical and operational impasse resulting from improved fortifications. However, a very different picture emerges further east, where, both in the Great Northern War (1700–21) and the War of the Polish Succession, there was more mobility and far more decisive warfare.

It is not clear that either situation should be used to characterize European warfare as a whole; and this is equally the case for World War One. It would be mistaken to exaggerate the fluidity of warfare then in eastern Europe, but it was sufficiently different to the situation on the Western Front to undermine any common portrayal of conflict. In addition, the conflict in eastern Europe confirmed assumptions about the way in which war (and not just defeat) could cause political breakdown. In Britain and France, there had been no such development; indeed, despite the repeated failure of military operations to secure their objectives in 1914–17 and the heavy costs of the conflict, both countries showed the adaptability and endurance of modern industrial societies. In Germany, this was true until 1918. There had been no quick victory, and therefore no quick war, but both sides had fought on, and for several years, in a fashion that had not been anticipated by most commentators before the war.

CHAPTER FOUR

# The Inter-war Years

Next to the almost miraculous change in the situation which it
brought about, the most remarkable thing about the battle of Warsaw
[1920] is that *it was a victory won not by fighting but by manoeuvre.*
Indeed, throughout the course of the campaign it is doubtful whether
any hard fighting in the sense understood by Western armies has
taken place. The tide of battle has surged backwards and forwards
more in response to psychological and emotional factors than to the
results of hard blows on either side, and the possibilities of
manoeuvre have once more reached a pitch of development that has
not been seen in Europe since the days of Napoleon.

Coming so quickly on the heels of the long stagnation, which was
the feature of the war on the Western Front, the antithesis is all the
more striking.       (Major-General Sir Percy Rawcliffe, Director of
Military Operations,  Report on the Franco-British
Mission to Poland, 1920, original emphasis)[1]


[T]he complete mechanisation of the army is not to-day, or in the
near future, a possible or desirable measure. It would demand a
highly specialised army trained and equipped for one contingency
only, viz. war in a European theatre and on ground suitable for its
employment.             (Committee of Imperial Defence. Defence
Requirements Sub-Committee, Report, 28 February 1934)[2]

Rather than seeing the military history of the period 1919–38 solely in terms
of the policies of the Fascist dictators in the 1930s and the run-up to World
War Two, it is also necessary to devote due weight to earlier warfare. The
Treaty of Versailles of 1919 included a clause that fixed the responsibility of

the war on Germany, and this war-guilt issue, and the associated reparations (financial retribution), were designed to discourage further aggression.[3] Similar clauses were included in the treaties with Austria and Hungary. In addition, the League of Nations was established in 1919 in order to maintain peace and deal with any unresolved peace settlement issues. It was the first pan-national organization with a global mission to prevent war.

However, from the outset, force was involved in the settlement of the new world order. Thus, in 1919, the Czech army took Slovakia from the Hungarians, and a German strike in the Sudetenland against the new state was harshly repressed; while the Romanians, with Czech support, suppressed the Communist regime in Hungary, advancing as far as Budapest. Also in 1919, the Poles took Vilnius/Vilna from Lithuania, while an Italian volunteer force seized the Adriatic port of Fiume. The Italians were driven from Albania in 1920, by armed local opposition as well as by international pressure. The peace settlement for the Turkish empire led to a bitter war, as Greek attempts to gain part of Anatolia were defeated.

The biggest war in the West was the Russian Civil War (1917–21). This began with efforts in 1917 to overthrow the provisional government, which had assumed power after the overthrow of Tsar Nicholas II in February. Conservatives and Bolsheviks (Communists) both attempted coups that failed, but the Bolsheviks were successful in seizing power in November (October in the Russian calendar). Initially, there was a coalition government but, the following spring, the Bolsheviks launched a drive for power that led, by June, to a civil war. The Whites (or conservatives) came to play a major role from November 1918, when Admiral Kolchak took power in Siberia. Intervention on behalf of the Whites by Britain, France, Japan, the USA and other powers was unsuccessful, in part because only limited resources were committed; this had much to do with the general unpopularity at home of intervention. Post-war demobilization and the financial burdens left by World War One placed obvious limits on interventionism; there was also unrest within the British army, which led the government to demobilize more rapidly than it had originally intended. Foreign intervention, however, was not central to the struggle in Russia. There was a lack of both agreed aims among the intervening powers and resolve: the forces actually committed were very small.

The failure of the anti-Bolshevik forces in Russia also owed much to their internal divisions and their political and strategic mismanagement. White governments were selfish, greedy and incompetent. This helped to alienate support, especially from the peasantry, who have emerged in recent work as crucial to the course of the conflict. Although this simplifies a very complex situation, success in the struggle between Bolsheviks and Whites depended on who was best able to avoid fighting the Greens, Russia's peasant armies, and, even more, on who was able to win some of their support.[4]

The White underestimation of Bolshevik tenacity was also important, as was Bolshevik determination and use of terror. The Bolshevik's central position was also crucial: they had control of the vital populous and industrial areas, including key arms factories around Moscow, and rail links. As a result, the Bolsheviks fought on interior lines. Similarly, in the Mexican Revolution of 1910–17, the Carranza faction came to a commanding position in 1916 in large part thanks to the dominance of the cities and the rail system, although the effective generalship of Alvaro Obregón was also important. In Russia, the Whites, by contrast, lacked manufacturing capacity.

The Bolsheviks ruthlessly mobilized all the resources they could for the war effort, although that also harmed their support. For example, in 1918, the Cossack Don Army was able to raise troops against the Red Army because of the nature of Bolshevik grain requisitioning. More generally, businesses were nationalized, grain seized and a firm dictatorship imposed, with opposition brutally suppressed. The secret police helped maintain control, but troops were also used to crush opposition within the Soviet-dominated zone.

By retaining control of St Petersburg and Moscow, the Bolsheviks could afford to trade space for time in what was very much a war of movement, and one in which cavalry played a major role. Although the Bolsheviks had some skilled commanders, neither side showed much strategic skill. Instead of manoeuvring to obtain the most favourable positions, both sides chose to fight where they encountered each other, and success usually came to the one that mounted the offensive. This included frontal assaults on positions, such as Frunze's successful storming of the anti-Bolshevik defences of the Crimea in November 1920. Morale and logistics played a major role in engagements. The Bolsheviks, who had destroyed the coherence of the Tsarist army in 1917 by challenging the disciplinary authority of officers, were greatly helped by the raising of a large conscript army in 1918;[5] their numerical superiority over the Whites was of great importance on a number of occasions early in the struggle and, more generally, in the later stages of the war. The Red Army grew rapidly, especially in early 1919, and heavily outnumbered the Whites in infantry and artillery, although not in cavalry. Furthermore, much of the army was dedicated to food requisitioning and otherwise maintaining the rest of the army in the field. Once the impact of desertion is also included, then the effective size of the army was not as large as total numbers might imply.

The forces opposed to the Bolsheviks included not only Whites, and, at times, Greens, but also the forces of non-Russian peoples, which had been brought under the sway of the Russian empire and had separatist agendas of their own. In addition, there were foreign forces. Although, in combination, this was a formidable array, each of the anti-Bolshevik forces had their own goals, and sometimes took non-cooperation as far as conflict.

The most effectual pressure was exerted by the Don Cossacks to the west of the Volga, and the Whites, both under Kolchak on the east of the Soviet zone,[6] and under Denikin from the Ukraine. By April 1919, Kolchak had overrun the Urals, in June Denikin captured Kharkov, and by October he was within 250 miles of Moscow, while Yudenich, another White general, who had advanced from Estonia, was close to St Petersburg. However, their fighting quality was indifferent. On 1 October 1919, Captain John Kennedy, an artillery liaison officer with the British Military Mission to South Russia attached to Denikin, recorded,

> In the morning the batteries go out, and take up positions, and are followed presently by the infantry. The guns then blaze off at maximum range into the blue, limber up and go on when the signal to advance is given – *followed* by the infantry, who don't like to get in front of the artillery . . . there is but little opposition beyond sniping from machine guns and rifles.

Ten days later, Kennedy attributed the guns firing at extreme range to their lack of infantry and cavalry protection. He was also unimpressed by the calibre and discipline of the officers.

Green forces, which rallied against the Whites, turned the tide, and Denikin's men were driven back across the Ukraine. Orel and Voronezh fell to Red units, who defeated the Whites at Kastormoe; this was a victory in which Red cavalry under Budënny played a major role. Yudenich's force included tanks with British crews, but they were unable to overcome defending infantry once their initial panic had been mastered, and Yudenich was driven back in late October. The unpopular Kolchak had already been repelled. In November 1919, his capital, Omsk, fell to the Soviets, and in January 1920 he was handed over by the Czech Legion. Kolchak's regime had been undermined by his brutality and rapaciousness, by its divisions, and by growing Green hostility.

Civilian hostility to conscription and requisitioning undercut the White effort. This was made clear by Kennedy in the months before Deniken's retreat to the Crimea in March 1920. On 11 October 1919, he recorded, "The Army lives on the fat of the land" and, on 14 February 1920,

> we are making a mistake in continuing to support Denikin. Denikin himself is about the only man connected with the movement with any high ideals. When he formed his Volunteer Army, he attracted to it and assimilated very undesirable elements, for instance all the unemployed Regular Officers of the old regime, who would have to work or starve if there were no fighting, and also all the old rotten aristocracy of Petrograd and Moscow and the big landlords . . . His army is one mass of corruption . . . Everybody wants somebody else to do the fighting . . . the disorganisation and confusion and corruption and speculation increases every day.
>
> It is a useful experience for us, in that we see how *not* to do everything connected with war.

On 17 March, Kennedy added "Denikin's robber bands and rabbles . . . They are all in a terrible state of disorganization".[7]

The Whites, now under Wrangel, advanced again into the Ukraine in June 1920, crossing the Dnieper in October, but were then defeated, in part because an armistice between the Bolsheviks and Poland agreed to in October had freed Soviet troops to attack. After heavy losses, Wrangel's force fell back into the Crimea and was evacuated by the French fleet in November 1920. In this campaign, the Red Army was helped by the Greens under the anarchist Makhno, but, once Wrangel was defeated, the Red Army attacked his forces. Widespread fighting across the Ukraine led, by August 1921, to Red success.

The defeat of the Whites helped make foreign intervention redundant, although the Japanese supported the Whites in Siberia until 1922, and Vladivostok did not fall to the Red Army until October of that year. Fourteen states sent troops and weaponry to help the Whites. British forces were sent to the Baltic, the Black Sea, the Caspian and to Archangel and Murmansk in northern Russia. The Americans and the Japanese deployed forces in Siberia, and the French in the Baltic and Black Seas and northern Russia. Other participants included Canadians, Italians and Serbs in northern Russia, former Czech prisoners of war to the east of the Soviet zone, and Finns, Letts, Poles and Romanians to the west. Although these forces were important in particular areas, they did not make a decisive impact in the war. Foreign forces had their own agendas to pursue and, aside from defeating Communism, some sought territorial gains.[8]

This was particularly so of the Poles. Marshal Pilsudski wished to return Poland to her 1772 borders, at the expense of Russia, a plan that entailed a federation including Belorussia, Lithuania and the Ukraine. This was not welcome to most of the population in these areas, but, in November 1918, the Poles occupied the western Ukraine and, in the following spring, Vilnius/Vilna in Lithuania. By the end of 1919, most of Belorussia had also been brought under Polish control. In 1920, Pilsudski negotiated an agreement with Ukrainian separatists by which they ceded the western Ukraine in return for his help in establishing a Ukrainian government in Kiev. The city fell to the Poles on 7 May, but, having defeated the Whites, the Bolsheviks were now in a far stronger position and with a battle-hardened army. Bolshevik forces cut the Polish lines of communication and, in June, the Poles were obliged to abandon Kiev and the Ukraine.

Once the Bolsheviks had gained control of the central areas of the old Russian empire, they moved on to the attack, as they had earlier done after the end of World War One; at that time they had advanced into areas occupied by the Germans, capturing Riga on 3 January 1919 and Vilnius/Vilna two days later. In early 1919, the Bolsheviks had managed to overrun most of Latvia, much of Lithuania and part of Estonia, only to be driven back by counter-revolutionary forces supported by German Freikorps and British naval pressure.[9] The Bolsheviks captured Minsk and Vilnius/Vilna in July

1920, and advanced into Poland. However, they were defeated near Warsaw between 16 and 25 August 1920 and then driven back, with the Poles winning fresh battles on the Niemen and at Szczara.

The Poles benefited from a lack of coordination among the mutually distrustful Bolshevik generals, the length of Bolshevik supply lines, the availability of French supplies and military advice, and an ability to gain the initiative and then to defeat the Bolshevik forces in detail. Ably commanded by Pilsudski, the Poles outmanoeuvred their opponents, who lost over 100,000 men. General Sikorski, the commander of the Polish Fifth Army, made good use of motorized infantry and armoured cars, providing firepower to supplement the cavalry. However, Polish campaigning had serious weaknesses, and, in part, the conflict was decided by which side was best able to cope with its deficiencies and to exploit those of its opponent. Major General Sir Percy Radcliffe ascribed the contrast between the operational mobility of the Polish campaign and the Western Front in World War One to the lower density of troops in Poland. This left the Poles weak, and, more specifically, without depth and reserves:

> Naturally the attempt to leave no portion of the front uncovered made the Polish forces hopelessly weak everywhere, without cohesion, depth or reserves, and with little more power of resistance than that of a line of seaweed floating on the tide.

A lack of training on both sides, especially in the use of the rifle, undermined the strength of the defensive. Radcliffe argued that Bolshevik armies were poorly trained, equipped and led, and had low morale. He suggested that, because the Bolsheviks advanced over a very wide front, they lacked depth and nearby reserves. In the Battle of Warsaw, for the first time in the campaign, the Bolsheviks came up against a continuous line of barbed wire that was moderately well defended. Despite their success, Radcliffe argued that the Poles lacked training, equipment, organization and good officers. As the terrain was ideal for cavalry, Radcliffe believed that the Polish cavalry should be equipped with machine guns, armoured cars and Ford vans. He also argued that they must have ample reserves echeloned in depth.[10]

In October, the Poles captured Minsk and advanced to within 90 miles of Kiev, before agreeing an armistice. The eventual Treaty of Riga, in March 1921, left Poland with some territory in Lithuania, the Ukraine and Belorussia.[11]

In Finland, independence had been declared in December 1917, but a Communist revolt began the following month. Anti-Bolshevik forces under Carl Gustav von Mannerheim, a Finn who had been a lieutenant general in the Russian army, defeated the Bolsheviks by the end of April 1918, although a treaty accepting Finnish independence was not signed until October 1920.

In the Caucasus, the British had played a role in protecting the states of

Armenia, Azerbaijan and Georgia, which had all become independent from Russia in May 1918. However, they withdrew their forces from late 1919, a withdrawal that culminated when the Black Sea port of Batumi was evacuated in July 1920. The Bolsheviks were able to benefit from the weakness of the local republics. They advanced into Azerbaijan in April 1920, into Armenia later in the year, and into Georgia the following February. Further east, Bolshevik forces under Frunze overran Central Asia in 1920, capturing Bukhara and Khiva. On the other side of the Black Sea, the Soviets were able to re-establish Russian control in Bessarabia.

At a very different scale, World War One also closed with another unsettled problem, this time at the opposite side of Europe. The Anglo-Irish war illustrated the difficulties of responding to guerrilla warfare and the effectiveness of terrorism. Conflict began in 1916 when a general rising was planned by the military council of the Irish Republican Brotherhood. There was supporting action in different parts of Ireland, but, due to divisions in the leadership, nothing of note. This ensured that the rising would fail militarily; instead, it became merely a bold gesture. About 1,200 rose in Dublin on Easter Monday, 24 April, and seized a number of sites, but they suffered from bad planning, poor tactics, and the strength of the British response, which included an uncompromising use of artillery. The insurgents were forced to surrender unconditionally on 29 April.

The firm British response, however, served to radicalize Irish public opinion. Martial law was declared, and a series of trials, 15 executions, and numerous internments provided martyrs for the nationalist cause. The Irish Volunteers were swiftly re-established and, by the end of 1917, began public drilling exercises. Political support for independence grew. A government proposal to introduce conscription in 1918 was very unpopular, and the war undermined support for the Home Rulers, who had sought autonomy within the empire.

Instead, in 1919, the Irish Volunteers, soon to rename themselves the Irish Republican Army (IRA), began terrorist activity. They were opposed to conventional politics, which they saw as likely to lead to compromise. British refusal to accept independence precipitated a brutal civil war in 1919–21, in which terrorism and guerrilla warfare destroyed the ability of the British to maintain control. In tones that were to become familiar from counter-insurgency operations elsewhere, Lieutenant General Sir Philip Chetwode, Deputy Chief of the Imperial General Staff, claimed that victory was possible but only if the army was given more power, including control of the police, and the full support of British opinion:

> [T]he full incidence of Martial Law will demand very severe measures and to begin with many executions. In the present state of ignorance of the population in England, I doubt very much that it would not result in a protest which would not only ruin our efforts, but would

be most dangerous to the army. The latter have behaved magnificently throughout, but they feel from top to bottom that they are not supported by their countrymen, and should there be a strong protest against severe action it would be extremely difficult to hold them.

It is possible that with a tough policy the rebellion could have been put down, but public opinion would not have stood for it. This indicates the weakness of liberal regimes in suppressing civil unrest and terrorism. Instead, there was a British withdrawal from much of Ireland, and a partition between a self-governing Irish Free State, and a mainly Protestant Northern Ireland, which remained part of the United Kingdom. The partition was opposed by much of the IRA, the anti-Treaty forces known as the Irregulars. They were unable to accept a settlement that entailed anything short of a united Ireland. The Irregulars mounted a terrorist campaign in Northern Ireland in 1921, and also fought the newly independent government in the South in 1922–23, in what was a more bloody conflict than that of 1919–21.

The IRA was beaten in both Northern Ireland and the Irish Free State. The Northern Ireland Police were given "special powers", and the National Army in the Irish Free State emergency powers. IRA terrorism led to a vigorous response from the Irish government, which executed 77 rebels and imprisoned 12,000. Thereafter, IRA terrorism remained only a minor irritant, in both North and South, until the late 1960s.[12]

The Russian Civil War did not play a major role in inter-war discussion of military capability, other than in Russia. Instead, there was a focus on the supposed lessons of World War One. The successes of infantry–artillery cooperation in 1918 were widely overlooked because of greater interest in the potential of mechanized warfare. In the 1920s and 1930s, the development of mechanized forces on land was accompanied by debate about their operational employment, in particular concerning new tactics of combined arms operations. In the last stages of World War One, a British colonel, J. F. C. Fuller, had devised "Plan 1919", a strategy based on a large-scale tank offensive designed to penetrate deep into opposing territory, rather than simply supporting an infantry attack on the front line. Fuller saw this deep penetration as leading to the disintegration of opposition cohesion, and an attendant demoralization that would compromise fighting quality. This offensive strategy, by its impetus, was designed to provide effective protection for the attacking power.

Following Fuller, Basil Liddell Hart, an ex-army officer turned military correspondent and ardent self-publicist, developed notions of rapid tank warfare, although he also argued that the infantry retained an offensive role. Publicly expressed in his pieces for the *Daily Telegraph* and *The Times*, Liddell Hart's ideas also had an influence on British armoured manoeuvres in the 1930s, while he and Fuller were cited by the Inspector of the Royal Tank Corps in his report to the 1926 committee on the reorganization of the cavalry.[13] Liddell Hart was particularly keen to advocate advances that did not entail frontal attacks: the "indirect approach", that emphasized manoeuvre, not attrition. In his *The Decisive Wars of History* (1929), Liddell Hart pressed the case for attacking the enemy where they were not expecting it, and for mechanized forces bypassing the flanks of enemy armies in order to hit their communications and bases, a theme he returned to in *The British Way in Warfare* (1932).

Liddell Hart was to exaggerate his influence, and to be accused of "misstatements, perversions of fact, half-truths, and quotations taken out of their context".[14] It has been argued that his ideas, along with those of other British exponents of tank operations and reports of British manoeuvres, did not influence German blitzkrieg tactics in World War Two to the extent that was once claimed.[15] These tactics were a development of mechanized warfare and of the offensive tactics employed by the Germans in 1917, and also drew on the emphasis on an effective combined arms doctrine developed under Hans von Seeckt, Commander-in-Chief of the Reichswehr in 1920–26.[16]

In Britain, Germany, Russia, the USA and elsewhere, there was intellectual enquiry about the nature of war-winning, attempts to develop operational doctrine, concern about ensuring manoeuvrability and what would later be termed "deep battle", and much interest in the potential of tanks, mechanized transport, and air-to-land and air-to-sea warfare, and in the enhanced communication capability offered by radio.[17] Enhanced firepower also attracted attention. In 1923, General Rawlinson called for "a centre to train all ranks in the scientific use of automatic weapons".[18] In practice, ideas advanced further than technological capability and resource availability, as was to be shown in the early land campaigns in World War Two.

Furthermore, in some states, inter-war investment in armed forces was too limited to permit an effective implementation of new doctrine, both in equipment and in training. This, for example, was a problem for the American army and for British preparations for amphibious operations,[19] although the Americans also found it difficult to develop appropriate combined arms doctrine.[20] In 1928, Montgomery-Massingberd, then head of Britain's Southern Command, wrote of developments with tanks, "The whole question is one of money". This was a matter not only of the choices involved in force structure, but also of the weaknesses of liberal democracy in not permitting effective rearmament until the danger was obvious, when it is generally too late. Montgomery-Massingberd also emphasized the problems of choice, not least in terms of the diversity of developing possibilities in mechanized warfare, and the sense of new potential:

> What we want most at present undoubtedly is light tanks or machine gun carriers, people are not however clear which will be best . . . It looks to me as if the cavalry will want the light tanks and the infantry the machine gun carriers. I don't think there is really very much difference between the two, except that the tanks will have more

armour and normally machine guns will fire from them, while it will
be the exception to fire from the machine gun carriers, and they will
normally be taken out and used on the tripod . . . The latest Carden
Lloyd tanks . . . a great advance . . . One trial machine did 49 miles
an hour, which for a track machine seems almost undreamable.[21]

British military commitments in the 1920s focused on the empire, and both
force structure and operational doctrine were affected by the Ten Year Rule
adopted by the British government in 1919, which argued that there would
be no major conflict for ten years, and, therefore, that the British did not have
to prepare for war on the Continent. The Chiefs of Staff did not initiate the
abolition of this rule until 1932: the Committee of Imperial Defence accepted
their recommendation in March of that year. Two years later, the Committee
noted of the rule, "It was under this assumption, which became gradually
untenable, that our present and exceedingly serious deficiencies have accumu-
lated". These deficiencies were made acute by the threats posed by Japan and,
in the longer term, Germany. The British failure to sustain the alliance with
Japan negotiated in 1902 had created a major problem for Britain in the Far
East. German rearmament already seemed a danger; and the Committee
argued that Germany could not be trusted and, instead, could become a
serious menace.[22] The collapse of the World Disarmament Conference in
1934 made the situation in Europe more menacing.

Nevertheless, imperial commitments remained important, and affected
force structure. The Committee responded to its critics in 1934, "it would not
be possible to organise a larger mechanised force than the one we recommend
below without upsetting the whole system by which our forces overseas are
maintained by the Home Army". The Committee proposed a tank brigade as
part of the expeditionary force, but argued that imperial tasks cannot "be met
by the creation of a highly specialised 'robot' army at home, even if that were
the best system for a continental war, itself a matter far from certain". The
Committee also argued that the infantry needed anti-tank guns and mechanized first-line transport.[23]

Similarly, political contexts placed the American military in a difficult
position. For example,

the US Army recognized the danger posed by Japan very early . . . But
a variety of factors – inadequate manpower and resources, changes in
weaponry and tactics, low budgets, public and political indifference,
intraservice and interservice dissension between local commanders
and Washington – all hindered the development of adequate defenses
for the Pacific territories . . . the army's failure to prepare the local
populations for their own defense . . . Challenged by a strategic
dilemma, army officers tinkered with technicalities . . . refused to
challenge their civilian superiors to provide realistic policies.[24]

A lack of funds was a major problem for the inter-war American military, but there were also limitations, if not deficiencies, in areas of doctrine and equipment. For example, tank warfare was given little role and no independence under the National Defense Act of 1920. Instead, tanks were allocated to the infantry, an allocation only challenged in 1931 when light tanks were allocated to the cavalry. It took the fall of France to the Germans in 1940 to lead to rearmament and to inspire the creation of the United States Armored Force.[25] Nevertheless, it would be inappropriate to adopt too critical an approach. The American army made a serious attempt to assess the lessons of World War One, and also devoted much attention to the military education of officers.[26]

The Spanish Civil War of 1936-39 seemed to offer the possibility of testing out new weapons and tactics and of learning military lessons. Germany, Italy and the Soviet Union played a supporting role in the conflict, each sending troops and supplies, and other powers followed with close attention. Thus, although to a more limited extent than is often imagined, the Germans used close air-support tactics and aircraft, including dive-bombers. They found that this required an effective ground–air liaison system, and developed one. These tactics were to be important in the early stages of World War Two.

It is therefore easy to adopt an approach to the period that focuses on new weaponry and related operational doctrines. Both were important, but it is also necessary to note the lack of clarity about what constituted military progress, the variety of responses and the role of political suppositions. To take the lack of clarity about what constituted military progress, lesson-learning and doctrinal innovation sound far more clear-cut and easier than is, in fact, the case; so also with the evaluation of the process. One particular problem concerns the assessment of "anti-" strategies and tactics. If, for example, the doctrine and technology of a period favours the offensive, then investing in the defensive can be seen as anachronistic, or, more favourably, as a way to try to lessen the impact of the offensive. In the latter view, it can be regarded as prescient, or even forward-looking.

By the 1930s, both Fuller and Liddell Hart had come to appreciate that tank offensives could be blunted by an effective defence, as was actually to be the case in World War Two. Enthusiasm for tanks became more contained than it had been in the 1920s. Furthermore, the military establishment remained committed to infantry. Field-Marshal Sir George Milne, Chief of the British Imperial General Staff, told a staff conference, in January 1930, that "the infantry soldier will be required in the wars of the future just as much as in the wars of the past. Of course the more armoured formations we can have the better it will be, but we always get back to the infantry soldier."

Three years earlier, in his "Address to the Officers of the Mechanized Force", Milne had detected, over the previous 30 or 40 years, a "gradual stabilization in the battlefield . . . If we had studied the Russo-Japanese War more carefully, we should have seen whither things were leading".[27]

Mechanization posed problems of equipment procurement and maintenance, both of which were costly, and also of training. The latter was linked to
a process of specialization, and thus distinction, within the military. The
British army committee that in 1938 recommended the merger of the Royal
Tank Corps and the newly mechanized cavalry noted that, in the past, troops
had been trained within their own regiments, but that "this system is
impracticable for a corps equipped with armoured fighting vehicles, and it is
clear that in future training will be necessary at a depot equipped with suitable
vehicles and staffed by technically qualified instructors".[28]

The search for a doctrine of rapid victory through utilizing the operational
possibilities of the new weaponry was at once a desire to respond to the
apparent possibilities of this weaponry and to avoid the devastation and
prolonged struggle of World War One. Thus, it was a search for a limited war
that could be effective, as opposed to what was presented as the ineffective
total conflict seen in World War One. At the level of control, the emphasis on
such operations suggested that war would be entrusted to trained, regular
forces under military command, rather than to mass armies in whose
direction civilian politicians played a major role.

Inter-war mechanization of armies led to a focus on the combination of
firepower and mobility. Changes and new doctrine made static defences seem
limited and cavalry appear redundant. The horse was increasingly replaced by
the motor vehicle. Surviving cavalry units sought to adapt. In 1939, the Polish
cavalry, about 10 per cent of the men under arms, was armed with anti-tank
weapons and heavy machine guns, and was trained to fight dismounted, the
horses being employed in order to change position after an action – in short,
for mobility, not shock action.[29] Arguably, horses still had a combat role in
modern warfare – to provide mounted infantry in difficult terrain; they were
widely used as such by the Red Army in World War Two.

The Polish example underlines the difficulty of deciding what lessons to
draw from recent conflict, as well as indicating the role of military politics in
the development of doctrine and organization. The Polish victory over Russia
in 1920, not least at Komarów, the last cavalry battle in Europe, led to a
mistaken confidence in the continued value of the methods used then. The
Poles did not match the mechanization of the German and Soviet armies in
the 1930s, in part because of a lack of financial resources. Sikorski pressed the
value of mechanized warfare and the tank, but he was out of favour with
Pilsudski, who was dictator from 1926, when he staged a coup, until his death
in 1935. Although, in the late 1930s, the Polish military came to understand
the value of armour, they were too far behind their rivals.[30] There had also
been resistance elsewhere to accepting the obsolescence of cavalry. Philip
Chetwode, Inspector-General of Cavalry in the British army, complained in
1921 "how much the apparent success of the cavalry in Palestine has
mesmerised them". He countered that if the Turks in 1918 had had gas, tanks,
planes and firepower, the cavalry would have achieved far less.[31]

At the same time, it is necessary to remember that the word "inter-war", with its suggestion of the need to prepare for World War Two, is misleading, especially for the 1920s. Even in the 1930s the configuration of powers in a major war was still very unclear, and this had major implications for strategy and thus for desirable force structure. In the 1920s, with the Soviet Union checked by the Poles, German armed forces limited by the Versailles Treaty, and Balkan tensions containable without war, the most pressing military problems for Britain, France and the USA appeared to be imperial: colonial in the case of the first two and within the informal American empire in the Caribbean and Central America for the third.

The political dimension in military investment decisions became more pronounced. This was caused by the range of investment options increasing in the inter-war period with the additional claims of air power and armour, creating inter-service disputes over the division of limited resources. Furthermore, there were competing domestic calls, and the situation was affected by the fiscal consequences of severe economic down-turns in the 1930s: the Slump and the Depression.

## The dictators and the military

Military build-ups were easiest for states that were autocratic and lacked powerful representative institutions and practices of political consensus. They could impose in peacetime an economy designed for war. Thus in the Soviet Union, following a war scare in 1927, there was a massive expansion of the armaments industry. This played a central role in the general drive to expand and modernize the economy and to develop industrial capability. Large numbers of aircraft and tanks were built. To a considerable extent there was a militarization of the economy.[32] Hitler publicly announced German rearmament in 1935. This was to break the provisions of the Versailles Treaty, and thereafter there was a rapid increase in German military spending. This was designed not only to increase the size of the armed forces, but also to ensure that they were the most modern in Europe and therefore able to give effect to Hitler's foreign policy goals. This increase helped to unbalance the German economy.

Opportunity to act was not enough. In Fascist Italy, Nazi Germany, the Communist Soviet Union, Hungary (a right-wing dictatorship), and even Japan, there was also a drive for radical revision of the post-war peace terms and international system.

Of the European revisionist powers, the armed forces in Italy were least under state direction. Mussolini benefited from the failure of the Italian armed forces to resist his seizure and consolidation of power, but, equally, he did not feel a need to transform them. The Italian armed forces had not suffered the traumatic experience of revolution, like those of the Russians and Hungarians, or defeat and enforced reduction, like those of the Germans, Austrians and Hungarians. They were not brought under Fascist control, and continued to owe allegiance to the Crown. Although Mussolini was Minister of Marine for most of the period, and in 1938 appointed himself "First Marshal" of the empire, with a military rank at least equal to that of Victor Emmanuel III, his control of the armed forces was limited and he had little power over senior appointments. Furthermore, the armed forces were not circumvented. The Fascist programme of 1919 had called for the creation of a National Militia, which was to have been the basis of a popular army under party control, and for the nationalism of all armaments factories, but this programme was not implemented once Mussolini gained power. Instead, he sought to develop the existing professional armed forces.

Like many politicians and commentators in the period, especially those on the political right,[33] Mussolini was fascinated by new technology, seeing machinization as an analogue for the powerful authoritarian progressivism he intended to introduce. He believed that the adoption of advanced weaponry would serve to enhance Italy's international position. He was particularly interested in air power, describing Italy as a natural aircraft carrier in the Mediterranean. He provided more men to support Franco in the Spanish Civil War than Hitler, and was in favour of bold, mechanized advances.[34] Reality did not measure up to Mussolini's bombast.

Mussolini's use of, and relationship with, the armed forces was typical of a number of inter-war autocratic regimes. In Hungary, the army was largely independent of political control. In contrast, in both Germany and the Soviet Union in the 1930s, dictators felt it necessary to seize a greater control over the forces, in order to ensure that they were loyal to them personally, rather than to any notion of national interests.

Hitler had not followed Ernst Röhm, who wanted to transform the *Sturmabteilung* (SA) movement he headed into a militia-type army that would incorporate the professional military and remove their independence.[35] This form of Nazi revolution was unacceptable to both Hitler and the army, but Hitler was still determined to control the latter. In 1934, on the death of President Hindenburg, Hitler combined the office of the President with that of the Chancellor, and thus became Supreme Commander of the armed forces. At the suggestion of the army leadership, who thought that it would bind Hitler to the army, an oath of unconditional loyalty to him as Führer (leader) of the German people was taken by every officer and soldier in the armed forces. The army's uniforms were altered to include the Nazi Party Badge. In 1938, Hitler removed the Minister of War and the army Commander-in-Chief, and took effective control of the entire military high command. No new Minister of War was appointed, and the War Ministry's Armed Forces Office was replaced by a Supreme Command of the Armed Forces, which would be easier for Hitler to control. In December 1941, Hitler also appointed himself Army Commander-in-Chief. The following year, he came to exercise a closer control over weapons production and development.

Hitler's determination to control the army reflected his need for it to support his aggressive policies, his determination to tolerate no other views, and his dissatisfaction with the attitudes and reliability of his senior military advisers and of the army leadership in general. Fritsch, the Army Commander, Blomberg, the Minister of War, and other senior colleagues had been against the dispatch of troops into the Rhineland in 1936, which had unilaterally abrogated the demilitarization of Germany's western frontier provided for under the Locarno Pact. In 1937, both Blomberg and Fritsch had made it clear that they were unhappy about Hitler's plans, specifically the risk of war with Britain and France, while Blomberg had stressed the strength of Czech fortifications as a reason for caution in going to war.

Indeed, in 1938, as war seemed likely as a result of the Czech crisis, Ludwig Beck, the Chief of the General Staff, prepared a coup in the event of war breaking out. Earlier that year, he had protested without success at the occupation of Austria. Blomberg proved unable to defend army interests against Hitler and, in 1938, was summarily removed when he made a questionable choice of wife. Falsely accused of being a homosexual, Fritsch was interrogated by the Gestapo and tried by court martial: a dramatic display of the army's subordination. Although he was acquitted, Fritsch was not restored to his post. Ten other generals (six from the Luftwaffe) were removed. The isolated Beck resigned in August 1938: his plot was not executed because of a lack of support from other senior generals, and because Britain and France negotiated the Munich settlement. Beck's emissaries to Britain seeking support had been rebuffed.

From the low base permitted under the Versailles settlement (100,000 men), Hitler built up the German military, although rearmament took time, not least in creating the necessary industrial capability. On 1 October 1934, he ordered a trebling of army size to 300,000 men, as well as the creation of an (illegal) air force. The Luftwaffe became independent from the army in March 1935, and its existence was publicly acknowledged that summer. The Four-Year Plan, initiated in 1936, was designed to ensure self-sufficiency and readiness to go to war in four years. Hitler set out to strengthen the German position by negotiating agreements with Italy and Japan in late 1936, and by constructing the West Wall fortifications to protect the western frontier. The aim of these enhancements was not to secure stability, but to provide strategic flexibility for German aggression. However, it was not as easy to create a war army as Hitler had envisaged. There was a shortage of the necessary trained troops and reservists, as well as of military stores and the relevant industrial capacity. The last was greatly helped by the seizure of Czech resources in March 1939; this doubled the amount of artillery. German rearmament had a "shop window" character and failed in many ways: there was little long-term planning.[36] The scale of rearmament was deliberately exaggerated to intimidate likely opponents.

In the Soviet Union, Stalin, who felt it necessary to terrorize the armed forces, moved with greater violence than Hitler. Claiming to discover a conspiracy between the Soviet and German armies, he had his military heavily purged in 1937. Marshal Mikhail Tukhachevsky, the talented commander of the Red Army, who was interested in mechanized warfare and seizing the offensive, and had been responsible for the creation of mechanized corps in 1932,[37] was shot; over half the remaining generals were killed (the rank itself had been abolished during the Revolution), and about 23,000 lesser officers were killed or dismissed, including many of the most experienced. An alternative basis of political power was thus ruthlessly crushed. Party control of the armed forces had been pushed hard from the outset, especially by Kliment Voroshilov. He became Commissar for War in 1925, a post changed to Commissar for Defence in 1934. Party control was strengthened with the reintroduction, in 1937, of the system of dual control introduced in the Civil War: all military orders had to be countersigned by a political commissar, and, the following year, military soviets of the Commander, Chief of Staff and a commissar were created to provide trusted leadership at army and corps level. Political commissars, however, were not noted for their military ability. They also played a major, but harmful, role on the Republican side in the Spanish Civil War.[38] In the Soviet Union, the purges led to the discrediting of the mechanized corps concept, but not of the cavalry, which had been built up in the 1920s and 1930s by Budënny, a protégé of Stalin.[39]

Despite the purges, the Red Army, making effective use of its tanks to carry out a full encirclement, heavily defeated Japan in fighting on the Manchurian/ Mongolian border at Khalkin-Gol (also known as the Battle of Nomonhan) in August 1939, although 34 per cent of the Soviet troops involved became casualties.[40] However, the loss of talented officers in the purges, and the promotion of men whom Stalin could trust, many of whom were mediocre and unwilling to challenge his views, ensured that the Soviet army was poorly led when it attacked Finland in 1939–40. The more general development of the entire army in the 1930s hindered its fighting quality, which became evident when Germany invaded in 1941. Training systems were poor, there were serious organizational weaknesses, and the expansion in size of the late 1930s had not been matched by a comparable increase in effectiveness.[41] As World War One indicated, this was a common problem with rapidly expanded large forces. The mechanized corps in the Red Army were unwisely disbanded in 1939, as the emphasis shifted from the large armoured formations advocated by Tukhachevsky to smaller units integrated with the infantry, a force structure also seen in France, which served her ill in 1940.

The desire to control the armed forces was particularly strong in totalitarian regimes intent on driving through major changes in society, but, more generally, the dictatorial nature of many governments led to a focus on the political position of the armed forces, or, as in Spain, the army created the regime. This was accentuated in the 1930s as economic problems provoked authoritarian solutions and a decline in liberal democracy. The attitude of the armed forces thus became crucial at the time of coups and seizures of power, for example those of Antanas Smetona in Lithuania in 1926, King Alexander in Yugoslavia in 1928, Antonio de Salazar in Portugal in 1932, Konstantin Päts in Estonia in 1934, and King Carol II in Romania in 1938. There was an army coup in Bulgaria in 1934, and the country became a military dictatorship under King Boris in 1935; Greece also became a military dictatorship in 1935. In March 1941, a military coup in Yugoslavia directed against the pro-German policies of the government led to a German invasion. Conversely, although the French officer corps was right-wing and anti-Communist, it did not react to the democratic creation of a Popular Front government in 1936. This owed much to the determination of the commander, Gamelin, who did not see himself as a military dictator.[42]

## The Spanish Civil War, 1936–39

General Miguel Primo de Rivera became dictator of Spain in 1923, after seizing power as the result of a coup. He was Captain General of Barcelona and was supported by military action in Zaragoza and Valencia; he also profited from King Alfonso XIII's refusal to back the civilian government. As with other coups, this was not a case of a united military seizing power. Instead, as was the norm, it was action by a determined minority, while the majority did nothing, that was crucial. Once in office, Primo de Rivera's efforts at military reform, in particular his attempts to remove superfluous officers, and his continued interference in military promotion, enraged much of the army. There was nearly a coup against him in 1926, and, in 1930, the prospect of yet another led the king to force Primo out.[43]

The instability generated by military involvement in politics is evident in the fact that the Spanish Civil War also began as a military coup in 1936. Opposed to the modernizing policies of the left-leaning Republican government and concerned about the possibility of a Communist seizure of power via the Popular Front after the narrow left-wing electoral victory in the hard-fought elections of the spring of 1936, a group of senior army officers, who called themselves the Nationalists, sought to seize power on 18 July. Their failure led to a bitter civil war, which only ended on 28 March 1939, when the Nationalists seized Madrid. Much attention has focused on foreign intervention. Indeed, this was important, even decisive at particular moments, for example in helping Franco transport his troops from the Army of Africa from Morocco to Spain by sea and air in 1936, a critical move for the Nationalist side. However, most of the ground fighting was waged by Spaniards.

The initial Nationalist rising was successful in some areas, but, elsewhere, Republican positions were preserved by workers or by loyal forces. Areas of control were consolidated on both sides during July as flying columns sought to suppress local opposition. By the end of the month, the country was divided into two zones, with the Republicans controlling the bulk of the population and industry, and backed by the navy and most of the air force, and the Nationalists, supported by most of the army's combat units, especially the Army of Africa, dominating the more rural areas. The Nationalists called up reservists where they could and organized the right-wing militias into army units. The Republicans found it far harder to organize an effective army, partly because of political differences, but also because they, especially their militias, lacked the necessary planned organization and discipline.

As a consequence, the Republicans lost the initiative and were unable to capitalize on the early difficulties faced by the Nationalists. Instead, Franco used the Army of Africa to overrun western Andalusia and to link up with Nationalists further north, storming Badajoz on 14 August 1936. Although Franco was able to fight his way close to Madrid by early November, he was stopped by the strength of the resistance around the capital, resulting in the war becoming both longer and more wide-ranging in its intensity. This put a premium on foreign help, but also on the resilience of the Spanish combatants.

A number of informed foreign commentators analysed the nature of the war. Fuller, then a retired major general and a newspaper correspondent, had marked sympathies with Franco, but this does not detract from the value of his observations. Having visited Franco's army, he sent a report to British Military Intelligence in March 1937:

It is in no sense a great war, a trench war or even a guerrilla war . . . a city war . . . main strength of the Reds was in the towns . . . had Franco a highly organised army and plenty of transport he could take Madrid. But he has not. For instance, General Queipo de Llano told me himself that, when he launched his advance against Malaga, he had only 28 lorries . . . Nothing like the full man power has been called up, in fact it cannot be, as the military organisation is not able to absorb more men . . . though the nominal front is immense . . . its garrisons are minute . . . The front is totally unlike the fronts in the World War. Not only is it in no way continuous, but, generally speaking, hard to discover, and during my journey, so far as I know, at times I may have been in Red territory . . . The villages normally are natural fortresses, generally walled all round, and whichever side holds them "holds" the intervening gaps as well. Immediately west of Madrid, and of course in other places also, actual trenches do exist. I visited the Madrid ones which were very sketchy . . . Though I was in this front line for an hour and a half only two Red shells were fired and a few rifle shots were heard . . . Of tanks I saw few: on Franco's side the Italian light tank is an indifferent and blind machine . . . Tank tactics are conspicuous only through their absence. Machines are generally used singly, or, if in numbers, they split up over a wide front. The result is that they are met by concentrated fire . . . In fact, there are no tactics, no proper training or maintenance. One of Franco's officers told me that the largest number so far used in an attack was 15! I do not think we have to learn from either tanks or anti-tank weapons in this war, because the basis of tactics is training, and this is mainly a war of untrained men with a sprinkling of foreign mercenaries.[44]

In April 1938, the British Assistant Military Attaché in Paris commented, after visiting Nationalist Spain,

Even a short visit brought out very clearly a number of singular features which characterise this war, a war in which the majority of the participants are almost entirely untrained, a war in which comparatively small forces are strung out on a vast length of front, a war in which modern weapons are used but not on the modern scale, and, finally, a war in which there have been more assassinations than deaths in battle . . . In view of these singularities, it will be obvious that the greatest caution must be used in deducing general lessons from this war: a little adroitness and it will be possible to use it to "prove" any preconceived theory . . . To anyone with experience of the Great War, the almost complete absence of warlike activities in all three sectors of the front visited was most striking . . . It seems that the battle only flares up intermittently, and then only on small portions of the front; for hundreds of miles the enemy is out of rifle shot . . . no attempt is made by either side to harass the other in his business of living and feeding . . . the paucity of artillery when an action does take place . . . very soon the full fury of the fight dies down; and the end is either a stalemate in the same positions or rapid advances.

The Attaché went on to ascribe recent successes by the Nationalists principally to "their ability to concentrate in secrecy a large preponderance of field artillery in the sector selected for the break-through". He noted that, in general, tactics were "largely based on Great War principles", with creeping barrages and trenches. The Attaché also commented on deficiencies, including "an incomplete and ad hoc organisation", poor transport and roads, and the conduct of the war "in an utterly haphazard way".[45]

These lofty remarks were somewhat harsh, and both sides proved able to adapt to circumstances. Thus, in his advance towards Madrid in 1936, Franco successfully motorized his force using buses and trucks that he had seized, and was therefore able to outflank larger Republican forces. Conversely, helped by Franco's decision to move first to relieve Toledo, the Republicans were

In Portugal, strikes in 1934 led to the deployment of troops. The same year, the army suppressed a miners' uprising in the Asturias region of Spain (they had earlier suppressed a revolutionary strike there in 1917). Franco played a major role in planning the operation. The ability of the miners to unite, seize weapons and defeat the local police provoked a military response, which was brutal. After the rebellion had been defeated, there was widespread killing of prisoners as well as of civilians. Already, in July 1931, artillery had been deployed against anarchist strikers in Seville. In Portugal, however, although Salazar's Estado Novo was authoritarian, it relied more on the Policia Internacional de Defesa do Estado, a very effective secret state-police force, than on the army. Similarly, in Spain the Civil Guards were widely used against strikers and anarchists in the early 1930s.

In the Soviet Union, the Red Army was used in 1921 to suppress brutally the uprising of both the garrison, workers and sailors at Kronstadt, who challenged the Communist monopoly of power, and the peasantry in the Tambov region[48] and a peasant uprising in western Siberia. In Germany, the army suppressed a number of Communist uprisings in 1920 and acted against Hitler's Munich putsch in 1923. Hans von Seeckt, the effective commander of the army in 1919–26, argued that the army must remain above party. There was no doubt, however, of its conservatism under Seeckt, himself a monarchist. He refused to move against the right-wing Kapp putsch of 1920. In January 1941, the Romanian army suppressed the powerful Iron Guards, a Fascist movement.

This process was not restricted to autocratic regimes. Their democratic counterparts also felt challenged by labour unrest. In Britain, 12,000 troops were deployed in Glasgow in 1919, as were tanks. There were extensive troop movements at the time of the General Strike in 1926 (although no use of force), while in France troops were used to try to keep order at the time of the Stavisky riots in 1934. Troops were deployed to deal with the Winnipeg general strike in 1919 and on a number of other occasions in Canada in the 1920s.

This civil dimension of military activity tends to be ignored in work on inter-war developments with its focus on machinization. Yet its importance is obvious for the interaction of the armed forces and society, and for the manner in which it affected military politics and force structures. This was not only true of authoritarian societies. Military loyalty was a sensitive issue in Britain, and in 1924 there was a serious political controversy when John Campbell, editor of the *British Worker*, published a piece pressing soldiers never to shoot at strikers. The Labour government's hesitation about prosecuting Campbell led to a vote of no confidence in the House of Commons. In September 1931, pay cuts imposed by the newly formed National Government resulted in the Invergordon Mutiny, in which sailors of 15 warships of the British Atlantic fleet, based at Invergordon, refused to go on duty. The Admiralty's willingness to revise the cuts ended the crisis in the fleet, but the whole episode helped cause a run on sterling in the foreign-exchange markets.

These were not only issues in Europe. The relationship between the military and the political process was a fraught process in Japan, where the army supported a militarism that challenged civil society and affected government policies, leading to what was called, by some, "government by assassination". Young naval officers assassinated the civilian Prime Minister in 1932 and young officers staged a revolt in Tokyo in 1936.[49]

## Latin America

There was also serious political instability in Latin America, not least as a consequence of acute economic pressures and social divisions, as well as of only limited support for democratic practices. The military served to suppress insurrections, and thus to enforce the social order. A peasant revolt in El Salvador was smashed with much slaughter in 1932 and the army was used against peasant opposition in Mexico in 1929 and Honduras in 1932 and 1937. The inability of rebels to confront the military directly[50] encouraged a brutal military policing that frequently relied on acts of terror. In 1923, Pancho Villa, who had been a revolutionary leader in Mexico over the previous decade, and an effective guerrilla leader, was assassinated in a plot in which the army was clearly implicated.[51]

The major inter-war conflict in Latin America was the Chaco War between Bolivia and Paraguay in 1932–35. This was not a war determined by resources: Bolivia spent nearly twice what Paraguay could afford, was more populous and had the latest weaponry, including aeroplanes. Despite this, it was defeated. Commanded by José Estigarribia, the Paraguayans were better-led militarily and politically, and they benefited from superior communications, and from understanding how to operate in the humid flood plains and how to fight a war of manoeuvre in the harsh, largely waterless, scrub terrain beyond the flood plains. Bolivian positions were encircled and their over-long supply lines were attacked. The Bolivians lacked the water for their larger army, which relied on tactics of mass attack. Invading Bolivian forces were defeated and pushed back into Bolivia, leading to the overthrow of President Salamanca in 1934, and a truce in which Paraguay was left in control of the Chaco; this was turned into a treaty in 1938.[52]

Although war in Latin America might be small in scale, the military played a major role in politics. In Chile, the army forced out the President in 1924, and in 1927 Carlos Ibánez, an ex-Colonel, then Minister of War, was elected unopposed with army support. The army intervened again in 1932 to guarantee the election of the President they had forced out in 1924. In Brazil, in 1930, the army removed the President and prevented the inauguration of the President-elect, instead putting his defeated opponent, Getúlio Vargas, into office. Supported by the army, Vargas crushed the "Constitutionalist" Revolt of 1932 and Communist uprisings in 1935, and in 1937 used troops to introduce a new constitutional policy, termed the Estado Novo or New State, in which he enjoyed near dictatorial powers. There were coups in Argentina in 1930 and Uruguay in 1933. The army overthrew the peasant-based government of El Salvador in 1931 and seized power in Cuba in 1933.

## Military tasking

In Latin America, as in Europe, the military benefited from the untrained and poorly organized nature of most domestic opposition. Furthermore, the opposition was often disunited, as for example in Germany in 1920 and in Asturias in Spain in 1934. Although veterans did play a role in some uprisings, many rebels lacked any experience of military training or organization. Furthermore, rebellions suffered from an absence of the logistical support that the military enjoyed.

Thus, military tasking varied considerably in the inter-war period. Aside from the colonial policing, counter-insurgency work and, in the case of Italy, conquest as discussed in Chapter 1, there were also domestic tasks; these certainly involved the preservation of order, but also, in some cases, involved seizing power. Preparing for a war with other European states was another priority, although one of varying importance and impact. It was far more important for the German forces, which represented a revisionist regime and lacked colonial commitments, than for their British counterparts.

The French devoted considerable effort to preparing for another war with Germany. This included the construction of the Maginot Line of fortifications to cover their eastern frontier,[53] and the build-up of their tank strength, but they also had major colonial commitments and, in order to be able to exert power in the Mediterranean, put strenuous effort into developing their navy. French military doctrine, drawing on the experience of World War One, emphasized the role of artillery. Tanks were seen as best integrated with infantry; not as a separate arm.[54] Montgomery-Massingberd, who visited France in 1935, commented on the strength of the fortifications facing Italy – "tunnelled as they are under 40 or 50 feet of rock, with embrasures for guns and machine guns covering every approach" – but he was also very impressed by French developments with mechanization. The Maginot Line was seen as offering protection and a support for operational mobility:

[M]y recollections of our attacks against strong lines during the war, even with masses of heavy guns and tanks, is that this frontier, in three or four years time will be practically impregnable, always provided of course that the French keep up their present garrison and maintain everything at the standard they are doing at present. Here again the underlying idea of economy in men so as to set free as many troops as possible for the mobile army.[55]

The French were not alone in putting an emphasis on fortifications. In Finland, the Karelian Isthmus was fortified in the 1930s in order to reduce vulnerability to Soviety attack, while reinforced concrete was used in forts on the Dutch New Holland Waterline.

## The coming of World War Two

In the late 1930s, the revisionist powers increasingly relied on force to achieve their goals. Hitler unilaterally remilitarized the Rhineland on 7 March 1936: it provided military protection for the Ruhr and was also a springboard for action against France. Far from responding forcefully against this breach of the Treaty of Versailles, the British sought to discourage the French from acting. In hindsight, Western passiveness marked a major step in Nazi expansionism, but, at the time, it was not seen in such a stark light. Furthermore, the very limited nature of Anglo-French military cooperation over the previous decade, and their lack of preparedness, were understood by contemporaries as a poor basis for joint action. But when Hitler occupied Austria on 12 March 1938, uniting it with Germany in the Anschluss (union) on 13 March, this was more than a revision of the Versailles settlement; it was a fundamental redrawing of the map of Europe.

The Versailles settlement had left to Czechoslovakia those parts of Bohemia and Moravia where there was an ethnic majority of Germans (the Sudeten Germans). This was unacceptable to Hitler, who sought the union of all Germans in one state and was determined to destroy Czechoslovakia, a democratic state that looked to other great powers for support. His threat to attack Czechoslovakia in 1938 led to the satisfaction of his territorial demands in a settlement negotiated with Britain, France and Italy; this was the Munich agreement of 29 September. Eventually, in March 1939, Hitler destroyed his victim, and was able to do so without encountering armed resistance, because Czechoslovakia had been much weakened by internal dissent between Czechs and Slovaks, and by the Munich agreement, which resulted in its loss of the frontier fortifications in the areas annexed by Germany. Hungary and Poland used the crisis to make gains at Czechoslovakia's expense in 1938, and, in March 1939, Hungarian forces occupied Ruthenia, the easternmost part of Czechoslovakia. Also in March, the Germans bullied Lithuania into ceding the city of Memel, where there was a vocal German minority, plus the surrounding area. In intimidating the other powers in 1938, Hitler benefited from their fear of war. In many respects, the Munich agreement was part of the legacy of World War One.

In April 1939, Mussolini invaded and annexed Albania. This followed on from his suppression of Libyan opposition and his conquest of Ethiopia. The Fascist glorification of war and the revived notion of rebirth through conflict, so widely held before 1914, came to have a greater impact on Italian policy, accentuating the consequences of an already extreme nationalism. Mussolini's rhetorical foreign policy placed an emphasis on force and power, often for their own sake. In Japan in the 1930s, there were those in the army who believed devoutly in the idea of war as "the father of creativity".

The dictators were increasingly acting as war leaders in peacetime. The systems they had created lacked effective institutional and political restraints or the facility to offer any reasonable range of policy options. In Germany, control and direction of foreign and military policy were monopolized by Hitler, whose long-term views interacted with the short-term opportunities and anxieties presented by international developments. Opportunities and anxieties do not exist in the abstract, but are sensed and created, and Hitler's ideology largely conditioned the process. Far from being a nihilist without plans, Hitler sought a war for the extirpation of what he regarded as a Jewish-dominated Soviet Union, which he felt would secure his notions of racial superiority and living space. To that end, Hitler aspired to control eastern Europe, end the threat of a war on two fronts by defeating France, and reach an agreement with Britain. The destruction of the Soviet Union was to be accompanied by the annihilation of the Jews, the two acts creating a Europe that could be dominated by the Germans, who were to be a master race over the Slavs and others.

This agenda began long before the outbreak of World War Two in 1939, with the violent suppression of political and economic freedoms, organizations and entities within Germany, including strikes, left-wing parties and Jews. Hitler might not have wanted a major conflict in 1939, and he thought that Britain and France would not come to the relief of Poland, but he anticipated such a war within six years, and planned his economy accordingly. Import-substitution policies were pushed actively from 1936, in order to reduce Germany's vulnerability to blockade. Hitler did not invent racialism, anti-Semitism, the notion of *Lebensraum* (living space) or aggressive warfare, but they were combined to genocidal effect and given dynamic force by his evil genius.[56] Hitler also believed that war was a necessary, and even positive, force.

Initially, the British and French governments had hoped that Hitler would be tamed by the responsibilities and exigencies of power, or that he would restrict his energies to ruling Germany. There was also a feeling in Britain that the Versailles terms had been overly harsh on Germany and that it was, therefore, understandable that Hitler should press for revision. It was anticipated that German revisionism could be accommodated, and that Hitler would prove to be just another episode in European power politics. Both Britain and France were unsure whether the Soviet Union was not a greater threat to the European system than Nazi Germany. Furthermore, in both Britain and France, pacifism was strong, and fiscal restraint even stronger, although, outside Europe, both powers used troops to sustain their imperial interests. The paramount nature of these interests pushed the response to Italy, for example over Spain, lower down the list of priorities.

The policy of the appeasement of dictators rested on the belief that it was possible to reach mutually acceptable settlements with them. The British government thought it both necessary and feasible to negotiate with Hitler, and it took time for the government to appreciate that this was both impossible and, indeed, dangerous.[57] Hitler wanted Germany to be a superpower, was happy to destroy both the balance of power and collective security in order to achieve this goal, and aimed at a new world order. By 1938, he appeared quite openly as a threat, and British intelligence, if anything, exaggerated German military capabilities *vis-à-vis* Britain and Czechoslovakia.[58]

Even if mobilized, however, Britain could do little in central or eastern Europe to stop him. Commenting on Hitler's threat to Austria, Harold Nicolson had noted in 1934, "We cannot send the Atlantic fleet to Linz". In 1938, the British service chiefs urged caution. They were conscious of Britain's numerous global commitments and warned about the dangers of becoming entangled in major military action on the Continent. Concern about the German air force, specifically the impact of German bombing, reinforced this caution. The "Note on the Development of the 'Army Rearmament Programme'", drawn up in May 1939 by General Sir Ronald Adam, Deputy Chief of the Imperial General Staff, recorded that, under the plan approved in April 1938, the Field Force was

> to be organised primarily, with a view to reinforcing the Middle East . . . The crisis in September 1938 emphasised the danger in the assumption that a Continental commitment was to be given a low order of priority. It also focused sharply the fact that, even when the programme was complete, our forces would be inadequate for a major Continental war.[59]

Anglo-French fears may have been excessive, given the weaknesses of the Nazi regime; of these, not least was a lack of enthusiasm among the German generals. It is too easy in hindsight, however, to criticize the leaders of the period and to underrate their genuine and understandable fear of causing a second "Great War". Germany may have been weaker than was thought, but was, nevertheless, determined to gain its objectives. Suspicion between Britain and France harmed cooperation against her.[60]

Once Hitler seized Bohemia and Moravia on 15 March 1939, and renounced all the guarantees he had earlier made in the Munich agreement, showing that his ambitions were not restricted to bringing all Germans under one state, Neville Chamberlain, the British Prime Minister, lost confidence in negotiating directly with Germany. He sought, instead, to create an alliance system capable of intimidating Hitler. Despite the resulting guarantees of British support to Poland and Romania, Hitler persisted with his plan for an attack on Poland. He believed that Britain and France would not fight, especially after he secured a non-aggression pact with Stalin, signed on 23 August, which reflected the failure of the Western Allies to negotiate an alliance with the Soviet Union. Indeed, the British Chiefs of Staff had advised that it would not be possible to offer Poland any direct assistance. Despite this, the German attack on Poland on 1 September 1939 led Britain and France to declare war on 3 September.[61] The resulting conflict was to test military systems across the world.

CHAPTER FIVE

# World War Two

World War Two is an umbrella term for a number of closely related struggles that, nevertheless, each had their own cause, course and consequences. Seen from the perspective of Italy or Iran, Japan or Jamaica, it can look very different. This chapter will look at why so many powers became involved and will then offer a brief narrative, and then an analysis. At the outset, however, it is important to note that study of the conflict is still very much in progress. In part, this reflects major lacunae in the documentation or scholarship, as – until recently – with the war on the Eastern Front. There, it is now possible to direct attention to important Soviet operations that failed and were subsequently ignored: for example, Operation Mars in November–December 1942, the Soviet Central and Kursk Front offensive of February–March 1943, and the Belorussian offensive of November–December 1943.

It is also now possible to re-evaluate positively the Red Army, and to suggest that it was a more effective fighting force than German commentators allowed, and that its victory was not simply a consequence of greater resources and willingness to take losses. Other campaigns of the war also require additional study. For example, there has been inadequate coverage of Japanese operations in 1941–42 and what they have to contribute to the understanding of amphibious warfare. In part, it is also necessary to re-examine widely held assumptions about the true character of the war.

## Political background

A war that began over Hitler's intimidation of Poland came to involve much of the world. This reflected the range of interests involved, the failure of the system of international adjudication and peace-making (the League of

Nations), and the vortex-like nature of war. In particular, the outbreak of hostilities led to a heightened pace of fear and opportunity. The unwillingness of the Germans to try to translate initial victories into a widely accepted peace ensured that the cessation of offensive operations with the fall of Poland did not lead to an end to conflict. Hitler had turned the defeat of Poland into an opportunity for better relations with the Soviet Union, but, despite Hitler's Reichstag speech of 6 October calling for peace with Britain and France, no real effort was made to negotiate one. Britain and France were determined to fight on, to prevent German hegemony, and this led Hitler to plan an attack on France eventually successfully launched in May 1940.

A year later, Hitler's overconfidence and contempt for other political systems, his belief that Germany had to conquer the Soviet Union in order to fulfil her destiny, and obtain *Lebensraum*, combined with his concern about Stalin's intentions, led him to attack the Soviet Union. Britain was undefeated, but it was no longer able to make any effective resistance to German domination of mainland Europe. Hitler was confident that the Soviet system would collapse rapidly and was happy to accept misleading intelligence assessments of the size and mobilization potential of the Red Army, although appreciable casualties were anticipated and the Germans deployed as many troops as they could for Operation Barbarossa. Hitler's refusal to accept what others might consider objective diplomatic and strategic considerations ensured that local wars he had won were, from 1941, transformed into a world war he could not win. Such adventurism and conceit rested on Hitler's warped personality and were also the product of a political-ideological system in which conflict and hatred appeared natural, and genocide all too possible.

The process by which the war spread is important, because the course of the conflict is inseparable from its politics, and those helped to frame strategic goals and planning options. The American President, Franklin Delano Roosevelt, had responded to the escalation of Japanese attacks on China with a speech urging "a quarantine of the patients in order to protect the health of the community against the spread of the disease". Such a policy eventually proved impossible for most of the world in the early 1940s. The vortex-like character of a major war can be seen at work in the extension of the German war, with, for example, the entry of Italy in June 1940 and the German attack on Yugoslavia and Greece in spring 1941, and also with the outbreak of war in the Pacific in December 1941. In the first case, German successes in 1939–41 led other states, willingly or otherwise, to become Axis allies and protégés, and to provide military resources to help the Germans, most obviously against the Soviet Union when Germany attacked it on 22 June 1941. Romania, Hungary, Slovakia and Finland all made major contributions to the war against the Soviet Union, while other allies, such as Italy, also sent troops. The composite force launched against the Soviet Union was similar in that respect to that led by Napoleon in 1812. Earlier, the neutrality of states such as

Denmark, Norway, Belgium and the Netherlands had been casually violated in 1940 to serve German strategic convenience.

Despite his alliance with Hitler, Mussolini had initially taken no part in the war, but in June 1940, after the defeat of France, he joined in because he feared that he would otherwise lose the opportunity to gain glory and territories: Mussolini sought gains from France and the British empire, and greater power in the Balkans. He felt that Italian greatness required a new imperial home that could dominate the Mediterranean anew, and, to this end, thought British defeat necessary. This policy, however, was not based on a reasonable assessment of the capabilities of the Italian military machine, and this failure was to lead to a series of disasters in 1940, when the British positions in Egypt and Greece were successively attacked.

It was not only the Axis powers, however, that led to a widening of the war in its early stages. Soviet aggression, most prominently the attack on Finland in November 1939, helped destabilize eastern Europe. The Soviets had first demanded 30-year leases on bases that would leave Finland strategically bereft and had then staged an incident that offered them a pretext for invasion. British plans to stage an "uninvited landing" in Norway, as a prelude to sending troops to help the Finns, was a response. They were not implemented, but, in 1940, the British mined Norwegian waters in order to prevent the transport of Swedish iron ore to Germany. This, however, was overshadowed by the surprise German invasion of Denmark and Norway that April, an invasion intended to end alarming British moves in Scandinavia, and to establish submarine bases from which to attack British shipping.

Like Hitler, the Soviet Union, Hungary and Bulgaria wished to revise the post-World War One peace settlement, while Italy and Japan were also dissatisfied powers. All had territorial motives for overturning the inter-national situation in 1939, but, in the case of Germany, Italy, the Soviet Union and Japan, there were also powerful psychological reasons – their political cultures rested on the idea of struggle and on defiance of the existing global order – although, whatever the long-term plans of the Soviet Union, it can be argued that in 1939–40 it was acting, in part, as a pre-emptive defender against the threat of German power. Furthermore, success encouraged intervention in the war. Mussolini hoped to follow up earlier German successes.

Having joined the war, it was difficult to leave it. Defeated France agreed armistice terms in June 1940. Part was occupied, the remainder becoming a neutral state with its capital at Vichy. This, however, was not accepted either by the Free French, who were determined to fight on, or by Britain. British anxiety about the fate of the Vichy French fleet at Mers-el-Kebir in French North Africa, and its possible effect on the Mediterranean balance of power, led to a demand that it scuttle, join the British, or sail to a harbour outside possible German control, and, when this was refused, it was attacked in July 1940. The death of 1,300 French sailors did not lead to a declaration of war, but it set a pattern for hostilities between Britain and Vichy, including the British invasion of Syria and Lebanon in 1941 and of Madagascar in 1942.[1] Both were motivated by fear – of German influence in Syria and of possible Japanese submarine bases in Madagascar – reflecting the way in which geostrategy could be a reason for action. Thus, the British also overthrew a pro-German government in Iraq in May 1941, and, that August, British and Soviet troops entered Persia in order to gain control of supply routes. Elsewhere, resistance ensured that conflict continued across much of the area already conquered by Germany, leading, in some regions, especially much of Yugoslavia, to civil war.

The collapse of France and the Netherlands to German attack in 1940, and the weakening position of Britain, already vulnerable in the Pacific, created an apparent power vacuum in East and South-East Asia, encouraging Japanese ambitions southwards into Indo-China and the East Indies, while leading the Americans to feel that only they were in a position to resist Japan. Japanese aggression and expansion in Indo-China helped to trigger American commercial sanctions, specifically an embargo on oil exports that was tantamount to an ultimatum, because, without oil, the Japanese armed forces would grind to a halt; so this, in turn, provoked the Japanese to act against the USA, in order to protect their position. They were confident of securing a rapid military advantage and hopeful that the difficulties of driving them back would dissuade the Americans from trying, despite their greater strength. As with Hitler and Britain and France, a conviction of the weakness of the opposing system led to a failure to judge resolve.

The issue of "cause" in the Pacific War is problematic. The Japanese were unwilling to accept limitations on their expansion in the Far East, unless fought to a stop, as by the Soviet Union in 1939, a defeat that led in April 1941 to a non-aggression pact between the two powers. At that stage, the Soviet Union was still in a non-aggression pact with Germany, to the anger of Japan, and Japan had not been informed of the planned German attack in June.

The Americans considered themselves entitled to react forcefully to events on the other side of the Pacific, a position enhanced by their control over the Philippines. This is not intended to imply any equality of action, responsibility or guilt between America and Japan, but simply to note that both had wide-ranging views on their own positions, interests, rights and views that it was difficult to accommodate through diplomatic means. Each was based on a different concept of "globalism": a sense of interaction with the outside world in which there was little room for mutuality.

Neither power wanted to fight the other, but the Japanese government and military, although divided, were determined to expand at the expense of others, particularly from 1940 in South-East Asia, which was to Japan "the southern resources area", and the American government was resolved to prevent them and unable to make an accurate assessment of Japanese military capability. The occupation of northern Indo-China in September 1940 led the Americans to limit trade with Japan, and the occupation of the south the following July led to a trade embargo and freezing of Japanese assets in America. They also demanded that the Japanese withdraw from China. The Japanese decided to launch a war if diplomacy failed to lead to a lifting of the embargo. In October, a hardline ministry under General Tojo gained power and, on 7 December 1941, the Japanese attacked Pearl Harbor without any prior declaration of war.

In part angered by American cooperation with the British against German submarine operations in the Atlantic, Hitler then declared war on the USA, in accord, he said with German obligations under the Tripartite Treaty (with Italy and Japan), although, strictly, the terms of the treaty did not require it. This was a crucial step that prevented any chance of the USA fighting only Japan. Hitler's motives for declaring war have been subject to considerable historical speculation. The declaration let Roosevelt off the hook, since he agreed with Churchill that Hitler was a greater menace than the Japanese, but not all American opinion shared this view. Aside from his declaration of war on the USA, Hitler was also foolish in not having earlier encouraged the Japanese to invade the Soviet Union.

The initial Japanese ability to mount successful attacks and to gain great swathes of territory in the face of weak and poorly led opponents, and to establish an apparent stranglehold on the Far East, did not deter the Americans from the long-term effort of driving back and destroying their opponents. The American government and American public opinion were not interested in the idea of a compromise peace with the power that had attacked Pearl Harbor. The lack of a realistic Japanese war plan in part arose from the confusion in Japanese policy-making, with differences between military and civilian politicians and between army and navy interacting with rifts over strategy.

## German advances, 1939–41

An understanding of the political background is important for any discussion of campaigning, although that, in turn, affected political decisions. World War Two began with a dramatic example of military effectiveness. The Germans lost fewer than 15,000 dead in a blitzkrieg that led to the rapid defeat of Poland, a state with armed forces totalling over one million men, although all bar 370,000 were reservists. The Germans greatly outnumbered the Poles in aeroplanes, tanks and other mechanized vehicles, enjoyed the initiative, and benefited from the long and vulnerable nature of the Polish frontier and the dispersed position of the Polish army, most of which was infantry. The Poles defended the full extent of their borders, which helped the

German penetration and encirclement strategy, rather than concentrating in the heart of Poland to attack German thrusts separately. By forcing the Poles into a war of manoeuvre, the Germans put them at a tremendous disadvantage. The Polish air force was destroyed, and the cohesion of the Polish army was destroyed: German armoured forces outmanoeuvred and isolated their dispersed military formations. Despite brave resistance, the German victory was total and rapid. Poland was invaded on 1 September, Warsaw surrendered on 27 September, and the last Polish troops stopped fighting on 6 October. The Germans took 694,000 prisoners and killed 70,000 Polish troops. A successful, although poorly executed, Soviet invasion of eastern Poland on 17 September in cooperation with the Germans had helped complete the picture of Polish vulnerability. The victorious German campaign helped to consolidate the position of generals who favoured rapid armoured advance and enhanced Hitler's self-confidence as a great strategist.

Britain and France had entered the war in support of the Poles, but were unable to provide assistance. Their failure to attack Germany during the so-called Phoney War of 1939–40 was due to limited preparedness and to military and political caution. The French needed two weeks to get their artillery out of storage. They advanced, but only five miles and with only nine divisions, in September 1939, despite the weakness of the opposing German forces, and then fell back after Warsaw fell. Chamberlain hoped it would be possible to intimidate Hitler by a limited war through blockade. The strategy was intended to put such pressure on Germany that either Hitler would be forced to negotiate, or it would lead to his overthrow. Hitler side-stepped or trumped this policy by destroying France in a seven week blitzkrieg in early summer 1940.

In contrast, the numerically superior Soviets attacked Finland in November 1939, but were at first singularly unsuccessful, suffering serious defeats, especially at Tolvayarvi and Suomussalmi in December. Their strategy was poor, characterized by an inadequate coordination of advancing forces, an underestimation of the fighting quality and mobility of the Finns, and Stalin's serious exaggeration of Soviet military capability and failure to commit adequate resources at the outset. Soviet flexibility could not match that of the Finns, who used ski battalions.

Eventually, in January 1940, the Soviets reorganized their forces and overwhelmed the Finns with numbers, focusing the attack in the south. They used their superior artillery in February and March to smash their way through the fortified Mannerheim Line, although only with considerable difficulty. The Finns were forced by a treaty of 12 March to cede territory as the price of peace. Nevertheless, Soviet casualties came to about 392,000 men. The combination of deficiencies in the Finland campaign with those in the attack on Poland in 1939 stimulated demands for military reform in the Soviet Union; pressure that was accentuated by evidence of German success.[2] In 1940, the Soviets also occupied Estonia, Latvia and Lithuania, with scant resistance from their vastly outnumbered and disunited forces.

Although the Greeks successfully repelled an Italian invasion from Albania launched in October 1940, the Germans were generally successful that year. They began with the conquest of hitherto neutral Denmark and Norway. The first fell on 9 April to a surprise attack in which the Germans made effective use of their air power. Airborne troops complemented those landed by ship. Thanks to tougher resistance and Anglo-French intervention, Norway took longer to fall, and the Germans lost about a quarter of their navy in the campaign, but, again, German air power made a great impact. The Germans were further helped by the distraction of their attack on the Low Countries and France in May, and the Allies evacuated Narvik, their last base, on 8 June. The following day, the Norwegian army accepted armistice terms.

Given the emphasis in discussion of the blitzkrieg on German weaponry and operational methods, it is worth noting the analysis of the campaign by General Auchinleck, who commanded the Anglo-French expeditionary force to Narvik. Auchinleck argued that German air power had been the leading factor, but he went on to discuss the importance of training and morale, factors that are generally underplayed due to the customary emphasis on weaponry:

> [G]enerally the morale of our troops was undoubtedly lower than that of the enemy. It is considered that this was due, first, to our inferiority of resources as compared with those of the enemy, particularly in the air. Secondly, it was due to the lack of training of the men as soldiers and a lack of adaptability which induced in them a feeling of inferiority as compared with the enemy. Thirdly their flanks and rear were continually threatened . . . our men for the most part seemed distressingly young, not so much in years as in self-reliance and manliness generally.[3]

The role of morale in the war has not been systematically studied, and this is a major problem in our understanding of particular campaigns.

A German blitzkrieg launched on 10 May 1940, overran the Netherlands, Belgium and France, and brutally exposed the military failure of the Anglo-French alliance, and, in particular, the quality of French military leadership. The French Maginot Line was outflanked when, in Operation Sicklestroke, the Germans advanced through the supposedly impenetrable Ardennes in southern Belgium and pushed across the Meuse at Dinant and Sedan on 13 May. Poor Allied strategy and a major intelligence failure led the Allies to move their strategic reserve into Belgium before they were aware of the main direction of the German attack. This mistake ensured that they were unable to respond adequately to the German advance, but so also did their doctrine, not least the failure to prepare for fluid defence in depth.

The Germans made effective use of their massed mechanized forces, especially tanks, and of tactical air support, particularly Ju-87 (Stuka) dive-bombers, gaining the strategic initiative against forces that were as numerous.

German Panzer (tank) divisions proved operationally effective as formations, maximizing the weapon characteristics of tanks. Handled well, as by the British at Arras on 21 May, Allied tanks could be effective, but, on the whole, the Germans controlled the pace of the armoured conflict, not least because their tank doctrine was more effective. The French attention to a continuous front greatly limited their ability to respond to the German breakthrough. German tanks broke through to reach Abbeville on 20 May and the English Channel the following day, cutting off much of the mobile Allied forces to the north. The tempo of the attack was far greater than in 1918, but the Germans were also more successful in maintaining supplies for their advancing units. Superiority in the air helped the Germans. The Allies had no equivalent to the Stuka dive-bomber, and the French and British air forces were outclassed by the German one.

Bravery, skill, luck, and the not fully explained German halt on the Aa Canal on 24 May, helped the British save much of their army (but not its equipment) in the evacuation from Dunkirk on 27 May–4 June, but the German achievement had been far greater than in 1870–71 and 1914. They pressed south into France, overcoming strong resistance on the Somme and the Aisne in early June. Thereafter, resistance rapidly collapsed. The French government left Paris on 10 June and the Germans entered the city on 14 June. The new French government asked for an armistice on 19 June and, on 22 June, accepted German terms. By then, German forces had captured Lyons and Vichy.[4] Under the settlement, a French government based in Vichy was left in control of south and part of central France, until it also was occupied by the Germans in November 1942. This success transformed the strategic situation in Europe and also changed the global position, as most of the French empire was under the control of Vichy. Thanks to their victory, the Germans were able to fight on and any successful challenge to them would now have to overcome German dominance of western Europe.

Furthermore, from bases from the Spanish border to the North Cape, German air power and submarines threatened Britain and her vital sea lines of communication and supply from the outside world. However, the blunting of German air power by British radar, effective and growing numbers of fighter aeroplanes, able command decisions, and high fighting quality in the Battle of Britain in July–September at least saved Britain. Hitler in 1940 called off Operation Sealion, his planned invasion of southern England – one that had been inadequately prepared.

This was not the limit of successful German advances at the expense of Britain. The Germans moved to repair the blow to their system represented by Italian defeats in the Mediterranean theatre, including the British success in December 1940–February 1941 in smashing an invasion of Egypt and then advancing into Libya. The British also defeated the Italians in Ethiopia. The Germans, however, sent forces to North Africa that, in March–June 1941, drove the British back into Egypt. They also rapidly conquered Yugoslavia and Greece in April 1941. The British intervened in Greece, but with inadequate air support, and were pushed out. The tempo of the German advance, especially its rapid use of airborne troops and armour, gained a decisive advantage over Germany's opponents.

The loss of Crete in May 1941 to German airborne attack was the last major defeat for an isolated Britain; her subsequent defeats occurred when she had powerful allies. Already, on 31 July 1940, Hitler had given orders for preparations for an invasion of the Soviet Union. These took precedence over the war with Britain. The German assault on the Soviet Union on 22 June 1941, the Japanese attack on the USA and Britain, and the German declaration of war on the USA that December, totally altered the situation. Thanks to the accession of the Soviet Union and, still more, the USA, the Allied system was far stronger economically than that of Germany. Furthermore, Axis hopes that their attacks would knock the Soviet Union out of the war and leave the USA unable to prevent the consolidation of a Japanese system proved misplaced.

Nevertheless, there were still major blows to come for the Allies. The Germans launched 148 combat divisions against the Soviet Union. They planned to concentrate between the Pripet Marshes and the Baltic, with much of the armour in Army Group Centre destroying opposing forces and then moving north from Smolensk to help Army Group North capture Leningrad. Army Group South was to capture Kiev and then encircle Soviet armies in the Ukraine, thus preventing these forces from falling back to defend the interior. In the next phase of the plan, forces from Leningrad and Smolensk were to drive on Moscow, while Army Group South advanced to Rostov in order to open the way to the Caucasus.

Along a 2,000-kilometre front, the Germans made major advances, inflicting heavy casualties and conquering the former Baltic republics, White Russia and the Ukraine. Soviet forces were numerous, but poorly prepared and deployed for the attack.[5] Stalin had ignored repeated warnings from the West and the advice of his own front-line commanders. However, the German infantry was not able to keep up with the armour, while the latter was insufficient in numbers and affected by fuel shortages and maintenance problems. The vastness of Russia, once again, drained an invader of energy. The vast distances of the Soviet Union were exacerbated by the primitive nature of the road network: the overwhelming majority of the roads were unpaved.

By early December, German troops were close to Moscow, after major victories in early October, but a successful Soviet winter counter-attack stabilized the situation. Aside from the impact of the fierce Russian winter, the Soviets benefited from superior supplies, not least as a consequence of serious limitations in German logistics, as well as from the improved situation of Soviet reserves made available by an effective mobilization scheme. Fresh forces were raised to replace those destroyed by the German advance.

German intelligence had grossly underestimated the number of divisions available to Stalin.

In addition, although Soviet casualties in the 1941 campaign were far higher than those of the Germans, the Soviets had, nonetheless, inflicted considerable losses on the Germans, losses that were to reduce the number of troops available for the 1942 offensive. Motivated by ideological and ethnic contempt, the Germans had underestimated Soviet capability, effectiveness and determination, and exaggerated the bad effects of Stalin's purges. Hitler also misjudged the ruthlessness and ability of Stalin to drive the Russian people into gargantuan efforts to build up their military capacity and commit to ferocious fighting.

The impact of the blitzkrieg was also exaggerated, because insufficient weight was devoted to the difference between winning frontier battles and the situation in the Soviet rear areas. Unlike in Poland in 1939, or France in 1940, the Soviet rear areas were not exposed to attack, and the continued determination of the Soviet army ensured that reserves were organized and deployed. The Germans were dazzled by the success of their frontier battles and deep penetrative thrusts (ignoring the fact that tens of thousands of Soviet soldiers were left behind, later to become very effective partisans), and failed to appreciate the resilience and productive capacity of the Soviet industrial regions east of Moscow, which were beyond their reach.

Furthermore, some Soviet forces fought well and effectively from the outset, especially the Southwest Front. This affected German strategy and accentuated the consequences of a prior failure to settle grand strategic choices. Instead of focusing on the advances on the planned axes, towards Leningrad and Moscow, Hitler diverted Guderian's panzers to effect an encirclement of Soviet forces in the Ukraine. This led to a major victory in September 1941, but one that delayed the advance on Moscow, fatally so. Meanwhile, the Soviet government had created an effective response system, that further ensured that the German timetable of victory was totally derailed. Having lost the border battles, Stalin pushed through a reorganization of the Red Army, including the creation of Stavka, a strategic high command. Soviet resources were mobilized, industries moved east, and the Soviet popular response focused on an appeal to patriotism rather than communism. The German underestimation of the Soviets was further seen in the success of the Soviet winter counter-offensive, which took the Germans by surprise. The Soviets initially made significant gains, leading the German high command to suffer a crisis. However, the offensive did not lead to a total defeat, in part because Stalin focused on a wide-front attack, which could not be sustained, and Hitler issued a "stand or die" order to his forward forces.

## 1942, the Axis held

The Japanese also made major gains after they launched their surprise attacks. Pearl Harbor had been bombed on 7 December 1941 in order to wreck the American Pacific Fleet (and gain time to build a defensive shield), but the bombers found battleships rather than the more crucial aircraft carriers, which were not in harbour. Three days later, Japanese forces landed on the Philippines, and Guam fell. Hong Kong was attacked on 8 December, and the remaining positions were forced to surrender on 25 December 1941. The main invasion of the Philippines was launched on 22 December and organized resistance came to an end on 6 May 1942. The surrender of "impregnable" Singapore to the Japanese on 15 February 1942, after British forces had been outfought in Malaya, destroyed British prestige in Asia: 130,000 British and Allied troops were taken prisoner. The British in Malaya had considerably outnumbered the Japanese, but the latter were better led, had the strategic initiative, fought "like fanatics",[6] used tanks and enjoyed air superiority. By the end of May 1942, the Japanese had conquered the Dutch East Indies and Burma: Batavia, the capital of Java, fell on 5 March and Rangoon, the capital of Burma, two days later. That summer, both Chinese and Soviet collapse appeared possible. The Japanese advance into Burma hit supply routes to China, although the Japanese did not press on to attack north-east India until March 1944. Aside from Japanese advantages, not least dominating the tempo of war, their conquests reflected the poorly prepared and coordinated nature of the opposition.

In 1942, the Germans had first to respond to Soviet counter-offensives in both the centre and the south as the Soviets took advantage of fresh troops, German exhaustion and the winter weather, for which the Germans were not prepared. The Germans relied on defensive "hedgehogs", based on the main communication nodes, and were able to prevent major breakthroughs. The poorly executed Soviet attempt to make one near Kharkov in May 1942 led to the encirclement of the attacking forces, and was a major failure that enabled the Germans subsequently to gain the initiative. The shift of the initiative to the Soviets, suggested by their winter counter-offensive, had been brought to an end.[7] Much of the responsibility was Stalin's: he failed to heed intelligence reports and overestimated the improvement in military effectiveness of the Red Army.

In June 1942, the Germans launched a fresh offensive against the Soviet Union. However, unlike in 1941, they were not able to attack along their entire front, while the Red Army was allowed by Stalin to fall back. Furthermore, poor direction by Hitler led to a division of German resources and, eventually, to an obsession with taking the Volga crossing-point of Stalingrad, rather than keeping the focus on the initial plan of destroying Soviet forces west of the Don and then moving into the Caucasus in order to capture the Soviet oilfields and possibly put pressure on Allied interests in the

Near and Middle East. The plan was always flawed, however, because it offered a massive flank in the north to attack by the Red Army.

The first section of the plan was achieved in July, when Soviet forces in the Don bend were destroyed and the Germans captured Rostov. To the east, German forces advanced to the Volga, which they reached to the north of Stalingrad, a major communications and industrial centre. Taking Stalingrad assumed a great and increasing symbolic importance for Hitler, who also hoped that Stalin would commit his forces to hold the city. Hitler's Verdun complex led to a concentration of military assets on what became a wrecked urban terrain (thanks in large part to German bombing), which turned out to be very difficult for the German attackers. More and more German forces were sucked into the battle and were expended in repeated attempts to seize individual complexes, especially the Tractor, Red October and Barricades factories. Armour and air attack could achieve little in the ruined terrain, and much of the fighting was very close range. Both sides used massive quantities of artillery.[8]

The British conquest of Iraq, Lebanon and Syria in May–July 1941, the Anglo-Soviet occupation of Persia from August 1941 and the British conquest of Madagascar in May–November 1942 ensured that the worlds of German and Japanese would be kept well apart and that the Allied world would not be fractured, but these operations were peripheral to the main campaigns.

As German and Japanese offensives were blunted in 1942, the long and stony path to victory appeared clearer. The Japanese found it impossible to retain the initiative successfully in the Pacific. Their move towards Port Moresby in New Guinea, which would have increased the threat of an attack on Australia, was postponed as a result of the Battle of the Coral Sea on 4–8 May, the first battle entirely between carrier groups. The American victory on 4 June over a Japanese fleet seeking to capture Midway Island and engage the Americans in a decisive battle, with the sinking of all four Japanese carriers, shifted the naval balance in the Pacific to the Americans. Both the initiative and the arithmetic of carrier power moved against the Japanese. The very extent of their conquests strained the capacity of their military to hold them, but in the Midway operation the Japanese had been hit by flawed preparation. This contrasted with the more effective repair effort that had returned damaged American carriers to service and with the American ability to intercept and decipher Japanese radio messages.

The Soviet counter-attack and (avoidable) encirclement of the German Sixth Army at Stalingrad in November 1942 was a crippling blow to Hitler's plans in Russia, and one that reflected the German failure to give due heed to Soviet capability. Launched on 19 November, the encirclement was complete on 23 November. Relief attempts failed and it proved impossible to provide sufficient supplies by air, although, looked at differently, the very attempt to mount a large-scale airlift testified to the advances made by air power, while what was transported helped keep the Sixth Army alive. The pocket was driven in by Soviet attacks, and by 2 February 1943 the remaining Germans had surrendered. The campaign was a triumph for Soviet offensive art, and was badly mishandled by the Germans, in large part due to poor direction not only from Hitler, who exaggerated the potential impact of his determination to hold out, but also from the Sixth Army commander, Paulus, who refused to allow a shrinking of the pocket that would have concentrated German forces. Aside from very heavy casualties, the Germans had lost a mass of material. The southern portion of their Eastern Front was left short of men and the initiative was lost. The units that had advanced into the northern Caucasus were now threatened with encirclement.

French North Africa was successfully invaded by Anglo-American amphibious forces in Operation Torch on 8 November 1942, and resistance by Vichy French forces was rapidly overcome. The aim was to squeeze the Axis forces from the west and east. On 23 October–4 November, German forces in Egypt were pushed back by British and Commonwealth forces under Montgomery in the battle of El Alamein. Skilful generalship, greater numbers of men and tanks, air support (and attacks on Rommel's vital petrol supplies from Italy), and the effective use of artillery broke the German–Italian army, destroying most of the German tanks and most of the Italian units. Rommel fell back across Libya (slowly pursued by Montgomery), reaching Tunisia in early February 1943. Going into World War One, strategists and field commanders had expected to bring matters to a head in one big battle on each front, only to find this elusive. In World War Two, there were clear turning points at Midway, El Alamein and Stalingrad.

## Allied advance, 1943

The Allies moved over to the offensive. Their insistence on an unconditional German surrender and the fanatical nature of Hitler's regime both ensured that it would be a fight to the finish and thus prolonged the war. Unconditional surrender was a response to the character of the Nazi regime, and serves as a reminder of the flawed political analysis of the German military leadership. Their willingness to accept Hitler not only morally corrupted them, as the military came to collaborate in Hitler's genocidal policies, but also led them into a conflict in which, from 1941, limited war and political compromise ceased to be options. As a consequence, the operational ability of the German military was linked to a task that risked, and in the end caused, not only their defeat but also their dissolution, along with the total conquest of Germany.

The war, in part, took on the character of attrition, on land, at sea and in the air. The high tempo of campaigning used up resources, but the availability of massive resources enabled the Allies to attack on a number of fronts at once. Resources were also important for specific types of operations. In particular, resources in the air and on land and sea, the development of amphibious vehicles and training and the building of aircraft carriers helped to make amphibious operations viable in both Europe and the Pacific. Large-scale amphibious attacks are among the most difficult forms of warfare to mount successfully, and are, therefore, rare. However, in this war, due to Allied domination of sea and air from late 1942, they were launched with great success in North Africa, Italy, the Pacific and, famously, Normandy.

After heavy fighting from February, the Germans had surrendered in Tunisia on 13 May 1943. Rommel had been reinforced by Hitler, ensuring a larger German defeat. The western and eastern Allied forces joined up in compressing the Axis army against the sea. The fighting in Tunisia showed the value of Allied numerical superiority and air support, but also showed that superior German generalship could still mount effective ripostes, particularly in the Battle of the Kasserine Pass in mid-February. Initially, the Americans did not fight well against the seasoned German veterans, and they suffered from ineffective leadership: poor communication, lack of cooperation and command rivalries. The Allies faced the difficulty of coordinating advances of disparate forces from two different directions – Libya and Algeria – but were helped by the movement forwards of their supply points, both ports and airfields, following the advance on land, and by the success of Allied anti-submarine operations, which helped secure Allied supply routes. Allied air and surface attacks and mining badly hit the flow of Axis supplies between Italy and Tunisia.

Allied forces landed in Sicily on 10 July 1943, and in Italy on 3 September. Amphibious power and air support allowed the Allies to seize the initiative. Italy surrendered unconditionally that month, although a rapid German response left them in control of central and northern Italy, and a series of hard-fought offensives were required to surmount successive defensive lines. The Po Valley was not occupied until April 1945. The Germans were helped by the narrowness of the front, the terrain and the winter weather, as well as by skilled leadership and the density of their forces on the east–west defensive lines that they successively adopted in Italy, especially the Gustav (Winter) Line in the winter of 1943–44 and the Gothic Line in the autumn of 1944.

This ended the brief opportunity for manoeuvre that the Anglo-Americans had had in the initial stages of the war in Italy, while German forces were dispersed throughout the peninsula. German counter-offensives, as in September 1943 at Salerno, and in February 1944 at Anzio, could be stopped with the help of sea and air bombardment, but it was more difficult to translate this superiority into success in offensive land operations. The pace of advance was slower than in France or eastern Europe, because in both the defensive density was lower, the front was wider and the terrain less difficult than in Italy. In the winter of 1944–45, the number of German divisions in Italy exceeded those of the Allies, although the Allies had superior material.

On the Eastern Front, the Soviets exploited the success of their Stalingrad counter-offensive, although Stalin's hope of trapping German forces north of the Caucasus, and of the rapid reconquest of the Ukraine proved wildly over-optimistic. Furthermore, Manstein, the German commander, proved skilful at mobile defence, successfully recapturing Kharkov in March 1943, the last German offensive victory in the east. In July 1943, the Germans launched their last major offensive of the war on a principal theatre of the Eastern Front: an attempt to break through the flanks of the Soviet Kurst salient and achieve an encirclement triumph to match Stalingrad. Hitler saw this as a battle of annihilation in which superior will would prevail, but the Red Army was now ready for such a challenge. Intelligence information forewarned the Soviets and they had prepared a dense defensive system, including extensive anti-tank defences, field fortifications and minefields, that provided a defence in depth and an artillery support system that inflicted heavy casualties when the Germans attacked on 5 July. Once the German armour had been weakened, the Soviets were better able to commit their tanks, which they did with some success from 12 July. In this, the largest tank battle of the war, the Germans had effective new tanks, the Panther and the Tiger, but the standard Soviet T-34 had been upgraded, and was used effectively at close range where it matched up well with the new German armour.

The Soviet counter-offensive, which finished on 27 August, regained all the lost territory and went on to make bigger gains. Further south, the Red Army had already launched an offensive that, by the end of December 1943, had recovered the Ukraine east of the Dnieper and Kiev, and created a powerful bridgehead across the river. This reflected the shift in the ratio of power between the German and Soviet armies, in particular the growing weaknesses in the tank- and air-strength of the former and the enhanced operational capability of the latter. This enhanced capability was inspired by Soviet theories of deep operations advanced in the 1930s, but now refined in the cauldron of war. The strategic initiative had passed to the Red Army as its strength, confidence and operational capability increased.

Also in 1943, the Japanese were pushed back at crucial points of their Pacific perimeter, losing both Guadalcanal and their position in eastern New Guinea. The fate of the former had been settled by American naval successes in November 1942, which compromised the ability of the Japanese to support their force on the island, and led to its evacuation the following February.

Heavy Japanese losses of aircraft and crew over Guadalcanal helped the Americans to seize the initiative the following year, as they began a process of island hopping in the Solomon Islands. Carriers played a major role, but so also did the creation and securing of airfields. In the Central Pacific, the Americans opened up a new axis of advance, directed at the Philippines, and captured key atolls (especially Makin and Tarawa) in the Gilbert Islands in November, although only after difficult assaults on well-prepared and highly motivated defenders. This success helped prepare the way for operations against the Marshall Islands, which were to be successfully attacked the following January; by April 1944, they had been brought under American control, although some isolated positions were still held by the Japanese. "Leap-frogging" such positions helped maintain the pace of the advance and reflected the extent to which the Americans had the initiative. In the Mediterranean, in contrast, where distances were far smaller and Allied air power weaker, the Germans were able to withdraw from strategically irrelevant Sardinia and Corsica in the autumn of 1943, after the invasion of Italy. In the Pacific, the ability to deploy carriers both in the Central Pacific and in the South-West Pacific, reflected the extent to which superior American resources permitted the simultaneous pursuit of more than one offensive strategy. During the war, the Americans deployed nearly 100 carriers of all sorts in the Pacific.

## 1944–45, Allies victorious

In 1944, far harder blows were delivered at the Axis powers. They failed to regain the initiative and continued to lose territory, and were also outfought. In the Pacific, the collapse of the Japanese empire was inexorable. Without air superiority, Japanese naval units were highly vulnerable. The Americans could decide where to make attacks, and could neutralize bases, such as Rabaul, that they chose to "leap-frog". This was part of the more general degradation of Japanese logistics. "Leap-frogging" lessened the extent of hard, slogging conflict. The synergy of American operations was matched in planning; bases from which Japan could be bombed increasingly became a priority, reflecting the role envisaged for the new, long-range B-29 bomber.

In June 1944, the American Pacific fleet covered an amphibious attack on the Marianas, leading to a struggle between carrier forces that devastated that of Japan. Saipan fell, and the Japanese cabinet resigned on 18 July. The resolution of the Japanese resistance was shown on Saipan, where nearly the entire garrison, 27,000 men, died resisting attack, and the island took three weeks to capture. On Tinian, where the Americans landed on 24 July, the Japanese also fought to the end, but the American attack was more effective and the island fell in a week, although, as elsewhere, for example on Guam, those Japanese who were not killed fought on until the end of the war and, in some cases, beyond it. Further south, mobility and firepower brought the Americans success in New Guinea.

The Americans used their naval and air superiority, already strong and rapidly growing, to mount a reconquest of the Philippines, which began in October, when Leyte was invaded, and continued in January when a large force was landed on the largest island, Luzon. In the battle of Leyte Gulf of 23–6 October 1944, the Japanese fleet was comprehensively destroyed, with the loss of four carriers, three battleships and 10 cruisers, and Japanese air power in and near the Philippines was badly hit. On land, the Japanese fought to the end, a sacrificial policy that matched the use of *kamikaze* planes against American warships, beginning on 25 October 1944. The Americans could choose where to land, but the fighting and logistical problems of operations on shore were both formidable, and Japanese determination to fight on lessened the value of deep penetration attacks. At the same time, the Japanese forces on the Philippines, which still totalled over 225,000 in February 1945, were able to make little effective contribution to the Japanese war effort, other than tying down Allied forces and causing casualties. However, this attritional end was an important Japanese goal.

In Burma, the Japanese were outfought on the ground. The simplicity of their determined offensive tactics were no longer adequate against better-trained British and Commonwealth troops able to control battles carefully and benefiting from high unit quality, and superior logistics, air power and artillery. The Japanese had succeeded in defeating a limited British offensive in the Arakan region, but their own invasion of north-eastern India was heavily defeated at Kohima and Imphal in March–July 1944. This provided a basis for the British invasion of Burma from December 1944, which led to a successful drive on the Irrawaddy valley, and a subsequent advance towards Rangoon, supported by an amphibious landing. Fighting in Burma was difficult; as Lieutenant-General Sir Henry Pownall wrote: "It is bound to be a slow business, I fear. That jungle is so infernally thick you literally cannot see ten yards into it, and to winkle out concealed Japs, one by one (and they have to be killed to the last man) is the devil of a business."[9]

In Europe, the seizure of the initiative by the Allies was also crucial, although Hitler and some of his supporters continued to believe in a Nazi victory. The Soviets pushed the Germans back across Russia, White Russia and the Ukraine, in an impressive series of offensives, and opened up the Balkans. Sevastopol surrendered on 9 May 1944, at the end of a rapidly successful conquest of the Crimea. The German Army Group Centre was destroyed in June–July with successful encirclement attacks. Romania surrendered in August, and Bulgaria and Finland in September. The need for the Germans to defend the entire front left them with few resources for staging counter-offensives. The Soviets also proved superior at operational art, and this enabled them to stage successful offensives focusing on manoeuvre warfare. This counteracted German tactical proficiency.

Further west, Anglo-American forces landed in Normandy on 6 June 1944. They benefited from absolute air superiority, which, combined with the efforts of the French resistance, helped to isolate the battlefield, and from a successful deception exercise, which ensured that the Normandy landing was a surprise. It proved difficult to break out of Normandy, but, greatly helped by air power, the Allies finally succeeded in doing so at the close of July.[10] The retreating Germans suffered heavy casualties in the Falaise pocket the following month, although the Allies failure to close it quickly was a major blunder, which possibly cost victory in 1944. Other Allied units liberated Paris on 25 August. The break-out from Normandy had been followed by a deep exploitation that matched earlier operations in North Africa, as well as the Soviet advance in 1944, but contrasted with Allied operations in Italy. The Allies had also landed successfully in the south of France in August.

The speedy liberation of France and Belgium created resupply problems over increasing distances and was followed by tough German resistance as the German border was approached, and a standstill over the winter. However, the impact on the manpower of the German army of continuous fighting in France, Italy and on the Eastern Front in the second half of 1944 had been heavy. In a meeting on 7 December 1944, Eisenhower, the Commander of Allied forces in the West, "emphasised the heavy rate of attrition they were forcing on the enemy, a rate very much greater than our own. He pointed out that the enemy could not afford losses on such a scale."[11] Nevertheless, the fighting quality the Germans showed in, for example, successfully resisting the Allied attack on Arnhem in September and in the Scheldt estuary in October–November 1944, as well as opposing the American advance in Lorraine that autumn,[12] indicated the extent to which defeat in Normandy had not destroyed the German war effort in the West and that there would probably be no sudden collapse once Germany was invaded.

After a German counter-offensive in the Ardennes was defeated in the Battle of the Bulge that December, speeding up the German defeat, Anglo-American forces advanced across the Rhine in March 1945, and reached the Elbe on 11 April. Against bitter resistance, the Soviets were victorious in the Vistula-Oder Offensive of January–February 1945, and the crowning Berlin Operation. They fought their way into Berlin, where Hitler committed suicide on 30 April. On 7 May 1945, the Germans surrendered unconditionally.[13]

Soviet strength had played a crucial role in the victory and the vast numbers involved on the Eastern Front identify it as the decisive theatre in the war against Germany. At no point after June 1941 was there less than two-thirds of the German army on the Eastern Front, and most of the time the percentage was larger than that. However, the Anglo-American achievement had been considerable, not least because of the range of their commitments against Germany, including not only in western Europe and the Mediterranean but also the Battle of the Atlantic and the strategic air offensive.

The Western Allies, particularly the Americans, also bore the brunt of the war with Japan. In early 1945, the Americans seized the islands of Iwo Jima and Okinawa in order to provide air bases for an attack on Japan. This bland remark gives no guidance to the difficulty of the conquests and the heavy casualties involved in defeating the well-positioned Japanese forces, who fought to the death with fanatical intensity for islands seen as part of Japan, although under heavy pressure from the attacking American marines with their massive air and sea support. The Japanese were also skilful defenders, well able to exploit the terrain, not least by tunnelling into Iwo Jima. This ensured that the bombing and shelling that preceded the landing of the marines on 19 February inflicted only minimal damage. As a consequence, the conquest of the island was slow and bloody, and much of the fighting was at close quarters. The Americans made extensive use of tank-mounted flame-throwers in order to clear positions. On Okinawa, the Americans dropped napalm into the entrances of Japanese positions.

The heavy casualty rate inflicted by the defenders, the vast majority of whom died in the defence,[14] led to fears about the casualties that an invasion of Japan would entail. This encouraged the use of the atom bomb. The homeland army was weak – poorly trained and equipped and lacking mobility and air support – but the atom bomb was seen as necessary both in order to overcome a suicidal determination to fight on and to obtain unconditional surrender.[15]

The war ended with the Japanese agreeing on 14 August 1945 to surrender unconditionally, just a few days after the dropping of two American atomic bombs. The Soviet Union had declared war on Japan and invaded Manchuria on 8 August, two days after the first bomb had been dropped on Hiroshima. The Japanese had been outnumbered in Manchuria, especially in tanks and aircraft, but they were also outfought. The Soviet forces were better trained and many had had combat experience in Europe. Soviet forces not only seized the initiative, but also advanced rapidly to envelop their opponents. Soviet armoured columns concentrated on advancing through the Greater Khingan Range of mountains, where the Japanese were weakly deployed. The Soviets also used airborne detachments to seize important positions. Their campaign bridged German blitzkrieg with Cold War Soviet plans for invasions of western Europe. Crucially, the Soviets had far more tanks, guns and aircraft than the Germans had in 1940.

## The analysis of victory

Allied victory can most easily be attributed to vastly superior resources, but much else was involved in ensuring success. In 1939–40, the Germans avoided the danger of encirclement and war on two fronts, and the other possibility – that Britain and France would be able to rest successfully on the defensive behind the Maginot Line while blockading Germany into a change of policy or leadership. The Germans were able to make the offensive work in both strategic and tactical terms. In mechanized warfare, the tactical potential of an offensive spearheaded by armoured forces with air support was amply displayed in 1939–40. Tanks could move across country, limiting the need to tie forward units to roads. The French had more tanks than the

Germans in 1940, and their tanks were, for the most part, heavier gunned and had more effective protection, although they were somewhat slower and had to turn in order to fire. Their lack of radios also created problems for French tanks: communication was by signal flag. However, aside from a poor overall strategy, the French failed to develop an effective doctrine for their armour. They persisted in seeing tanks as support for infantry, and most French tanks were, accordingly, split up into small groups for use as mobile artillery, rather than being used as armoured divisions for their shock value. Tactics and operational control and coordination were more important for success than the technological capabilities of the weapon.

Nevertheless, some commentators remain excessively under the spell cast by the sheer shock and drama of the first blitzkrieg campaigns in 1939 and 1940, and have therefore overrated the impact on war of German military methods, which represented more of an improvisation than the fruition of a coherent doctrine, even among the Germans. Blitzkrieg never existed as a unified concept, and the term was not favoured by the Germans.[16] It is better to employ phrases such as "the effective use of air and mechanized forces".

Analysis of the German campaigns in the early stages of the war qualifies some popularly held notions. German offensive strategy worked best if the opponent was poorly prepared to contest a rapid advance from a number of directions (Poland 1939, Yugoslavia 1941), or lacked a strategic reserve (Poland 1939, Yugoslavia 1941), or if the reserve was inadequate and/or poorly directed (France 1940). The Poles and the French placed the bulk of their forces too far forward. This provided an opportunity for outmanoeuvring, fixing and surrounding or destroying these forces, the strategy attempted against France in 1914. In addition, the distances in Poland and north-east France that the advancing Germans had to overcome were relatively short.

As far as the France campaign is concerned, the effectiveness of the blitzkrieg must not be exaggerated. Much of the German army still walked. The key element was the tactical and operational use of the armoured tip of the army rather than its overall weight. There was a massive French intelligence failure and totally inadequate forces in the Ardennes. Morale counted as well. German morale was high, and French morale on the whole poor. When the French fought well, however, the weaknesses of the blitzkrieg tactical system were demonstrated. At Gembloux on 14–15 May, a French artillery–infantry defence, particularly the French artillery, was effective.[17] When the British counter-attacked, as they sometimes did, they disrupted the German advance considerably. But they were poorly commanded and, for many, their heart was not in the fight. In the end, getting the army out of France became paramount.

The deficiencies of their opponents ensured that insufficient attention was devoted to the limitation of the German military machine for offensive operations. Aside from flaws in strategy and command, seen for example in the planning and execution of the attacks on Poland, Norway and France, the Germans were deficient in mechanized (or at least motorized) infantry, logistics, artillery support, and effective ground-support air power. Basically, they were not ready when war broke out in 1939.

These deficiencies became more apparent and important when the Soviet Union was attacked in 1941. Initially, the speed of the German advance impressed observers. Thanks to developments in weaponry and road- and bridge-building, an army taking the offensive could advance more rapidly than ever before, especially, as with the Germans, if tank units were able to operate with open flanks and unconstrained by the need to wait for support, and, thus, by the lower speed of supporting artillery and infantry.

However, the Germans had not planned adequately for a sequence of campaigns and a long war. The space of the Soviet Union had not been conceptually overcome. Space was a force-multiplier for the defensive and, as such, an aspect of the reserve. The existence of such a reserve in 1941, and the fact that it was ably deployed, ensured that the initial success of the offensive could not be sustained. German war-making, with its emphasis on surprise, speed, and overwhelming and dynamic force at the chosen point of contact, was designed for an offensive strategy that was most effective against linear defences, not against defence in depth that retained the capacity to use reserves.

In addition, there were tactical problems with mechanized assaults, not least the difficulty of maintaining infantry support. It could be risky if too wide a gap opened up. Infantry support was important for countering anti-tank guns, which the Soviets used skilfully. This was not only an issue in the Soviet Union. Major-General Eric Dorman-Smith, who served as second in command to Auchinleck with the British Eighth Army in North Africa, was scathing about British generalship:

> In the Middle East Command, during the autumn of 1941, there arose the tactical heresy which propounded that armour alone counted in the Desert battle, therefore British armour should discover and destroy the enemy's equivalent armour, after which decision the unarmoured infantry divisions would enter the arena to clear up what remained and hold the ground gained.

Dorman-Smith contrasted this with Rommel's Afrika Korps, and its tactical preference for a "mixed formation of all arms", and attributed British deficiencies to the sway of generals with a cavalry background: "the romantic cavalry mystique of horsed warfare" led to "basic tactical fallacies . . . the dichotomy between the unarmoured infantry divisions and the relatively 'un-infanterised' armoured divisions".[18]

In February 1945, Auchinleck's successor, Montgomery, then commander of the 21st Army Group, argued that close cooperation with infantry was needed in order to overcome anti-tank guns: "I cannot emphasise too strongly that victory in battle depends not on armoured action alone, but on the intimate co-operation of all arms; the tank by itself can achieve little".[19] This had been demonstrated the previous year in Normandy, where tanks had failed to achieve what the Americans, British and Germans had expected from them. This was more than a matter of difficult terrain; there were also serious operational limitations for tank warfare.

Soviet doctrine, with its emphasis on defence in depth and its stress on artillery in defence and attack, proved effective once the initial shock and surprise of the German attack had been absorbed. The Soviets responded rapidly in order to rebuild their forces. The Germans were not simply thwarted by the size of the Soviet Union, the delay in launching the 1941 offensive, the onset of winter and maladroit intervention by Hitler – they were also defeated in battle. Once their advances had been held, the Germans suffered from the absence of sufficient manpower, artillery and supplies. Stabilizing, let alone advancing, the front proved an enormous strain on resources. Once the psychological shock of the blitzkrieg had been overcome, and effective anti-tank weapons reached the battlefield, then the defence could again cope with the offensive, beginning with the successful defence by the Red Army in late 1941. The Germans presented their attack in terms of rapidly advancing armour, but most of the German troops were slow-moving infantry, dependent on horse-drawn transport. In addition, in contrast to the relatively small size of the crucial field of operations in Poland and northern France, the Germans were handicapped in the Soviet Union by the length of the front and the area they had to advance across. Their logistical support could not keep up. The German leadership was dangerously overconfident. At Stalingrad in 1942, the attacking Germans were fought to a standstill despite a massive commitment of resources.

World War Two reverted to a prolonged struggle of attrition, although there was usually much more movement than in World War One. The Germans proved formidable foes on the defensive, but were outnumbered and outfought. When the Germans resumed the attack with the Kursk offensive in the summer of 1943, the Soviets were able to thwart them, despite the sophistication of their tanks.[20] The Red Army proved adept at developing good cooperation between armour, artillery and infantry, and at making the latter two mobile, successfully executing a strategy of encirclement, as in the right-bank Ukraine Campaign of early 1944, around Korsun-Shevchenkovski. In addition, advancing Soviet forces proved able to split opposing armies. The Soviets achieved what has been seen as their own blitzkrieg, especially in the breakthrough attacks in March and April 1944, which drove the Germans back across the Bug, Dniester and Prut, and those in June–September 1944, which overran Belorussia (White Russia) and took the Soviets close to Warsaw, destroying much of the German Army Group Centre. This was a triumph for operational skill. The Germans were outgeneralled and outfought, with the Soviets using effective deception to disguise their plans and skilful infantry tactics.[21]

In less than two-and-a-half years' fighting, the Red Army drove the Germans from the Volga to the Elbe, a distance greater than that achieved by any European force for over a century, and one that showed that a war of fronts did not preclude one of a frequent movement of these fronts. Furthermore, this was not simply an advance on one axis. Indeed, the scale of the Soviet achievement can be grasped by considering their advances on their flanks. These included the clearing of most of the Baltic states in late 1944, and the defeat of the German army in Moldavia in August 1944, followed by the overthrow of Romanian resistance and the invasion of Bulgaria, which led to the seizure of power by the Communists and their allies. The Soviets went on in October to invade Slovakia and to overrun much of eastern Hungary, although Budapest did not completely fall until 13 February 1945, showing that Stalingrad was not the only city that could be bitterly defended. However, as with Stalingrad, a German attempt to relieve a surrounded force failed.

Soviet operational art towards the end of the war stressed firepower, but also employed mobile tank warfare: attrition and manoeuvre were combined in a coordinated sequence of attacks that reflected operational skill. This can be seen in the conquest of Poland, much of which was completed in January 1945: the Soviets used large numbers of tanks, which were able to exploit opportunities prepared by short and savage artillery attacks. The individual Soviet tank armies gained space to manoeuvre and this prevented the Germans from consolidating new positions. Breslau, the fortified capital of Silesia, held out, but the Soviets were able to establish bridgeheads across the Oder at the start of February 1945. For forces that had broken through their opponents, mobility enhanced the ability to prevent their opponents from falling back in order. Mobility replaced the new front line of World War One advances with the open battlefield, in which retreating opponents had to rely on defensive hedgehog positions that could be encircled, if the momentum of the offensive could be maintained. The limit of the new advance was often that of maintaining petrol supplies, as in the Soviet advance through Poland in early 1945. Also, a continued use of frontal attacks was, by Western standards, wasteful of manpower.

The Red Army's record was not one of invariable success from late 1942. This emerges clearly from Glantz's study of Operation Mars. Launched in November 1942 on the central front west of Moscow, this was the counterpart of Operation Uranus, the Soviet Stalingrad counter-offensive. Planned and directed by Marshal Zhukov, Mars failed and was covered up. Zhukov provided a wholly inaccurate and incomplete account in which he ignored the deluded character of the planning and the defective execution. The premature commitment of the Soviet armour into too small a bridgehead prevented the subsequent forward movement of supporting artillery. As a result, the exploiting forces had to engage a counter-attacking enemy without proper artillery support. Furthermore, repeated, costly frontal Soviet attacks quickly led to the combat exhaustion of units. Soviet forces lost about 100,000 killed and about 235,000 wounded. These men were forgotten in the Soviet portrayal of a continuous and heroic march to victory from late 1942.[22]

The fighting quality of German units operating against Allied forces in 1943–45, in North Africa, Italy and western Europe, was high, and sometimes higher than that of their attackers, as with the struggle between British and German armour in Normandy in 1944. However, aside from the quantity of Allied resources, there was also an improvement in Allied capability, for example in ground-support aircraft, which was to have a devastating impact in the battle for Normandy. The Allies were also helped by a less difficult logistical situation than that in eastern Europe. They faced problems with logistical support after their break-out from Normandy in 1944, but not on the same scale or with effects that were so dire. The Allies drove the Germans from Normandy to the Elbe in less than a year. As in 1918, there was no stab in the back: the Germans were beaten, and recent work has qualified earlier suggestions that their fighting quality was far higher than that of the Allies.[23]

In the Solomons and Midway in 1942 and in Burma in 1944, the Japanese discovered that it was difficult to sustain success once the dramatic advances of the early stages of the conflict had passed. They were overconfident and poorly prepared for a long struggle, not least due to a lack of necessary resources, and also suffered from a long-standing failure to reconcile army and naval objectives, priorities and methods. The fighting quality of Japanese units could not compensate for the number of their opponents and their successful mobilization of greater resources. Japanese army and naval tactics and force structures have been seen as overly dogmatic and mistaken. The army was wasteful of troops in attack and had a poor logistical system, while the navy overrated battleships and underrated submarines. Against mobile Soviet forces, the Japanese also proved deficient in both 1939 and 1945.

When the Soviets invaded Manchuria in 1945, they deployed 1.5 million troops, 4,370 aeroplanes, 5,500 tanks and 28,000 pieces of artillery. It would be absurd to ignore the role of resources, troops, *matériel* and funds, as well as the more basic resources of population, raw materials and industrial plant. Not all states, however, responded to the need for resources with a similar level of effectiveness. In both world wars, the Germans knew that they were most likely to win through a rapid offensive war, because they could not match the industrial, financial and demographic resources of their opponents, hence their emphasis on surprise, "will power" and knocking a major opponent out of the conflict. But none of this worked once the Allies had extended to include the USA and had mobilized their superior capacity to produce and overwhelm the enemy with military hardware and munitions.

In World War Two, the Germans tried to mobilize their massive industrial base for a long period of fighting from 1939, an extensive conversion of industrial capacity to war production beginning with the outbreak of hostilities. However, they faced many difficulties, not least too many competing agencies being involved, especially in 1939–41. Their highest level of armaments production did not come until September 1944, despite devastating Allied bombing, towards the close of the war, when the rationalization plans of Albert Speer, who had been appointed Minister for Armaments in 1942, came to fruition. In addition, unlike their opponents, the Germans failed to mobilize female labour thoroughly.

They preferred to use slave labour, an inefficient as well as cruel policy: millions of foreign workers, especially Soviet, Polish and French, were brought to Germany, while, elsewhere in occupied Europe, workers were forced to work in often brutal conditions in order to produce resources for Germany. Aside from prisoners of war, 5.7 million foreign workers were registered in the Greater German Reich in August 1944; combined with the prisoners of war, they provided half the workforce in agriculture and in the manufacture of munitions.[24] Furthermore, the Germans failed to exploit mass-production techniques as successfully as their opponents, because they put a premium on responding to military requests for custom-made weapons, rather than on mass production of a more limited range of weapons.

This reflected a military culture that emphasized duty and tactics, not logistics (nor indeed intelligence), a political culture in which there was a reluctance to understand the exigencies and potential of the economy, and a simple expectation that it would produce resources as required without consultation and to order. The Germans were also fascinated with potent weapons – moving towards bigger and bigger tanks and guns – rather than with weapons that were less effective individually, but easier to produce in mass. Hitler's interventions in the allocation of resources for weapon production and, subsequently, in the use of weapons, were frequently deleterious. He was convinced that, late in the war, Germany would suddenly produce a wonder weapon that would win the war; such a weapon existed in the atom bomb, but Germany missed the chance of developing it.

Nevertheless, however inefficient, the German regime was able to direct and enforce a major expansion in the war economy, and a devotion of activity and production to the war, with personal consumption levels pushed down below those in Britain and the USA. Italy was less effective than Germany: "The terms of war had changed [since 1918] beyond the ability of Italy's military institutions to follow either materially or culturally".[25]

The Germans, like the Japanese, gained control over the resources and labour forces of areas they conquered or that were allied to them: for example, the coal and industry of north-east France, and the oil of Romania and the Dutch East Indies. Oil was crucial to warfare on land, at sea and in the air. Japan, in particular, suffered from oil shortages, but these also affected

Germany, leading Hitler to try to advance on the Soviet oilfields at Baku in 1942. However, the value of German gains were lessened because they were oilfields that the Germans had been able to tap prior to the war. In 1941, the Germans overran Estonia when they attacked the Soviet Union, but from 1935 they had already been the largest purchaser of oil from Estonia's oil-shale fields. More generally, despite Soviet reluctance to fulfil German requirements,[26] under the Nazi–Soviet pact of 1939, the Germans had enjoyed access to Soviet raw materials in a relationship that was ruptured by the German invasion in 1941.

Thus, German policy helped threaten its resource basis. This was also true of its policies within its areas of conquest. The cruel nature of Axis control dissipated support and, instead, encouraged resistance and labour non-cooperation; for example, policies of compulsory labour, including the deportation of workers to work in Germany, met with opposition, as in Belgium. Large numbers of German troops were deployed in order to limit resistance operations or to prevent their possible outbreak. On 1 January 1944, German, Bulgarian and quisling forces in Yugoslavia amounted to 360,000 men. Furthermore, the horrendous programmes of genocide pursued by the Germans absorbed resources that might otherwise have been devoted to the war. Thus, trains were used to transport victims to the concentration camps, rather than to move military supplies.

In contrast, the dynamic of American resource build-up relied on lightly regulated capitalism, not coercion. Having had cool relations with much of American business during the 1930s, Roosevelt turned to them to create a war machine, a task that was doubly difficult because there had not been a military build-up in the 1930s comparable to that of the Axis powers. The American army was in a particularly poor state, and smaller in 1939 than that of Portugal. In 1939, Congress agreed a major increase in military expenditure. Part of this was directed at creating a larger manufacturing base for war material. The War Resources Board was established in 1939, in order to ready industry for a war footing, and the Office of Production Management under William Knudsen, head of General Motors, followed in 1941. Major changes resulted as aircraft and ship productive capacity and production increased. The populations of Washington, Oregon and, in particular, California, where many of the plants were located, rose greatly; by the end of the war, eight million people had moved permanently to different states.

Some of the internal migrants were African-Americans: about 700,000 African-American civilians left the South, especially for California. The opportunities that war industrialization provided for African-American workers helped loosen racial, as well as gender and social, relations, although much segregation remained and racial tension led to serious outbreaks of violence, particularly in Detroit in 1943.[27]

There was also an attempt to create new communication routes that would be outside the range of submarine attack. Pipelines were laid from Texas to the industrial centres of the North East, including the "Big Inch" from Houston to New York, in order to lessen coastal shipping. The coastal inland waterway system was improved. In 1942, the Alaska Highway was built in order to provide an overland route to the American bases there.

Turning to business for cooperation in rearmament led to a lack of coordination, but this was rectified by the establishment of the Office of War Mobilization in May 1943. Furthermore, the Americans benefited from their already sophisticated economic infrastructure, which helped in the adaptation of the economy for war production. Although care is needed before pushing any comparison too far, there is a parallel between the operational flexibility that the Americans frequently displayed in combat, and that of their economy.

Phenomenal quantities of weapons and weapons systems were produced, and the USA surmounted the domestic divisions of the 1930s in order to create a productivity-oriented political consensus, which brought great international strength. The resources, commitments and pretensions of the federal government grew greatly, and taxes and government expenditure both rose substantially. Government spending totalled $317 billion and nearly 90 per cent of this was on the war.

In the USA, the attitudes and techniques of the production line were focused on war. The Americans produced formidable quantities of munitions – $186 billion worth – and an infrastructure to move them. In 1941–45, the USA produced 297,000 aeroplanes and 86,000 tanks. Aside from massive resources, especially oil, and the fact that their industry was not being bombed as those of the other combatants were, the Americans benefited from a relative lack of need for imports, which contrasted greatly with the situation in Japan and Britain. In turn, American industry produced massive quantities of goods for allies. These made a significant impact in particular operations: in North Africa in 1942 the British benefited from American tanks.

Production of weaponry was closely linked to the objective of movement. American forces were motorized to an extent greater than those of any other state, and this was not only a question of the armour. Infantry and artillery were also motorized. This was intended to allow for "triangular" operations in which the opposing force was frontally engaged by one unit while another turned its flank, and a third, in reserve, was poised to intervene where most helpful.

The capability of the American war economy was amply shown in shipbuilding. The global scope of Allied power depended on American shipbuilding. Most of the 42 million tons of shipping built by the Allies during the war was constructed by the Americans. Many were Liberty ships, built often in as little as ten days, using prefabricated components on production lines. All-welded ships replaced riveting, speeding up production. Despite losing oil tankers with a total tonnage of 1,421,000, mostly to submarines, the tonnage of the American oil tanker fleet rose from 4,268,000 tons in 1942 to 12,875,000 tons in 1945. The flexibility of American society helped directly: by 1944, 11.5 per cent of the workers in the shipbuilding industry were women.[28]

American production helped counteract the serious problems created by the boldness of Allied strategic planning, which had paid insufficient attention to logistical realities. This was a particular problem in Churchill's case; his emphasis on the Mediterranean had serious logistical implications. The American preference for concentrating on a cross-Channel invasion of France was more appropriate in terms of logistical capability.[29] Like America, Canada benefited in its wartime industrial mobilization from its distance from the combat zone. Thanks to production for the war, Canadian gross national product more than doubled in 1939–45, while federal government expenditure rose from $680 million in 1939 to $5,136 million in 1945. The War Measures Act was used to regulate industrial activity and the Wartime Prices and Trade Board set wages and prices and allocated scarce commodities.[30]

Soviet industry also displayed considerable adaptability. From the late 1920s, the Soviets had developed industrial production and mining in or east of the Urals, which was beyond the range of German air attack. This looked back to a long tradition of production in the Urals, but was stepped up under Stalin such that about one-third of coal, iron and steel production was there. The Ural metallurgical industry proved of particular importance during the war. Major new industrial capacity was also developed near Novosibirsk in south-western Siberia, and new plants were built in Soviet Central Asia. It was particularly in the Soviet Union that the mobilization of resources involved a marked degree of direction of the economy. Already an autocracy, where economic planning and the brutalization of society were mutually supporting, the Soviet system sustained the war effort despite the loss of many of its leading agricultural and industrial areas to German advances in 1941 and 1942. Indeed, although production statistics should only be used with care, in the first six months of the war the Soviet economy lost areas producing 68 per cent of its iron, 63 per cent of its coal and 58 per cent of its steel, as well as 40 per cent of its farmland, including, in the Ukraine, much of its most fertile area. These losses were but part of the profound wartime disruption caused by unexpected invasion.[31]

The Americans and Soviets concentrated on weapons that were simple to build, operate and repair and enjoyed overwhelming superiority in the quantity of resources, and in most cases also in their quality. Allied artillery was more intensive and overwhelming in firepower. The British and the Americans were very keen on using big artillery bombardments, and the Germans had no real answer. The best German tanks were technically better in firepower and armour in 1944, but the unreliability and high maintenance requirements of the Tiger tank weakened it. German tanks were complex pieces of equipment, and often broke down. Most German armour was no better than, and often inferior to, Allied armour. The "quality gap" that favoured the Germans was closed by late 1944 and 1945, as new Allied tanks appeared. In eastern Europe, the impact of German long-range anti-tank guns was lessened by the close distances of actual engagements.

Allied resource superiority affected the conduct of the war. For example, as the Americans advanced across France in 1944, they did not storm villages and towns where they encountered resistance. Instead, they stopped, brought in aerial, armour and artillery support, and heavily bombarded the site before moving in, with scant loss of American life.

The importance of industrial resources lent point to strategic bombing, and ensured that victorious powers sought to seize industrial plant. They also had a role in the planning for the invasion of Germany. In his General Situation memorandum of 21 January 1945, Montgomery wrote, "The main objective of the Allies on the western front is the Ruhr; if we can cut it off from the rest of Germany the enemy capacity to continue the struggle must gradually peter out".[32]

The Allies also benefited more than their opponents from the provision of munitions and other supplies to members of the alliance under strain. Large quantities of Anglo-American supplies were provided to the Soviets. They helped compensate for particular deficiencies. Thus the American Jeep provided a valuable degree of mobility. There were also important exchanges of knowledge. The Tizard mission sent to the USA in 1940 provided valuable British technology, including a prototype cavity-magnetron. This was central to the development of short-wave radio.[33]

Science was deployed by the powers, but with differing results. For example, the Germans experienced a great shock when they discovered that the British were using microwaves. Until then, German scientific orthodoxy was sceptical of their value and no priority had been given to the production of the transmitting valves necessary for microwaves. In contrast to the Allied teams of scientists, who were free to handle their own affairs, the German technical staff were frightened of being proved wrong and being exposed to ridicule. Science was indispensable for the rapid development of radar, evolving from the rather crude Chain Home (CH) stations to the sophisticated magnetron. Microwave radar was the most effective counter to the U-boat because the Germans were not able to develop suitable counter-measures in time. They were, however, more successful in interfering with Allied offensive radar, thus introducing the new technique of electronic warfare in which attackers and defenders strove to outwit each other.[34] Nevertheless, accurate attacks on pinpoint targets could only be made after post-war scientific advances.

The role of resource availability and utilization in determining the result of the war is capable of different interpretations. The availability of vast resources did not overcome the contingent in the short term, and the long term is really only a series of short terms. In addition, the contingent fact of war helped mould the long-term resource base, socioeconomic structures and political cultures of the combatants.

The conflicts also included multiple contingencies and counterfactuals,[35] such as: what if Hitler had not declared war on the USA; or what if Stalin had acted on his fears about being left in the lurch by the Western Allies and had settled with Hitler? This is a reminder of the danger of basing an account of the conflict preponderantly on resource availability. Assessing the resources available to both sides is a misleading approach, because it underrates the contingent nature of the "sides".

This can be taken further by focusing on areas and groups that offer a different perspective to that of the "macro-scale", for example Albania, for which the official socialist view of the war actively propagated during the Hoxha regime, was so politicized as to lessen greatly its value. Instead, it is important to stress the role of the early non-Communist resistance movements, and to note the extent to which the Germans, in 1943–44, were initially more effective than the Italians (who occupied the country in 1939–43) in winning support. Opposition to the Serbs proved popular with some, but, ultimately, the Germans failed to maintain order in Albania and Kosovo through the use of Albanian forces. Furthermore, their attempt to do so compromised the groups with whom they allied. The experience of first Italian and then German rule undermined the position of the pre-war political and social elites, and thus helped Hoxha, the Communist resistance leader, to consolidate his position.[36]

The role of the resistance in Albania is a reminder that, even in a conflict dominated by the great powers and their resources, it is necessary to remember the role of non-regular forces. This was of particular importance in the internal conflicts of the inter-war period discussed in Chapter 4, but World War Two showed that such forces could play a role in resisting occupying regular forces after the defending regulars had been defeated. In part, there was also the dimension of civil conflict, as in Albania and Yugoslavia, resistance groups fought each other, a situation that bridged to the post-war world in Greece as one of the groups allied with the returning exile government and the other resisted it. In Yugoslavia, the Communists, led by Tito, competed with the Chetniks under Mihailovitch. The Chetniks derived from sections of the Yugoslav army. The situation in the Balkans was made more complex by frequently ambivalent relations between sections of the resistance and the occupying power. This was accentuated by the reliance of the Germans on local allies, a reliance that was pushed by the need for troops on the Eastern Front. In Yugoslavia, a full-scale civil war between Communists and Chetniks began in November 1942.

There were serious rivalries elsewhere in occupied Europe, but also a high level of activity directed against the Germans and their local allies. In Poland and occupied areas of the Soviet Union, there was extensive partisan activity, helped by the vastness of the area in question, the nature of the terrain – for example the Pripet Marshes – and the harshness of German rule. Initially, Soviet opposition came from units of the Red Army that had been cut off by the German advance, and from units from the People's Commissariat of Internal Affairs (NKVD, secret police), but, with time, partisan support became far more widespread. The better-armed Germans were generally able to defeat partisans in open conflict, as when they suppressed uprisings in Warsaw, Slovakia and the Vercors plateau in France in 1944. Furthermore, many areas under partisan control were so because the Germans chose not to deploy troops to occupy them.

However, the resistance still achieved much. Most important, as with the Allied air offensive, was the diversion of large amounts of German resources to dealing with the threat, as well as the need to adopt anti-partisan policies that affected the efficiency of German rule and economic and transport activities. The Allies also benefited from large quantities of crucial intelligence, for example on defences, troop movements, bomb damage and the development of German rocketry. In addition, considerable damage and disruption were inflicted by sabotage and by guerrilla attacks. This was most useful when coordinated with Allied operations, for example, fighting near Kursk in 1943, while, in 1944, the cutting of transport links by which the Germans might move troops complemented the Allied air offensive in preparing for the Normandy landings.

The role of the resistance is a reminder of the mistake of considering strength in terms of regular forces. It also testifies to the character of total war. The occupation of territory and use of its resources were not enough for the Germans, especially in eastern Europe. Instead, the genocidal thrust of German policy affected regular army as well as SS units. Brutalized, the defeated were not prepared to accept the verdict of battle, so that German occupation practices encouraged resistance. German behaviour, "entirely void of military logic", was the consequence of a war of annihilation, in which killing became an end in itself.[37]

The Germans were far less successful in developing a resistance movement as the Allies advanced. The speed of the Nazi collapse was important, but so also was the absence of unoccupied bases from which resistance could be encouraged and supplied. Nevertheless, the Werewolf movement did inflict some damage in 1945 and 1946, killing collaborators and Allied officials and troops.[38]

It is appropriate that this chapter ends with resistance activity, because it captured the way in which the war affected the people of Europe. Denmark, for example, might have fallen to the Germans in a day but, during the war, thousands of attacks were launched by the resistance, hitting the rail system and tying up many German troops in defensive tasks, although the Norwegian resistance was more effective. Such action was to encourage post-war North Atlantic Treaty Organization (NATO) planners, fearful of Soviet invasion, to develop resistance networks and facilities. Equally, resistance activity reflected the diversity of a war that can only be simplified at great cost, not only to any account of developments but also to their analysis. It is necessary to remember that the combatants not only had different under-standings of what victory entailed, with a consequent impact on political and military strategy, but also that their operational methods reflected this, and indeed were in part shaped by war aims.[39] The conflict became less fluid than it had been in its first two years, because Hitler's mindset and the Allies' response helped ensure that the war ended through unconditional surrender, rather than the unilateral negotiations that might, otherwise, have been a response to his failure to defeat the Soviet Union in 1941. This helped to give an attritional character to the later years of the war, but, even then, differences in war aims, operational culture, force structure and resource availability combined to ensure great diversity in conflict.[40]

# CHAPTER SIX
# *Naval Power and Warfare*

War will come like the Day of Judgement . . . there will be no more
time for building submarines than there will be for repentance . . .
The finality of a modern sea fight – once beaten, the war is finished.
(Sir John Fisher, First Lord of the Admiralty, 1904)[1]

What is it that the coming of the submarine really means? It means
that the whole foundation of our traditional naval strategy, which
served us so well in the past, has been broken down! The foundation
of that strategy was blockade. The fleet did not exist merely to win
battles – that was the means not the end. The ultimate purpose of the
fleet was to make blockade possible for us and impossible for our
enemy.
(Memorandum, "The oil engine and the submarine" [1912?],
among the material relating to the Royal Commission on Fuel
and Engines, 1912, in the papers of Vice-Admiral John Jellicoe,
Commander of the Second Division in the British Home Fleet)[2]

It may appear questionable to separate out this topic and the air power
discussed in the next chapter, but they can be submerged unless they receive
separate attention and can also be segmented if they are divided up among
chronological chapters. However, if separate chapters are found for the naval
and air dimensions, it is unclear where they should best be located. Any choice
has drawbacks, and it is necessary to consider the following in part in light of
the chronological chapters.

## Naval power before World War One

The processes of technological development, machinization, and doctrinal discussion described for land warfare in Chapter 2 can also be seen with navies. The causal relationship between the three is less clear, and it is possibly best to think in terms of a mutually sustaining development. At the same time, it is important to avoid any linear account of development, because that neglects the role of doctrinal debate and of disagreements about particular technologies. More generally, the absence of conflict between the major powers ensured that technologies and theories could not be adequately tested. It was unclear how far, in the event of war, it would be possible for any navy to realize the command of the sea that was discussed by contemporaries. It was also unclear how far the earlier limitations that powerful navies had encountered in preventing commerce raiding, and in ensuring amphibious capability, had been overcome.

The most important consequence of the absence of major naval conflicts after 1805, when collated with the radical technological developments in warships after 1850, was that a high degree of uncertainty grew up about the likely nature of naval combat, of the strengths and weaknesses of the new ship types, and about what effect all this might have on the organization of fleets, tactics, strategy and maritime dominance. States watched each other keenly in terms of technological innovation, and worried about the best places to put their money.

The size and cost of major warships increased significantly. The tension between armour and armament, weight and manoeuvrability, not least the mutually interacting need for more effective guns and stronger armour, led to changes in hull materials. Wooden-hulled ironclads were quickly superseded in the 1860s. The wrought iron navy was followed in the late 1870s, after experimentation with iron and wood armour, by one using compound armour plate: the iron and steel navy. In the leading navy, the British navy, large hull components, like the keel, stern post, and stern, continued to be iron until the 1880s, but there were also moves towards the first all-steel battleships in the 1870s.

Ship designers faced the problem that was to afflict tank makers: juggling the three desirable, but mutually antagonistic, qualities required of a weapons platform – speed, armament and armour. One could only be enhanced at the expense of the others because of the weight problem. More generally, in the 1870s and early 1880s, "no coherent, practical strategy [in ship design] was possible given the crucial disharmony between the aims of the policy makers and the technologically circumscribed means with which they had to carry them out" and the rapidity of technological development.[3]

Ship design also had to adapt to important changes in armament. In place of warships designed to fire broadsides came guns mounted in centreline turrets, which were able to fire end on, as well as to turn. Firing armour-piercing explosive shells, guns became more effective. It took much less time and effort to sink a steel battleship with high-explosive armour-piercing shells, than a wooden ship of the line with cannon. Guns also became more rapid.

However, some commentators wondered if battleships had a future in the face of torpedoes, which developed from the 1860s with the invention of a submerged torpedo driven by compressed air and with an explosive charge at the head; torpedo boats followed in the late 1870s, with Thornycroft's *Lightning* (1876) providing the model. The first warship sunk by a self-propelled torpedo was a Turkish screw gunboat, sunk by the Russians in 1878. There were also developments in mines and with submarines, although undersea technology posed particular problems. The first steam-powered submarine, the 30-ton *Resurgam*, was launched by George Garrett in 1879. Working with the Swedish arms manufacturer Thomas Nordenfelt, Garrett began work in 1882 on the *Nordenfelt I*, a 60-ton submarine, the first to be armed with self-propelled torpedoes. The French *Gymnôte*, which was powered by an electric battery and completed in 1888, was the first truly operational submarine. Submarines were most interesting initially to weaker navies looking for cheap weapons to threaten or sink the great ships of the big navies, and for *guerre de course* (commerce warfare).

Concern about torpedoes was but part of a wider sense of uncertainty about the role of large warships. In the 1880s, Admiral Théophile Aube and the French Jeune École provided an ideology for battleship opponents that gained at least some support in every navy. They pressed for unarmoured light cruisers that would use less coal and be faster and more manoeuvrable, able to protect sea lanes and attack the commerce of opponents. Aube also favoured the torpedo boat, and claimed that it nullified the power of the British battleship.[4] These ideas also had an impact outside France. By 1888, Germany had commissioned 72 torpedo boats and developed the manufacture of good torpedoes. This interest in an alternative to the battleship looked towards later German interest in the submarine.

Doctrine was linked to strategic need, and thus geopolitics. The Jeune École were pressing the case for a force structure and doctrine able to counter British naval superiority. The development of global trade and of the colonial empires of the Western maritime states helped lead to an emphasis on the value of large navies (but not necessarily large battle fleets), as in Philip Colomb's *The Protection of our Commerce and Distribution of our Naval Forces Considered* (1867). Concern with trade as well as status led the Germans to develop their fleet so that, by 1883, Germany had the third largest armoured fleet in the world. Nevertheless, in Germany, there was uncertainty about whether to concentrate on battleships, cruisers or torpedo craft. This contributed to (and reflected) what was in the 1880s and early 1890s a divided navy, lacking clear objectives and decisive leadership, and German battleship building fell behind that of other powers, so that Italy passed her in armoured tonnage in 1885 and Russia in 1892. The situation did not change until Alfred von Tirpitz became Chief of the Imperial Naval Office in 1897.[5]

Consideration of the strategic importance of trade could lead to states' adopting either an offensive or defensive approach, depending on the vulnerability of their trade compared with others. The French saw themselves facing the British with their superior naval resources, but with a greater reliance on overseas trade. In consequence, they had favoured commerce raiding. Aube's *La Guerre Maritime et Les Ports Françaises* (1882) and *De la Guerre Navale* (1885) were the latest iteration of this policy. German interest in cruisers developed in the 1880s as their overseas empire developed, and there were new sea routes to defend.

The British had to defend their massive overseas trade and the sea routes to their global empire and be ready to face all comers, and so had to build the biggest navy in the world, and have the highest rate of expenditure on the navy. Indeed, throughout the 1880s, British expenditure was close to the combined figure of the next two high spending powers, France and Russia. Unlike France, but like the USA and Japan, Britain was not threatened over land, and so all three could concentrate their defence spending on their navies. The British navy was helped by its peacetime victory in the competition with the French for naval enhancement in the 1860s, and also by the consequences of the Franco-Prussian War for French military priorities: there was a determined effort to strengthen both the army and the fortifications facing Germany.

The year 1887 was the only one between 1858 and 1922 in which no country laid down an armoured warship, but, in the 1890s, there was a renewed emphasis on battleships in naval doctrine. In part, this reflected growing awareness of the possibility of a "counter-tactic" to the torpedo, specifically torpedo nets, and thick belt armour around the waterline, as well as electric searchlights and quick-firing medium-calibre guns that could provide a secondary armament for use against torpedo boats. Finally, there was the development of the originally specialist torpedo boat destroyer, or all-purpose "destroyer" as it later became. In part, changes in warship capability were crucial. Despite the earlier appearance of steam, iron armour and breech-loading guns, the true ocean-going modern (all-steam) battleship did not really emerge until the 1890s.

The marine turbine engine had been invented by Sir Charles Parsons in 1884, new water-tube boiler technology of the early 1880s was introduced in larger ships, and nickel-steel armoured warships were developed in the 1890s after trials in America in 1890 had shown that carbon-treated nickel-steel was more effective in resisting fire than compound armour. Nickel-steel was improved in 1892 when the German Krupp works introduced a process of "gas cementing". It gave added protection without added weight, encouraging the construction of bigger ships, a process that required a sophisticated shipbuilding industry and much expenditure. This protection was a necessary response to the development of chrome steel shells and armour-piercing shell caps, while the latter had increased the effectiveness of major pieces of naval ordnance, and thus provided a greater role for large ships able to carry such guns. In 1890, the British introduced a more powerful "smokeless" powder, cordite, which had a nitroglycerine base. In the 1890s, the British built battleships of the *Majestic* class: the first ships carrying cordite-using big guns mounted in centreline turrets.

British naval construction was driven by closer Franco-Russian cooperation, which included an alliance in 1892, and by the expansion of the Russian navy. From the 1900s, British concern swung towards the German naval expansion that had begun in 1898. In addition, the Anglo-French Entente Cordiale of 1904 marked a fundamental shift in British policy. This also affected British naval deployment and grand strategy. Whereas any conflict with France and Russia would require squadrons around the world, not least in the Mediterranean and the Pacific, confrontation with Germany ensured a focus on home waters, although it is important not to exaggerate the degree to which the main fleet was concentrated there.

Confrontation with Germany encouraged an emphasis on battleships, rather than cruisers. Sir John Fisher, who became First Sea Lord in 1904, had originally planned a focus on battle-cruisers, a new type of ship designed to have more firepower than existing battleships or cruisers, but to be quicker than battleships due to turbine engines and reduced armour. The latter was seen as acceptable, as superior firepower would enable the battle-cruiser to outgun battleships from a distance. However, the Entente Cordiale, which was followed by the Anglo-Russian *rapprochement* of 1907, led to an emphasis not on the global range offered by battle-cruisers but on the new battleship, HMS *Dreadnought*, which Fisher had seen as a one-off.[6] HMS *Dreadnought*, launched in 1906, was the first of a new class of all big-gun (12-inch) battleships, and the first capital ship in the world to be powered by the marine turbine engine. Completed in one year, her construction reflected the industrial and organizational efficiency of British shipbuilding.[7]

Advances in machine tools, metallurgy and explosives ensured that more accurate guns, capable of longer ranges and supported by better explosives, could be produced. The development of optical range-finders improved accuracy. The net effect of technological change was to ensure the need for frequent retooling in order to retain competitive advantage. This placed a serious burden on government finances. In the later nineteenth century, warships became obsolete far more rapidly than in the past. The dreadnought revolution, for example, led to a spiralling of costs as each naval power rushed to acquire the expensive new type.

More sophisticated equipment led to a need for better-trained officers and sailors and, therefore, to the creation of new colleges and training methods. The Americans founded a Naval War College at Newport, and the naval strategist Alfred Thayer Mahan (1840–1914) lectured there from 1885 and was twice its president. It also became more important to ensure continuity in service in navies, because of the more complex training required, and this led to the development of career conditions and structures.

Greater naval capability was designed both to meet actual threats from other naval powers and to overawe them so that actual conflict was prevented. The balance of naval power changed significantly in the last decades of the nineteenth century, and the traditional ranking of Britain, France and Russia was challenged by the emergence of Germany, the USA and Japan; even Italy and Austria developed naval strength significant enough to matter in the global balance.

Naval rivalry focused on competition between battleship numbers and power. Indeed a cult of powerful battleship fleets developed at the close of the century. This owed something to Mahan, whose lectures, published as *The Influence of Sea Power upon History, 1660–1783* (1890), and other works, emphasized the importance of command of the sea, and saw the destruction of the opponent's battle fleet as the means to achieve it. Commerce raiding was presented as less important; and, as a consequence, he put an emphasis on battleships, not cruisers. Mahan's views were widely disseminated – both Kaiser Wilhelm II and Tirpitz read his 1890 book and it was published in German and Japanese in 1896 – and encouraged the process of big-ship construction, which affected many states, including some not generally seen as naval powers, such as Austria.[8]

The naval position of the USA was transformed. The American navy developed a concept of offensive sea control by a battleship fleet, and pressed successfully for the launching and maintenance of an offensive battle fleet in peacetime. America also developed a military–industrial complex, and a chain of protected bases from the Atlantic to the Pacific via Panama, in order to be able to support a large fleet in the Pacific.[9] There was no comparable commitment to the untested submarine.

The case for the battleship was underlined by the Sino-Japanese War of 1894–95. The Battle of the Yalu on 17 September 1894 was the first high seas encounter between fleets of warships since 1866. The two Chinese battleships engaged took a terrific pounding, but did not sink. Their performance helped turn the Japanese back towards the battleship and armoured cruiser and away from French-designed "protected" cruisers, which were the core of their fleet in 1894–95. The battle also showed that the line-ahead formation permitted a greater efficiency of fire and gave commanders greater tactical control once a battle began. The Japanese decision to fight in two separate squadrons rather than a single line supported the argument that a fleet commander should delegate authority to subordinate squadron commanders. The cruisers making up the vanguard of the Japanese force were similar in speed and firepower, underscoring the importance of homogeneity in a line of battle.

The Sino-Japanese War was rapidly followed by two other conflicts in which naval power played a major role: the Spanish–American War of 1898, in which the Americans invaded Cuba and the Philippines, and the Russo-Japanese War of 1904–1905. Spanish squadrons were destroyed by more heavily gunned American squadrons in Manila Bay on 1 May 1898 and off Santiago, Cuba, on 3 July.[10] The Battle of Tsushima (27–8 May 1905) was the only example of a decisive clash between modern battleships in the twentieth century. Superior Japanese gunnery combined with tactical effectiveness and greater speed led to very heavy Russian losses: six battleships and two cruisers were sunk, four battleships were captured, and one battleship and three cruisers were scuttled to prevent capture. The Japanese only lost three torpedo boats. In the battle, Japanese gunners scored hits on Russian battleships from unprecedented distances, as they had earlier done at the Battle of the Yellow Sea (10 August 1904). In both battles, big 12-inch guns inflicted the damage.[11] This led many to conclude (correctly) that future battleship engagements would be fought at great distance, reinforcing the case for the heavily armoured, "all-big-gun" battleship soon to be embodied in the *Dreadnought*, and causing more attention to be directed towards fire control in the years before 1914.

This was not the sole novelty of the war. Instead, it offered examples of new technology, although not of the use of the submarine. The Japanese used torpedoes for their surprise attack at the outset of the war on the Russian squadron in Port Arthur. Destroyers were used in combat for the first time. In addition, during the war, both sides lost battleships to mines. Tsushima was rapidly followed by the end of the war, with Japan victorious. This appeared to vindicate Mahanian ideas: a high seas encounter would occur, it could be a decisive battle, and would then affect the fate of nations.

The importance of naval power was again shown in the Italian–Turkish war over Libya of 1911–12. The Italians were able to convoy their landed force and reinforcements, and to intimidate the Turkish fleet into staying within the Dardanelles. Smaller Turkish naval units elsewhere were destroyed or captured. In 1912, the Italian fleet attacked Turkey's Aegean possessions, occupying Rhodes and Kos, and also bombarded Beirut, Smyrna and the Dardanelles.

Competitive emulation between navies set the pace. The *Dreadnought* was faster and more heavily gunned than any other battleship then sailing, and made the earlier arithmetic of relative naval capability redundant. It encouraged the Germans to respond with the construction of powerful battleships: four were begun in the summer of 1907. Theirs was a naval race with Britain, and Germany built the world's second largest battle fleet. However, as the British were determined to stay ahead, and willing to pay to do so, German shipbuilding simply encouraged the laying down of more dreadnoughts. The naval race continued because attempts in 1909–10 and 1912 to negotiate a treaty fixing the ratio of strength between both navies failed, although it has been argued that the Germans had given up on the naval arms race by 1912 as they were running out of financial resources to keep up. They also began to focus on land warfare more emphatically, believing a war in Europe to be imminent.

By the outbreak of the war, the British had 21 dreadnoughts in service, the Germans 14, and 12 and 5 respectively were under construction, although numbers were to be affected by Britain seizing ships being prepared for delivery to Turkey and Chile. The British had also more battle-cruisers (8 compared to Germany's 4) in service. Germany's failure in this race ensured a shift to advocacy of submarine warfare. France, in contrast, focused on land competition with Germany, especially as a consequence of improved relations with Britain from 1904, and by 1914 France had dropped from second to fifth among the world's navies.[12] Similarly, Austria and Italy engaged in a naval race. Other countries, including France and Russia, also swiftly built or ordered dreadnoughts. The Americans laid down their first dreadnought in 1906 and had four finished by the end of 1910, while Japan laid down their first two dreadnoughts in 1909. Such ships were seen as crucial to great-power status.[13] These battleships were to play a role in World War One, although less so than had been anticipated.

## Naval warfare in World War One

The Battle of Jutland of 31 May–1 June 1916 between the main British and German fleets was not to be the Trafalgar hoped for by naval planners, and there was no decisive clash between the British and German fleets in the war. Similarly, there was no decisive battle in the Adriatic between the Austrians and the Italians or, further east, involving the Turks. However, that did not mean that naval power was unimportant. Thanks to the navy, the British retained control of their home waters and were, therefore, able to avoid blockade and invasion, to maintain a flow of men and munitions to their army in France unmolested, to retain trade links that permitted the mobilization of British resources, and to blockade Germany;[14] the very serious impact of the last was lessened by Germany's continental position and her ability to obtain most of the resources she required from within Europe.

Although the British lost more ships and men at Jutland, the Germans had been badly damaged,[15] as was their confidence: "more important was the spectre of irresistible coercive power which mere glimpses of the Grand Fleet had left in the minds and memories of German officers". Thereafter in the war, the German fleet sailed beyond the defensive minefields of the Heligoland Bight on only three occasions, and on each occasion the High Seas Fleet took care to avoid conflict with the British Grand Fleet.[16]

It is easy to derive a picture of relative naval capability from the result of engagements, but it is also necessary to make due allowance for other factors, not least command decisions. Thus, the caution of Jellicoe, the commander of the Grand Fleet at Jutland, possibly denied the British the victory they might have obtained had the bolder Beatty, commander of the battle-cruiser squadron, been in overall command, although Jellicoe did not need to win this battle – only not lose it: it was famously remarked that he could have lost the war in an afternoon. Informed contemporaries felt that the quality of command was important. Thus Kitchener observed in 1915, "In the solution of the Dardanelles much I fear depends on the Navy. If we only had Beatty out there I should feel very much happier".[17]

Britain's supply system, that of a country that could not feed itself, an imperial economy that relied on trade, and a military system that required troop movements within the empire, was challenged by surface raiders, but these were hunted down in the early stages of the war. The East Asiatic Squadron under Vice Admiral Maximilian Graf von Spee was the leading German naval force outside Europe at the outset of the war. It sailed to Chile, where a weaker British force was defeated off Coronel on 1 November, with the loss of two cruisers. Spee then sailed on to attack the Falkland Islands, but Fisher had sent two battle-cruisers there to hunt down Spee, and he was defeated on 8 December, although only after a prolonged chase that practically exhausted the magazines of the battle-cruisers. Thereafter, the Germans only had individual warships at large and these were eventually hunted down, although not before the *Emden* had inflicted some damage (and more disruption) on shipping in the Indian Ocean.

Britain's economy was challenged more seriously by submarines, which were also a major threat to warships. Indeed, the British Grand Fleet was obliged to withdraw from the North Sea and Scapa Flow in the Orkneys in 1914 to new bases on the north-west coast of Scotland due to the threat of submarine attack: it did not return to Scapa Flow until 1915, when its defences had been strengthened. There had been considerable speculation prior to the war about the likely impact of submarines, but scant experience on which to base discussion. In 1901, H. O. Arnold-Forster, Parliamentary Secretary to the Admiralty, was interested in how best to counter submarines:

[T]he submarine is, in fact, the true reply to the submarine . . . That provided we are as well equipped in the matter of submarines as our neighbours, the introduction of this new weapon, so far from being a disadvantage to us, will strengthen our position. We have no desire to invade any other country: it is important that we ourselves should not be invaded. If the submarine proves as formidable as some authorities think is likely to be the case, the bombardment of our ports, and the landing of troops on our shores will become absolutely impossible. The same reasoning applies to every part of our empire which is approachable by water only.

The following year, Sir John Fisher, then Second Sea Lord, saw submarines as an instance of the competitive enhancement of weaponry that he felt Britain had been falling behind in, like, for example, the introduction of both wireless and the gyroscope:

> The great principle to be invariably followed by us is that no naval weapon of any description must be adopted by foreign navies, without exhaustive trials of it on our part, to ascertain its capabilities and possibilities in a future naval war, and to make provision accordingly. We cannot afford to leave anything to be a matter of opinion which affects, in the slightest degree, the fighting efficiency of the fleet.[18]

Submarines had not featured prominently in naval operations over the previous decade, in, for example, the Russo-Japanese or Balkan Wars. Indeed, their potential had been greatly underestimated by most commanders.[19] Admiral Tirpitz, the head of the German navy, was a late convert to submarines. Nevertheless, Fisher was concerned about the vulnerability of battleships to torpedoes, and this led him to emphasize flotilla defences for home waters. Britain, which had only launched its first submarine in 1901, had the largest number – 89 – at the outbreak of World War One. Although the Germans stepped up submarine production once war had begun, relatively few were ordered, and most were delivered behind schedule, in part because of poor organization and a concentration of industrial resources on the army.[20]

In September 1914, the first warships sunk by submarines in the war included three British and one German cruiser. German submarines swiftly affected the conduct of operations. Concern about submarines led Jellicoe in 1915 to observe, "I am most absolutely adverse to moving the Battle Fleet without a full destroyer screen".[21] Submarines benefited from an increase in their range, seaworthiness, speed and comfort, from improvements in the accuracy, range and speed of torpedoes, which, by 1914, could travel 7,000 yards at 45 knots, and from the limited effectiveness of anti-submarine weaponry. In October 1916, Jellicoe wrote that the greater size and range of submarines and their increased use of the torpedo, so that they did not need to come to the surface, meant that the submarine menace was getting worse.[22] They came to play a major role in naval planning, both strategically, in terms of trying to deny bodies of water to opponents, and tactically, with the hope that, in engagements, opposing warships could be drawn across submarine lines, a tactic used by the Germans in 1916. Balfour, then First Lord of the Admiralty, wrote in November 1916, "the submarine has already profoundly modified naval tactics . . . It was a very evil day for this country when this engine of naval warfare was discovered".[23] During the war, the Germans sank 11.9 million tons of allied shipping at the cost of 199 submarines; most of this was commercial shipping, however – *guerre de course* was the submarine's most productive métier, not attacks on warships.

Their growing importance was seen in November 1916, when the Germans risked an entire squadron of capital ships to salvage a submarine. On 2 February 1917, they introduced unrestricted submarine warfare. Serious losses were inflicted on Allied, particularly British, commerce, in large part due to British inexperience in confronting submarine attacks. Once unrestricted submarine warfare had been launched, this was part of a deliberate campaign to starve Britain into submission, and a reflection of the failure of the Germans to win victory at Jutland. The objective was total war, even if the Germans lacked the submarine fleet to achieve this objective. In the spring of 1917, British leaders, including Jellicoe, were pessimistic about the chances of success against the submarines. The initial rate of Allied losses was sufficiently high to threaten defeat. However, product substitution and enhanced agricultural production helped Britain survive the onslaught, while convoys proved effective.

The introduction by the British, in May 1917, of a system of escorted convoys, cut shipping losses dramatically and led to an increase in the sinking of German submarines. Convoys might appear such an obvious solution that it is surprising they were not adopted earlier, but there were counter-arguments, including the number of escorts required, the delays that would be forced on shipping and the possibility that convoys would simply offer a bigger target. They were resisted by the Admiralty for some time as not sufficiently in touch with the bold "Nelson touch". Although in the first four months of the unrestricted submarine attack the British lost an average of 630,000 tons, only 393 of the 95,000 ships that were to be convoyed across the Atlantic were lost.[24] Convoys reduced the targets for submarines and ensured that when they found them they could be attacked by escorts. They also benefited from the "shoal" factor; when they found a convoy submarines only had time to sink a limited number of ships. In coastal waters, convoys were supported by aircraft and airships, and this forced the submarines to remain submerged, where they were much slower.

Convoys limited the potency of German attacks, but mines sank more submarines than other weapons. They played an important role in the war, but have been underrated in favour of more spectacular weapons. Mine barrages limited the options for surface and submarine vessels. The Allies laid massive barrages across the English Channel (at Dover), the North Sea (between the Orkneys and Norway) and the Straits of Otranto in order to limit the operational range of German and Austrian forces. Particular operations were also affected by mines. The British naval attempt to force the Dardanelles on 18 May 1915 was stopped by mines after three battleships were sunk, and three more were badly damaged.

The naval experts had been aware of the hazards posed by the mines and shore batteries of the Dardanelles, not least because before the war the British naval mission had provided advice on mine-laying, but their caution was thrust aside by Churchill, the First Lord of the Admiralty, who was a keen advocate of the scheme for a naval advance on Constantinople.[25]

The Dardanelles offensive also led to the arrival of German submarines in the Mediterranean. They sank two British battleships in the Dardanelles campaign itself, and went on to attack shipping in the Mediterranean. This led to the laying of mines in the Straits of Otranto, in order to keep the submarines in their Adriatic bases. The campaign also led British submarines to pass through the Dardanelles and to operate in the Sea of Marmara.

There were important improvements in mine technology during the war, although these are apt to be overlooked. By the end of the war, magnetic mines had been developed and were being laid by the British. Command and control was another area of naval operations to benefit from technological improvement. As on land and in the air, developments with radio made it easier to retain detailed operational control. Directional wireless equipment aided location and navigation, while radio transmissions changed from a spark method to a continuous wave system.

The struggle between Britain and Germany dominates discussion of World War One at sea, but naval operations involving other powers were also extensive. The decision of Italy to abandon its allies in the Triple Alliance, with whom they had agreed a naval convention in 1913, and, instead, to join Britain and France in 1915, ensured that the Mediterranean was dominated by the Entente powers, with Austria and Turkey unable to contest their dominance. The small German squadron in the Mediterranean in 1914 took shelter with the Turks. A French squadron at Corfu and most of the Italian fleet at Taranto confined the Austrians to the Adriatic, and prevented them from breaking out into the Mediterranean. Due to submarines, the French and Italians withdrew their major ships from the sea.[26] In the Black Sea, the Russians had more warships than the Turks, and from 1915 blockaded the Bosporus. They also used the navy from 1916 to help operations in the Caucasus.[27]

In contrast, in the Baltic, the Russian fleet was weaker than the forces the Germans could deploy if they moved in some of their High Seas Fleet units from the North Sea via the Kiel Canal. This encouraged Russian caution, which was also in keeping with long-established Russian doctrine and the emphasis in the Baltic on local operations. Tsushima was scarcely an encouragement for bolder operations. The Russians laid extensive minefields to protect the Gulf of Finland and staged raids into the southern Baltic in order to mine German shipping routes. The Germans, in turn, laid mines.

The Japanese, who fought on the Allied side, used their navy in their successful attacks on Germany's Chinese base of Tsingtao in 1914 and on German bases in the Pacific, escorted British convoys from Australia, hunted German surface raiders and, in 1917, sent warships to assist the Allies in the Mediterranean. The Americans used their fleet to help protect communication routes across the Atlantic, and ultimately sent ships to serve in the Mediterranean. The major battleships they had built were not used in battle.

Although the extension of air power to the sea made scant impact on the course of the war, naval capability was affected by it; Britain took the lead and, in July 1918, conducted the first raid by land planes flown off an improvised aircraft carrier. In the following month, British seaplanes eliminated an entire naval force: six coastal motorboats. In September, HMS *Argus*, an aircraft carrier capable of carrying 20 planes, with a flush desk unobstructed by superstructure and funnels – the first clear-deck aircraft carrier – was commissioned by the British, although she did not undergo sea trials until October 1918.

Although the war was not settled (or apparently settled) by a major naval battle, as navalists claimed the Spanish–American and Russo-Japanese conflicts had been, it was one in which the overwhelming naval power of the Allies had played a crucial role. Without this power, the alliance could not have operated: it would have lacked operational reach and the ability to move and use resources across the Channel and the Atlantic.[28]

## Inter-war developments

At sea, air power was restricted in the 1910s and 1920s by the difficulty of operating aeroplanes in bad weather and the dark, by their limited load capacity and range, and by mechanical unreliability, but improvements were made, especially in the 1930s. The Americans and Japanese, although not so much the British, made major advances with naval aviation and aircraft carriers.[29] Germany, Italy and the Soviet Union, however, did not build aircraft carriers in the inter-war period, and France only had one, a converted dreadnought-type battleship. Britain's carrier construction therefore gave an important added dimension to her naval superiority over other European powers.

Whereas naval air power in Britain lacked a separate institutional framework, because the Fleet Air Arm was placed under the RAF between 1918 and 1937, and the RAF was primarily concerned with land-based aeroplanes, and had little time for their naval counterparts,[30] in the USA there was a very different situation thanks to the Bureau of Aeronautics of the American navy. This stimulated the development of effective air–sea doctrine, operational policies and tactics. Aside from developments in aircraft carriers, there were also marked improvements in aircraft. Thus, the Americans benefited from the development of dive-bombing tactics in the 1920s and, subsequently, of dive-bombers. These proved more effective than aircraft launching torpedoes.[31] Air spotting for naval gunfire also developed in the 1930s.

As had been the case before World War One, there was a drive to develop naval strength and weaponry, but there was controversy over the potency of different weapons systems in any future naval war. The respective merits of air power, from both aircraft carriers and shore-based sites, surface gunnery and submarines were all extensively discussed, as well as their likely tactical and strategic combinations. Although some theorists argued that battleships were now obsolete in the face of air power and submarines, big surface warships had a continued appeal and not simply for the European powers. Indeed, there was opposition to a stress on carriers becoming the key capital ship; in the 1930s, both the Americans and the British put a major emphasis on battle fleet tactics based on battleships. This was not simply a sign of conservatism; indeed, the British displayed adaptability in their tactics.[32] The Germans were also fascinated by battleships.

The role of such ships was enhanced by the absence of a major change in battleship design comparable to those in the late nineteenth century and 1900s. Indeed, with the arrival of the dreadnoughts, battleship architecture had reached a new period of relative stability. The USS *New York* (BB-34) of 1914, *Texas* (BB-35) of 1914, and *Nevada* (BB-36) of 1916 participated in the D-Day bombardment in 1944. The *Texas*'s ten 14-inch guns could fire 1½ rounds per minute; each armour-piercing shell weighing 1,500 lb. There was still great interest in such weaponry, both for ship destruction and for shore bombardment.

Nevertheless, there were considerable efforts to strengthen battleships in order to increase their resistance to air attack. Armour was strengthened, outer hulls added to protect against torpedo attack, and anti-aircraft guns and tactics developed. This is a reminder of the danger of assuming that a weapons system is necessarily static.

At the same time, the likely geostrategic character of any future major conflict ensured that there would be different requirements to those on the eve of World War One. In particular, the focus was less on the confined waters off north-west Europe and, instead, on the vast expanses of the Pacific. Even before the close of World War One, there had been an awareness that new technology was likely to lead to a very different naval situation in any future conflict. In May 1918, Balfour argued that a peace settlement that left the Germans with colonies would pose a great problem:

> a piratical power, prepared to use the submarine as Germany had used it in this war, and possessed of well placed bases in every ocean, could hold up the sea-borne commerce of neutral and belligerent alike, no matter what were the naval forces arrayed against it.[33]

The following year, an Admiralty memorandum warned that the British navy was likely to be weaker than that of Japan in the Far East. It suggested that using Hong Kong would expose the fleet and, instead, that Singapore should be developed as a base, as it was sufficiently far from Japan to permit reinforcement without peril.[34]

The Americans were increasingly concerned about Japanese intentions and naval strength. Furthermore, there were specific American interests in the western Pacific, including the territories of the Philippines, Guam and Samoa, trade, and a strong commitment to the independence of China. This led to planning for war with Japan, planning that was a bridge from the naval thought of the Mahanian period to the strategy pursued in World War Two. Plan Orange of 1924 called for the "through ticket": a rapid advance directly from Hawaii to Manila, a decisive battle and then starving Japan by blockade. This plan was followed by greater interest in a slower process of seizing the Japanese islands in the Pacific – the Marshalls, Carolines and Marianas – which they had gained in the World War One treaty settlement. These would provide the Americans with forward bases, and deny them to the Japanese. Without control of this area, it was argued, a naval advance to the Philippines would be unsuccessful.[35]

The Armistice had been followed by the surrender of the German fleet to the British. The Germans ceased to be a significant naval power, but the British accepted naval parity with the Americans, the leading industrial and financial power in the world. Both states accepted the fact of Japanese naval power in the Pacific. A 5:5:3 ratio in capital ship tonnage was agreed in the Washington Naval Treaty of 1922,[36] which, more generally, comprised an agreement to scrap many battleships and to stop new construction for ten years. The latter was extended by the London Naval Treaty of 1930. In the 1922 treaty, the quotas for France and Italy were 35 per cent of the capital ship tonnage of Britain. The treaty also limited warships other than capital ships to 10,000 tons and 8-inch guns (reduced to 6-inch in 1930), and this ensured that in the inter-war period there was a building of cruisers that met these limits, rather than of the battleships built prior to 1914.

Despite British efforts in 1922 and 1930, there were no limitations on submarines, although the Treaty of Versailles had banned Germany from using them. The French were keen to prevent limits on submarine warfare and built the most in the 1920s.

Jellicoe argued that submarines destroyed the feasibility of close blockades, forcing a reliance for trade protection on convoys protected by cruisers. He was concerned that Britain had insufficient cruisers both to do this and to work with the battle fleet in a future war. Admiralty concern about limitations on the size and number of ships was also expressed by Admiral Sir Charles Madden in a meeting of the Cabinet Committee preparing for the 1930 London Naval Conference held at 10 Downing Street in December 1929. He

> explained that it was not possible to build a battleship of less than 25,000 tons with the necessary quantities of armament, speed and protection, which would include an armoured deck of 5" and 6", to

keep out bombs and plunging shell, and have sufficient protection under water against mines, torpedoes and bombs . . . The Admiralty required a sufficient number of cruisers to give security to the overseas trade of the Empire against raiding forces of the enemy and a battlefleet to give cover to the trade protecting cruisers.

If battleships were done away by agreement, the Empire would still need a covering main fleet, and if these vessels were of the same size as the cruiser, it would entail a still heavier commitment than that of the existing battlefleet . . . unlike any other nation, we had to dissipate our cruiser strength to protect our dominions and colonies, and our vital lines of communication.[37]

The problem with negotiating parity agreements was that every naval power had different force requirements to meet its strategic needs; for example the Americans needed far fewer cruisers than the British.

The likely character of a major future war led to a new geography of commitment and concern that was reflected in the development of naval bases, for example those of Britain at Singapore and the USA at Pearl Harbor on the Hawaiian island of Oahu. In addition, it was envisaged that there was a far greater role for aircraft carriers in the Pacific than in the North Sea and the Mediterranean. As tensions mounted in the Far East in the 1920s and, even more, 1930s, with Japanese expansionism at the expense of China and an increase in the size of the Japanese navy, so it was necessary to plan for conflict across very large bodies of water. This accentuated the problems for powers with commitments in both Atlantic and Pacific, for they had to think about how best to distribute naval forces, and how vulnerabilities should affect policy. The British planned to send much of their fleet to Singapore in the event of war with Japan. In October 1932, the Cabinet decided to proceed with the completion and defences of the naval base at Singapore.[38]

In 1935, in the Second London Naval Conference, Japan demanded higher naval ratios. The American rejection of Japanese naval superiority in the Pacific led to the collapse of the conference, the unilateral Japanese disavowal of existing limits and the launching of the Marusan Programme of shipbuilding, designed to achieve superiority over British and American fleets.[39] By 1940, the Japanese fleet, however, was only 7:10 relative to the American. The Vinson–Trammel Act of March 1934, followed by the "Second Vinson Act" of May 1938 had set out to rearm the American navy, and remedy an earlier situation in which there had been a failure to construct what was allowed by the Naval Conferences. In July 1940, Congress passed the Two Ocean Naval Expansion Act, which was designed to produce a fleet larger than that of the second- and third-ranking naval powers combined. This would enable the Americans to wage naval war against both Germany and Japan.

At the same time, the development of the German and Italian navies suggested that both powers might contest European waters. Under the Anglo-

German Naval Treaty of 1935, the Germans were to have a quota equivalent to that of France or Italy under the 1922 treaty, with a surface fleet up to 35 per cent the size of that of Britain, although the submarine fleet could be the same size. Hitler ignored these restrictions in his naval build-up. Like Stalin, Hitler was fascinated by battleships to the detriment of smaller, frequently more effective, warships, while the Japanese also built the largest capital ships in the world, the "super-battleships" *Musashi* and *Yamato*, which were to be sunk by the Americans in 1944 and 1945.[40] Germany only had 57 submarines at the outset of World War Two.[41] Mussolini was also keen to develop the Italian navy.[42]

At the same time, the British were aware that any war would bring the threat of both air and sea attacks on their communications. The February 1934 report of the Defence Requirements Sub-Committee of the Committee of Imperial Defence noted of the navy: "The greatest potential threat lies in the acquisition of submarines and aircraft by Germany".[43] They were therefore prepared for a far more varied conflict than what might result from a German battle fleet offensive alone. Due to the time taken to build ships, the British would also know some years ahead whether or not Germany would have a battle fleet.

## World War Two

Naval conflict played a greater role in this war than in World War One, because the Pacific, for the first time, became a major war theatre, the conflict in the Mediterranean was more important because of the North African and Italian campaigns, and the Germans made a more serious and sustained effort to cut routes across the Atlantic. In addition, the German success in overrunning France in 1940 ensured that the subsequent defeat of Germany would entail a major amphibious invasion of occupied western Europe, a task that had not been envisaged prior to the war, which helps explain the limited nature of British amphibious preparations. There was great pressure on naval resources, especially prior to America's entry into the war. In September 1941, the First Sea Lord complained of a shortage of cruisers, adding "the destroyer situation is even worse", when explaining why he could send none to the Far East.[44]

There was no major clash between warship fleets in the Western hemisphere, in part because the Germans divided their powerful fleet and relied on squadron moves and raids, rather than on fleet actions. The most well known of these raids, that by the *Bismarck* in May 1941, led to the sinking of the largest inter-war British warship, the *Hood*, commissioned in 1920; but the *Bismarck* was eventually crippled by airborne torpedo attack (26 May) and was then sunk (27 May).[45] More generally, the war showed the vulnerability of surface ships to air power, and this led the Germans to withdraw their major warships from Brest in February 1942. Norway was an important base for operations against British convoys taking supplies to the Soviet Union, but the inroads of German aeroplanes and submarines were not matched by surface ships. Instead, the German warships fell victim, the *Scharnhorst* to an escorting British fleet on 26 December 1943, and the *Tirpitz*, which had sailed to Trondheim in January 1942, to British planes on 12 November 1944.

The German submarine assault on the North Atlantic was very serious for the British. Submarines were more sophisticated than in World War One, and became yet more so during the war. A battle of technological innovation ensued. In 1943, the Germans recalled their submarines in order to fit *schnorkel* devices, which allowed them to recharge their batteries while submerged, thus reducing their vulnerability to Allied air power, while the Allies introduced more powerful depth-charges, ship-borne radar, and better asdic detection equipment. In 1943, the Germans also introduced the T5 acoustic homing torpedo, at once sinking three escorts.

The years 1940–41 and 1942–43 were crisis periods for the Allies, with them experiencing severe ship losses. In the winter of 1940–41, Britain was put under great stress. Technology was a minor factor in defeating the submarines during that winter: instead, an increased number of escorts and more aircraft, over and ahead of convoys, were critical. In 1942–43, a fierce debate raged in London, with the Admiralty demanding more air cover from the RAF. However, using long-range aircraft for anti-submarine patrols was opposed by Sir Arthur Harris, who pressed for a concentration on bombing Germany.[46] The allocation of resources involved difficult debates over strategy.

The Allies really won the battle of the Atlantic in 1943. U-boat crews then and thereafter suffered very heavy losses: 754 out of the 863 submarines in commission were lost and 27,491 crew were killed. A range of factors helped the Allies win, including greater resources, effective anti-submarine tactics by both convoy escorts and aircraft, enhanced anti-submarine weaponry, such as improved asdics and better depth-charges, and signals intelligence. As a consequence, the number of submarines sunk per year was much greater than in World War One, while the percentage of Allied shipping lost was less. Land-based Liberators were the key to closing the mid-Atlantic air gap in the spring of 1943.[47]

Strategy, tactics and resources were all important, and helped to explain the greater success that the Allies enjoyed in preserving sea links across the Atlantic compared to the Japanese failure in the same period to protect their routes. The Japanese were less effective at convoy protection and anti-submarine warfare and devoted fewer resources to them, not least through not providing adequate air cover. In addition, they achieved little with submarine warfare, partly because they insisted on hoarding torpedoes for use against warships. Despite initial problems with their torpedoes, which, for example, affected operations off the Philippines in the winter of 1941–42, effective long-range American submarines sunk 1,114 Japanese merchantmen, and forced the Japanese to abandon many of their convoy routes in 1944. The Japanese failed to build sufficient ships to match their losses, their trade was dramatically cut and the Japanese imperial economy was shattered. The USA thus became the most successful practitioner of submarine warfare in history. The submarine assault was also supported by mining by naval aircraft.[48]

Carrier-based planes became crucial in naval actions. This was true of the British pursuit of German warships in the Atlantic and nearby waters. More generally, air power played a central role in opposing German submarine operations. It was also vital to the Pacific War, which began when Japanese aircraft from six carriers sank five American battleships at Pearl Harbor (7 December 1941),[49] both in conflict between fleets and in support of amphibious attacks. The effective use of air power and the development not only of carrier tactics but of successful air–naval cooperation were instrumental in the defeat of Japanese forces. Multiple tasking included fighter combat to gain control of the skies, dive-bombing and torpedo-attack to destroy ships, and ground attack to help amphibious operations.

The Americans developed self-sufficient carrier task-groups (supported by at-sea logistics groups), which did not depend on a string of bases. This permitted the rapid advance across an unprecedented distance, with a lot of island hopping that destroyed any hope that the Japanese might retain a defensive perimeter in the Pacific. Thus, in the Battle of the Philippine Sea in June 1944, an American fleet with 15 carriers and 902 aircraft devastated its Japanese opponent, which had 9 carriers and 450 aircraft, and this enabled the Americans to overrun the Marianas, a decisive advance of Allied power into the western Pacific. The Japanese navy lacked the capacity to resist the effective American assault, and also suffered from poor doctrine and an inadequate understanding of respective strategic options.

Although carriers were the key, battleships, cruisers and destroyers also played major roles, not least in shore bombardment. There were also clashes between surface ships. Thus, on 14 November 1942, off Guadalcanal, the radar-controlled fire of the battleship *Washington* pulverized the Japanese battleship *Kirishima*. Destroyer torpedo attacks could also be very effective, as when used by the Japanese off Guadalcanal on 13 and 30 November.[50]

Both in the Pacific and in Europe, the Americans acquired great experience in ship-to-shore operations. The war saw amphibious operations of an hitherto unprecedented scale and complexity, with close coordination by air, land and sea forces. All major powers practised such operations, but the scale varied greatly. The Germans focused on short-range invasions, most obviously of Norway in 1940. Their strength on land and their weakness relative to the British navy ensured that most German invasions were land attacks. The

Soviets subordinated naval units to land operations, and their amphibious advances, for example against the Japanese in the Kurile Islands and southern Sakhalin in August and early September 1945, were small in scale. In contrast, the Americans and the British used amphibious operations as the building blocks of strategy. Specialized landing vessels were developed: not only seagoing ships, but also smaller landing craft, and truly amphibious vehicles. This enhanced the tempo of amphibious assaults.

Air power was also very important to the naval war in the Mediterranean. There, sea lanes were crucial to both the British and the Axis war effort. Early in the war, successful British attacks on the Italian fleet, involving both surface ships and aeroplanes, combined with the failure of the large Italian submarine force to make a major impact, ensured that the British became the leading naval power in the Mediterranean. The attack on battleships moored in Taranto (11 November 1940) possibly inspired the Japanese attack on Pearl Harbor a year later.[51]

British prominence was further secured by the fate of the French navy after the fall of France to the Germans. The fleet was left under the Vichy French regime, and British uncertainty about the ability of the Vichy government to keep it out of German control led to a destructive attack on the North African squadron at Mers-el-Kebir near Oran on 3 July 1940. One French battleship was sunk and two were damaged. When the Germans occupied Vichy France in November 1942, the remainder of the fleet was scuttled at Toulon (27 November). The British position in the Mediterranean was then challenged by German air and submarine forces. Equally, Allied surface ship, air and submarine forces sought to limit the operational possibilities and resupply capability of Axis land forces. They failed to prevent the German conquest of Crete in 1941, but hung on to Malta, and, in 1943, succeeded in crippling the supply routes to Rommel's army in Tunisia, building on earlier efforts in 1940–42 to cut supply routes to Libya.[52]

The position of Japan in the summer of 1945 was an indication of the great value of naval power. Although the Japanese still ruled large areas in East and South-East Asia, these forces were isolated. American submarines operated with few difficulties in the Yellow and East China Seas and the Sea of Japan. Carrier-borne planes attacked Japan, while warships bombarded coastal positions. The Americans could plan where they wanted to mount an invasion. Just as the Battle of the Atlantic had ended in Allied triumph, the naval war in the Pacific had been decisively won.

## After World War Two

In the post-war world, part of the importance of air and later sea, more specifically submarine, power lay in their role as delivery platforms for nuclear bombs and later missiles. The Americans commissioned the *Ethan Allen*, the first true fleet missile submarine, in 1961. The previous July, off Cape Canaveral, the USS *George Washington* was responsible for the first successful underwater firing of a Polaris missile. Other states followed. The first British Polaris test missile was fired from a submarine in 1968, and the French commissioned their first ballistic missile submarine in 1969. However, it would also be misleading to focus on such a narrow definition of capability. In particular, it is necessary to consider the wide range of functions that were discharged by both services. This was particularly true of air power, which, in some respects, complemented or even superseded its naval counterpoint, as in the dispatch of troops to distant trouble spots.

Nevertheless, naval power also had an increasing attraction as colonial positions were challenged and, later, as states sought to project their strength and to influence newly independent "Third World" countries. The sea was a safer, and less contentious, dimension than land for a number of reasons, both political and military. Power deployed over the horizon was less conspicuous and vulnerable. In part, navies benefited from the degree to which irregular forces operated far less at sea than on land. In addition, at sea, it was easier to distinguish and assess other vessels, and thus to avoid the situation on land in which guerrillas could be indistinguishable from the civilian population. The sea, in short, could be known. Naval power offered reach, mobility and logistical independence, and provided a dynamic quality that was lacking from fixed overseas garrisons.

From 1945, the Americans dominated the oceans to a degree unmatched in history, although in 1949 their navy found its programme rejected and its major construction project cancelled, in favour of the Air Force's plans for strategic bombing.[53] Nevertheless, technology combined with economic resources to give their fleets a strength and capability that the British navy had lacked even at the height of its power. The Americans were able to deploy and apply a formidable amount of naval strength in the Korean and Vietnam Wars. Aside from the firepower of naval ordnance and aircraft, the fleet provided amphibious capability, shown, most significantly, in the Korean War, by the Inchon landing in September 1950 and the Hungnam evacuation three months later, and also logistical strength. Most of the men and supplies that crossed the Pacific Ocean to Korea and Vietnam came by sea. In the Vietnam War, there was an additional commitment and capability, that of riverine warfare. This was part of the interdiction process designed to prevent the movement of supplies to the Viet Cong.[54] However, naval and/or air power can rarely win wars; the killer punch has to be administered by an army.

The building of new ships and the upgrading of weaponry and communications kept the Americans in the leading position. During the period of the so-called "balanced navy", from 1949 to 1968, the navy emphasized force projection, specifically an amphibious capability able to seize and hold forward bases and intervene throughout the world; an ability to hold sea lanes to critical theatres, especially Europe – a task that led to anti-submarine requirements; and a role in aerial and later ballistic attack on the Soviet Union. Thus, the emphasis was not on a Mahanian focus on fleet engagements at sea. In 1962, the navy successfully isolated Cuba during the missile crisis, enforcing the blockade and deploying a total of 183 warships.[55]

American naval strength was challenged in the Cold War both by the growth of rival navies and by the development of anti-ship weaponry, specifically missiles. Thus, in 1967,the destroyer *Elat*, the Israeli flagship, was sunk by Soviet missiles used by the Egyptians. The build-up of the Soviet fleet that began in the 1950s under Admiral Sergei Gorshkov quickly made the Soviet Union the world's number two naval power, a position eased by the wartime destruction of the Japanese navy and the post-war decline of the British navy. Lord Mountbatten, then British First Lord of the Admiralty, wrote in 1956, "The Navy has begun to assume its new streamline form for the atomic age", but streamlining was followed by repeated adjustments downwards due to financial stringency.[56] No other western European navy, however, rose to a comparable position. Wrecked in the war, the French navy and its infrastructure were revived in the early 1950s, in part with American help, but this was compromised by Franco-American differences and French naval construction and deployment were reduced in the late 1950s.[57] The Canadian navy, which had been the world's third largest in 1945, continued thereafter to develop the anti-submarine capability it had rapidly expanded to provide during World War Two, although now the goal was Soviet threats to Canadian sea routes. In the 1970s, however, expenditure fell rapidly.[58]

Naval force structure and doctrine changed greatly after 1945. The age of the battleship passed, as those built in the inter-war period were scrapped, to be followed by others launched in wartime. Commissioned in 1946, the British *Vanguard* was the sole European battleship commissioned after the war, and was scrapped in 1960. In the Suez crisis of 1956, the French *Jean Bart* became the last European battleship to fire a shot in anger; although American battleships remained in use, including off Lebanon in the 1980s and in the Gulf War of 1990–91.

The decline of the battleship focused attention on carriers. Three French carriers operated off Vietnam against the Viet Minh in the 1946–54 war, one British carrier was deployed during the Korean War, and three British and two French carriers in the Suez Crisis. The British increased the capability of their carriers, with the angled flight deck, the steam catapult and, in 1960, the first vertical/short takeoff and landing (V/STOL) aircraft, based on carriers. These did not require fleet carriers, and in 1966 the British cancelled a planned one, the CVA-01, preferring, instead, to rely on smaller carriers.

America dominated carrier capability, and also integrated carrier strength into other military purposes. Thus, in the 1950s and early 1960s, American carriers were assigned strategic bombing duties. The most extensive use of carriers was during the Vietnam War. The absence of hostile submarine attacks provided a mistaken impression of the general invulnerability of carriers, but, nevertheless, in this conflict they were able to provide a nearby safe base for operations over both North and South Vietnam. Improvements in supply methods since World War Two, for example re-supply from other ships, ensured that carriers were able to stay at sea for longer. During most of 1972, no fewer than six carriers were on station, and, that summer, an average of 4,000 sorties were flown monthly.[59]

Although the Chinese and Japanese were to become major naval powers in the last quarter of the century, the limited number of states with any significant naval effectiveness, prior to that, helped ensure that the sea was essentially used for sea-to-land operations, rather than contested between marine powers.

There were no major naval conflicts in the three decades after the Second World War. The wars of decolonization were waged on land. There were hostilities at sea in the Arab–Israeli Wars of 1967 and 1973, and the Indo-Pakistan conflicts of 1965 and 1971, but they were limited. These were wars waged between contiguous states, and most of the fighting took place on land.

As a consequence, the Cold War saw a naval race that was unmediated by conflict. It was a high-cost exercise and one that, as a result of submarines and air power, was more complex than at the start of the century. It became necessary both to devise counter-measures and to ensure that the various forces that could operate on, over and under the sea cooperated effectively. America's naval position was affected by the development of a Soviet fleet designed to support Soviet interests across the world, and to challenge the deployment of American and allied forces. The traditional doctrine of Soviet naval power had emphasized support of land forces in the Baltic and Black Seas and the quest for naval superiority in these areas. However, Soviet forces based in these seas could only gain access to the oceans through straits and shallow waters, where they were vulnerable. A similar problem affected the naval base of Vladivostok on the Sea of Japan. As a result, the Soviet navy developed their Northern Fleet based at Murmansk. It became the largest Soviet fleet, with a particularly important submarine component. This obliged NATO powers to develop nearby patrol areas for submarines and underwater listening devices, and also to develop a similar capability in the Denmark Strait between Iceland and Greenland and in the waters between Iceland and Britain, through which Soviet submarines would have to travel *en route* to the Atlantic.

The Soviet navy also developed an important surface fleet, especially from the 1960s. This included missile cruisers. In 1967 and 1973, the Soviet navy was able to make substantial deployments in the eastern Mediterranean in order to advance Soviet views during Middle Eastern crises.[60] Soviet naval development led the Americans, from 1969, to focus on planning for naval conflict with the Soviets, rather than amphibious operations. The emphasis was on being able to destroy Soviet naval power in battle and in its home waters.[61] This led to a focus on big aircraft carriers and large submarines, both intended to attack the Soviet fleet.

The last decade of the century was to witness the rapid decline of the Russian navy after the collapse of the Soviet Union and to leave the USA as an even more prominent foremost naval power. This outcome had been less clear in the early 1970s, but, even then, the Americans were helped not only by greater naval resources and superior infrastructure, but also by more operational experience. Naval capability was very different to that on land because fewer states wielded naval power. As a consequence, it was easier to think in terms of a hierarchy of strength, although issues of force structure, operational effectiveness and political combination ensured that this was more than a matter of counting warships. More generally, American naval policy, like that of other naval powers, reflected not simply an "objective" assessment of interests and threats, but also "culturally-situated images of world politics . . . and of the military objectives of war".[62]

CHAPTER SEVEN

# *Air Power and Warfare*

Great activity has been displayed in the development of aircraft during the year, particularly in France and Germany. The main feature in the movement has been the increased importance of the aeroplane, which in 1909 was considered to be of minor military value. This was due partly to the surprising success of the aeroplane reconnaissances at the French manoeuvres, and partly to the successive disasters of the Zeppelin dirigibles [gas-filled airships] . . . Aviation schools have been started in almost every country.

(British report on changes in Foreign Armies during 1910)[1]

The predominant factor in the recent operations has been the effect of air power. In the operations which culminated in the evacuation of Bodo the enemy [Germany] had complete initiative in the air, and used it, first, to support his troops –
a)  By low-flying attacks
b)  By bombing
c)  By surprise landing of troops by parachute and from seaplanes
d)  By supplying his advanced detachments by air.
And, secondly, to deny us the use of sea communications in the narrow coastal waters in the theatre of operations.

The actual casualties caused to troops [British and Allied] on the ground by low-flying attacks were few, but the moral effect of continuous machine-gunning from the air was considerable. Further, the enemy made repeated use of low-flying attacks with machine guns in replacement of artillery to cover the movement of his troops. Troops in forward positions subjected to this form of attack are forced to ground, and, until they have learned by experience its comparative innocuousness, are apt not to keep constant watch on the enemy. Thus the enemy was enabled on many occasions to carry out forward and outflanking movements with impunity.

The second effect of low-flying attacks was the partial paralysis of head-quarters and the consequence interruption in the exercise of command.

Thirdly, low-flying attacks against transport moving along narrow roads seriously interfered with supply, though this was never completely interrupted.

Bombing was not effective against personnel deployed in the open, but, this, again, interfered with the functioning of headquarters and the movement of supplies.

The enemy's use of aircraft in these two methods of offence was obviously most closely co-ordinated with the action of his forward troops, and showed a very high degree of co-operation between his Air Force and his Army . . . Surprise landings from aircraft had far-reaching effects owing to the ability they conferred on the enemy to outflank positions or take them in the rear . . . The enemy's ability to supply detachments by air enabled him to neglect or overcome many of the obstacles put in his way by demolitions . . . the enemy's supremacy in the air made the use inshore of naval vessels of the type co-operating with this force highly dangerous . . . the first general lesson to be drawn is that to commit troops to a campaign in which they cannot be provided with adequate air support is to court disaster. (General Auchinleck's report on the Norwegian operation, 13 May–8 June 1940)[2]

## Pre-1914

Manned heavier-than-air flight, first officially achieved by the American Wright brothers in 1903 (there were several significant predecessors), led the British press baron, Lord Northcliffe, to remark, "England is no longer an island". Flight had had an earlier role in warfare with balloons, but its capability was now transformed. Imaginative literature, such as that of H. G. Wells, had prepared commentators for the impact of powered, controlled flight. It developed rapidly. In 1908, one of Count Zeppelin's hydrogen-filled dirigibles or airships flew 240 miles, and, the following year, Louis Blériot made the first aeroplane flight across the English Channel.

Aviation rapidly became a matter for international competition and military interest, with air power used in both the Italian War of 1911–12 and the Balkan Wars of 1912–13.[3] By 1914, the European powers had a total of over 1,000 aeroplanes in their armed forces: Russia had 244, Germany 245, France 141, Britain 113 and Austria about 55. Initially, the focus was on aeroplanes as a means of reconnaissance and artillery spotting. Some military leaders and thinkers, such as, in 1910, General Ferdinand Foch, Director of the French École Supérieure de la Guerre, argued that air power would only be a peripheral adjunct to the conduct of war. The previous year, when the Chief of the Imperial General Staff sought the advice of General Sir Ian Hamilton on the likely effectiveness of dirigibles and planes, he met with a sceptical response. Hamilton was unimpressed about the likely effectiveness of bombing: "The difficulty of carrying sufficient explosive, and of making a good shot, will probably result in a greater moral than material effect".[4]

Others were convinced that air power would play a more central role, and there was considerable interest within the military in the possibilities of air power. In 1910, an American admiral, Bradley Fiske, felt able to propose that the defence of the Philippines should be left to air power. Fiske sought to develop torpedo-carrying planes.[5] There was grave concern in Britain in 1909 and 1913 about the possibilities of an airship attack and the bombing of defenceless strategic targets and cities. In 1911, Britain established an air battalion, and, in 1912, the Royal Flying Corps.[6] The French Directorate of Military Aeronautics was created in 1914.

## World War One

In the war, aerial warfare involved aeroplanes and dirigibles, especially the German Zeppelins, which attacked Antwerp, Liège and Warsaw in 1914, and, from January 1915, Britain. The material damage inflicted by Zeppelins was relatively modest. A total of 51 attacks on the British Isles (208 sorties) during the war dropped 196 tons of bombs, which killed 557, wounded 1,358 and caused £1½ million worth of property damage. Such attacks on civilians were a preparation for a new type of total war, in which the centres of opposing states could be attacked.

Zeppelins were also capable of long-range missions. The longest was that of the L59, sent in 1917 from a base at Jamboli, Bulgaria, in order to carry supplies to German forces in East Africa. When recalled by radio, L59 had almost reached Khartoum, and it returned safely to Jamboli.

Aeroplanes performed a number of functions. Reconnaissance was the most important, and, even at the close of the war, a large percentage of the aircraft in service were reconnaissance and observation planes; this was particularly true in France and Germany. Aeroplanes reported the change of direction of the German advance near Paris in 1914 and helped the Germans in the Tannenburg campaign. The Turkish columns advancing on the Suez Canal in 1915 were spotted by British planes. In 1914 Jellicoe warned that "the German airships will be of the greatest possible advantage to their fleet as scouts".[7] Aeroplanes came to replace the reconnaissance functions of cavalry. Aerial photo-reconnaissance also developed, leading to the production of accurate maps. Tactical reconnaissance was also significant, especially artillery spotting, although the balloon was the most important means of aerial observation in the war and played a key role in artillery direction.

Aerial combat helped to deny those opportunities to opponents. Thus air superiority operations were seen as having value. The Germans sought to deny the Allies air space over their positions in order to hinder their ability to plan attacks effectively. In turn, when mounting offensives, as against Verdun, the Germans sought to gain air superiority. Conversely, the Allies sought to gain superiority in order to provide another dimension for their offensive operations. A failure to do so helped provide the Germans with valuable indications of the preparations for the Somme offensive.

Aeroplanes were also used for bombing. In September and October 1914, the British Royal Naval Air Service conducted the first effective strategic bombing raids of the war, when planes carrying 20-pound bombs flew from Antwerp to strike Zeppelin sheds at Düsseldorf and destroyed one airship. Strategic bombing was also directed against civilian targets. In 1917, as a counterpoint to unrestricted submarine warfare, twin-engined German Gotha bombers flew over the North Sea, beginning aeroplane strategic bombing of Britain with attacks on London. This encouraged the establishment of the Royal Air Force by the British on 1 April 1918. It was designed to surmount the deadlock of the trenches by permitting the destruction of the enemy where vulnerable.[8] However, the actual damage inflicted by British bombing raids in 1918 was minimal and many planes were lost. Similarly, Austrian and Italian raids across the Adriatic had little effect.

Ground-attack also developed as part of the enhancement of aeroplane military effectiveness during the war. The Allies used this technique at the Somme in 1916, and the British, in a more sophisticated fashion, at Passchendaele in 1917, and in support of tanks at Cambrai that year. In 1918, the Germans used ground-attack squadrons to support their offensives on the Western Front. The capability and range of ground-support operations expanded. German aeroplanes destroyed moving French tanks in Champagne, and the British used air strikes in their advance in Palestine. Supply links came under regular attack, inhibiting German and Austrian advances in 1918. At the same time, anti-aircraft capability increased considerably, and, in 1918, the German Air Service's anti-aircraft guns shot down 748 Allied aircraft. Aside from the guns, there were specialized spotting and communication troops, as well as relevant training, manuals and firing tables.

The ability of aeroplanes to act in aerial combat was also enhanced. Increases in aircraft speed, manoeuvrability and ceiling made it easier to attack other planes. Synchronizing gear, developed by Anthony Fokker, and modelled on a French aircraft shot down by the Germans, was used by the Germans from 1915 and copied by the British. It enabled aeroplanes to fire forwards without damaging their propellers. The Fokker Eindekker aircraft, which the Germans deployed from mid-1915, gave them a distinct advantage, and enabled them to seek the aerial advantage over Verdun. The eventually successful French attempt to contest this reflected their deployment of large groups of aircraft and the fact that they now also had planes with synchronized forward-firing machine guns, all of which allowed them to drive off German reconnaissance airplanes. In turn, in the winter of 1916–17, the Germans gained the advantage, thanks in part to their Albatross D-1, only to lose it from mid-1917 as more and better Allied planes arrived. Despite this, the Germans did not lose in the air as they were to do in World War Two, and this, in large part, indicated the relatively more limited capability of World War One aircraft. There was also a development in tactics during the war. Aeroplanes came to fly in groups. Formation tactics developed. Aeroplanes also became the dominant aerial weapon: their ability to destroy balloons and airships with incendiary bullets spelled doom for these, especially Zeppelins.[9]

The role of air power ensured that aeroplane production rose swiftly, although Russia failed to develop an adequate aircraft industry, and in Britain, in the early stages of the war, "the imposition of a virtual state procurement-based monopoly succeeded in suffocating design initiative . . . inflexible standardisation service procurement had to be opened again to the free market: the military-industrial complex had to be restored".[10]

In 1914, the British Royal Aircraft Factory at Farnborough could produce only two air-frames per month, but their artisanal methods were swiftly swept aside by mass production. Air power also exemplified the growing role of scientific research in military capability: wind tunnels were constructed for the purpose of research; strutless wings and aeroplanes made entirely from metal were developed. Engine power increased and size fell. The speed and rate of climb of aeroplanes rose.

By the close of the war, the extent and role of air power had been transformed. By 1918, the British had 22,000 aeroplanes, and, that September, a combined Franco-American-British force of 1,500 was launched against the Germans in the Saint-Mihiel Salient, the largest deployment thus far. The war ended before the British could use the large Handley Page V/500 bombers they had built to bomb Berlin.

The sense of what air power could achieve had also expanded. In 1915, the British Committee of Imperial Defence had considered using long-range British planes based in Russia and dropping incendiary bombs to destroy German wheat and rye crops.[11] However, this was not feasible. More generally, at this stage, many of the hopes of air power were based on a misleading sense of operational and technological possibilities. For example, the British exaggerated what their bombers had achieved, and it has been argued that this greatly affected inter-war discussion of strategic bombing, leading to a misrepresentation of its potential.[12]

## Inter-war developments

The role of air power in World War One led to major interest in developing its potential, which accorded with a more general fascination with the transforming character of flight.[13] Air power was seen as a war-winning tool and also as the best way to avoid the drawn-out attritional character of conflict on the ground seen in the recent war. Advocates, such as Guilio Douhet and William Mitchell, claimed that wars could be won through air power. In his *Il Dominio dell'Aria* [*The Command of the Air*] of 1921, Douhet, who had been appointed head of the Italian Central Aeronautical Bureau in 1917, claimed that aeroplanes would become the most successful offensive weapon, and that there was no viable defence against them. Air power was seen as the best way to overcome the impasse of trench warfare and to deliver the effective total war that was required. He pressed for air forces to be independent, rather than under army or naval command, and argued that air power could be used to attack enemy communications, economies and populations rather than the enemy fighting forces. Emphasizing the value of wrecking enemy morale and creating a demand for peace, Douhet advocated the use of gas and incendiary bombs against leading population centres. However, his influence on the development of strategic bombing was marginal.

The emphasis on the potency of strategic bombing led Douhet to devote little interest to air power as a means to support land or sea operations.[14] The same was true of British airmen. They argued that bombers would be able to destroy opposing economies and, more particularly, that large bombers would be able to fight off fighter attack and thus not require fight escorts.[15] As a consequence, the RAF had twice as many bombers as fighters for most of the inter-war period. These bombers were seen not only as likely to be effective in war but also as a deterrent against attack. Priorities were not changed until 1938.

Mitchell, Assistant Chief of the American Air Service, 1919–25, had been the senior American air commander in World War One, and was to be the leading American air theorist in the inter-war period. His three books, *Our Air Force: The Key to National Defense* (New York, 1921), *Winged Defense* (New York, 1925) and *Skyways* (Philadelphia, 1930), made successively greater claims for air power. Again the emphasis was on strategic bombing, not on support for land or sea operations. Strategic bombing was seen as the best way to harm an opponent's ability to wage war. Mitchell was also interested in large-scale maritime operations. He claimed that air power had made battleships obsolete, and to try to prove his point sank the former German dreadnought *Ostfriesland* in 21½ minutes' bombing in 1921, although the value of this demonstration was lessened as the battleship was anchored and therefore an easy target. Mitchell's emphasis on air power led him to press for an independent air force, and he became critical of aircraft carriers as he feared they would make it harder to wage a unified air war under a single air command.[16] The National Defence Act of 1920 had placed air power under the Army Air Service.

The American Air Corps Tactical School developed a policy of high-flying daylight precision bombing designed to damage an opponent's industrial system. This later greatly influenced American policy in World War Two, but, in practice, precision was to be difficult to achieve and bombing did not have the intended incisive strategic effect.[17]

It was anticipated that attacks on civilian targets would play a major role in future conflict. The major impact on public morale of German raids on London in World War One seemed an augury. Fuller predicted that air attacks on London would lead the people to demand that the government surrender. In 1923, the Steel–Bartholomew plan proposed a coordinated system of fighter bases, anti-aircraft ground defences and an Observer Corps to protect London against possible French attack.[18] The British feared an aerial "knock-out-blow". In the 1930s, it was believed, in the words of the ex- and future Prime Minister Stanley Baldwin, in 1932, that "the bomber will always get through".[19] Air Commodore L. E. O. Charlton developed these themes in *War from the Air: Past-Present-Future* (1935), *War over England* (1936), and *The Menace of the Clouds* (1937). The destructiveness of bombing was also the theme of *Flying* (New York, 1933) by Major-General James E. Fechet, former head of the American Air Corps. Air defence came to be a major issue in the 1920s and 1930s, with its own doctrine, technology and organization.

The increasing size of planes also led to interest in the use of airborne troops. A number of powers, especially the Soviet Union and Germany, trained parachute and glider-borne units. There were also developments in air transport: in 1935, the Soviets moved a 14,000-strong rifle division by air from near Moscow to the Far East, while, in 1937–38, they practised dropping artillery and tanks by parachute.

The potential of air power was speculatively investigated in other ways in the inter-war period. There was a growing interest in jet aircraft, rocketry and space flight, especially in Germany, where the Space-Flight Society was founded in 1927, and, in the Soviet Union, Konstantin Tsiolkovsky (1857–1936) developed a theory of rocket flight that encouraged the use of liquid propellants for rockets. Other work led to the development of the Soviet Katyusha multiple rocket launcher. In 1930, Frank Whittle, a British RAF officer, patented the principles that led to the first gas turbine jet engine, which he first ran under control in 1937. His innovation was rapidly copied, and the Germans, in 1939 and the Italians, in 1940, beat the British jet into the air. More significantly for the short term, there was an improvement in the flying standards and combat characteristics of planes in the inter-war period. This was particularly so for fighters in the mid- and late-1930s, as wooden-based biplanes were replaced by all-metal cantilever-wing monoplanes with high-performance engines capable of far greater speeds. The range and armament of fighters, and the range, payload and armament of bombers all increased.[20] Improvements in fighters began to undermine the doctrine of the paramountcy of the bomber. The introduction of radar on the eve of the war was another blow.

The creation of air forces was a major institutional change in the organization of war. It institutionalized a commitment to air power, that, in turn, was a cause of heavy expenditure. As a result, there was pressure in Britain from the army to end the independence of the air force and, instead, to give both army and navy their own forces.[21] Although the creation of independent air forces in Britain led to an exaggeration of the potential of air power, in Britain, the Air Ministry was more moderate in its claims than independent air enthusiasts,[22] while the inter-war use of air power had already suggested that it might be less effective than its protagonists claimed.[23] However, the conflicts of the 1920s and 1930s offered only limited guidance because they did not happen between equally balanced air forces, and rapid technological developments soon outdated experiment. In addition, it is not clear that the conflicts were adequately analysed. For example, the spectacular terror bombing of civilian targets, such as Madrid (1936), Guernica (1937) and Barcelona (1938), by German and Italian planes sent to help Franco's Nationalists in the Spanish Civil War did not actually play a significant role in the result of the conflict.

However, it captured the imagination of many, sowing fears that the bombing of civilian targets would be decisive in a future war. This affected British thinking at the time of the Munich crisis in 1938. The concentration on air defence led to a misapplication of scarce resources. As World War Two was to show, Douhet had exaggerated the potential of bombing (as well as underestimating the size of bomber forces required), and underplayed the value of tactical air support.

The Germans prioritized their air force (Luftwaffe) once Hitler came to power and spent about 40 per cent of the defence budget on it accordingly in 1933–36, but the German air industry did not develop sufficiently to support an air force for a major conflict. The Spanish Civil War also suggested to the Germans that large long-range bombers were not necessary: they used dive-bombers, instead, and developed dive-bombing tactics. Seeking a strategic bombing force that could act as a deterrent, Germany had initially led in the development of the four-engine bomber – the "Ural" or "Amerika" bomber – but had only prototypes. The capability to produce the engines necessary for the planned heavy bombers was lacking. More generally, there were problems with the availability of aviation fuel for the air force, and also a preference for numbers of planes as opposed to a balanced expenditure that would include investment in infrastructure, for example logistical provision, especially spares. This owed much to the poor quality of leadership.

Hermann Goering, Air Minister and Commander-in-Chief of the Luftwaffe, was not interested in the less glamorous side of air power, and this helped to weaken the Luftwaffe in the subsequent war. Goering was also less than careful in his appointments. Ernst Udet, whom he made Technical Director, was overly interested in dive-bombing. Goering's concern for plane numbers helped to lead, in 1937, to the abandonment of the four-engined bomber programme, as it was easier to produce large numbers of twin-engined bombers. Furthermore, the search for a force structure that would make blitzkrieg a success, a search made necessary by Hitler's preference for quick wars, led to a lack of support for strategic bombing, which was seen, instead, as a long-term solution. Blitzkrieg entailed no obvious requirement for a strategic bombing force.[24]

The ability to learn lessons about air support from the Spanish Civil War was limited by inter-service rivalry and the nature of air-force culture, especially in Britain, where there was a major commitment to strategic bombing as a way to break the will of an opposing population.[25] In particular, there was resistance to the possibilities of ground-support operations on the part of those committed to strategic bombing, while the need to provide fighter escorts for bombers was not appreciated by the British or the Americans until they suffered heavy casualties in World War Two.[26] Lessons were also not drawn from the Sino-Japanese War, which began in 1937. For example, the battle of Shanghai in 1937 showed that Chinese losses made during the day could be regained at night when Japanese air power was less potent.

In France and the Soviet Union the stress was on tactical doctrine and force structure. Both the British and the French devoted attention to fighter defence in the late 1930s, seeing this as a necessary response to German power. The British developed two effective monoplane fighters, the Hawker Hurricane and Supermarine Spitfire, and, alongside early warning radar, they were to help rescue Britain from the consequences of devoting too much attention to bombing.

## World War Two

Much of the debate about air power in World War Two revolves around its use in strategic bombing,[27] but it would be inappropriate to thus limit discussion. Air power also provided a long-range form of artillery, especially useful against communications and against concentrations of vehicles, but also at sea. By interdicting rear zones, air power could prevent resupply. The Germans and Soviets stressed the tactical employment of air power, and developed aviation technology and operational doctrine accordingly. As a consequence, neither air force was suited to strategic air campaigns, although, for other functions, German air power proved flexible and without a limiting dominant doctrine. Large numbers of aeroplanes were used to support or help repel major offensives, such as the battle of Kursk in 1943,[28] and considerable effectiveness in joint operations was developed.[29] Germany did not have a strategic air arm, while the Soviet air force was largely an extension of the army. Furthermore, the Germans were affected by a lack of raw materials and engine manufacturing technology. Nevertheless, the Luftwaffe was successful in Poland in 1939 and in Scandinavia and France in 1940, although, in each case, it benefited from launching surprise attacks that destroyed some of the opposing planes on the ground, although this has been exaggerated and it is more pertinent to note the losses of opposing air forces in aerial combat.

Although much of the older literature describes the Luftwaffe as a close air-support or tactical air force it is possibly better to describe it as an operational air force. Air superiority was a crucial goal and tactical air-support duties were less important. The Luftwaffe favoured gaining general air superiority and big "terror" bombing raids, and saw little merit in battlefield air support, and certainly not in close air-support. Most of the Luftwaffe was not designed to act as a tactical close support force. The much vaunted Ju 87 Stuka was not a dedicated close air-support bomber, although it came to be used as such, especially in the Soviet Union. In hostile skies, and without guaranteed friendly air superiority, the Stuka was a death-trap.

The Luftwaffe fought the Battle of Britain in 1940 with aeroplanes with limited range, which was a key reason why it lost the battle. In addition, the Germans had not planned for such a campaign because they had not anticipated its necessity. Aside from a lack of preparation for a strategic air offensive, the relationship between air attack and invasion was left unclear until late in the campaign. Although the Luftwaffe was instructed to help prepare the way for Operation Sealion, the planned invasion, Luftwaffe commanders were increasingly concerned to attack the British air force and its supporting infrastructure in order to prepare the way for reducing Britain to submission by a bombing war on civilian targets. Aside from these general limitations, the Germans were affected by a series of major problems, including a lack of sufficient trained pilots, and limitations with their planes (bombers' load capacity and range too small, fighters too slow) and tactics (fighters forced to escort bombers; failure to understand role of British radar). The Germans had also lost many planes and pilots during the Battle of France. Despite these deficiencies, the Germans outnumbered the British on the eve of the battle. Furthermore, there had been heavy losses of British planes in the Battle of France, and the factories where new planes might be manufactured could now be bombed as a result of German conquests, although in the event it was a shortage of pilots rather than of planes that threatened Britain's survival.

Initial German attacks on the British air force and its airfields inflicted heavy blows, especially on pilot numbers, although, fighting over Britain, the British air force benefited from the support provided by the ground control organization and could more often recover any pilots who survived being shot down. Once the Germans switched in early September 1940 to bomb London and other cities (the Blitz), the pressure on the RAF diminished, although the strain on the British people of coping with the Blitz was heavy.

On 17 September, Operation Sealion was formally postponed. Irrespective of the serious problems that would have faced any invasion, not least insufficient naval resources and preparation, it could not be allowed to go ahead without air superiority.[30] The different force structures and operational doctrines of the two air forces are a reminder of the role of choice in the use of resources and thus of the danger of simply quantifying the latter in order to assess capability.

The extent to which air power played only a supportive role on the Eastern Front reveals the limited effectiveness of air power on ground operations conducted on a massive scale. Nevertheless, the Allied use of bombers in both an interdiction role over France prior to D-Day in 1944 and a ground-support tactical role over Normandy thereafter was a clear example of air power having a significant impact on ground operations. The interdiction role made it difficult for the Germans to supply their forces, and, in part, justified the pre-war arguments of John Slessor, who had been RAF Director of Plans.[31]

Close air support was employed to great effect by the US Marines in the Pacific and the US Army in Europe. In the Normandy campaign, planes were used in ground-support both against specific targets and for "carpet-bombing", as in advance of American troops in Operation Cobra. Ground-support air attacks helped the Allies regain the initiative in the Battle of the Bulge in December 1944, although they had to wait for the weather to improve; Hitler had deliberately launched the attack when bad weather promised protection. The dependence of air operations on the weather was shown the following February, when rain and mist affected Allied aerial support for 21 Army Group in its operations west of the Rhine.[32]

The effectiveness of Allied ground-support air power owed much to the longer-term process of gaining a degree of air superiority over the Luftwaffe.[33] In "Some Notes on the use of Air Power in support of Land Operations and Direct Air Support", Montgomery argued in December 1944 that:

> Present operations in western Europe in all stages have been combined Army/Air operations . . . the overall contribution of the Air Forces to the successes gained has been immense . . . The greatest asset of air power is its flexibility . . . A retreating enemy offers the most favourable targets to air attack . . . The moral effect of air action is very great and is out of proportion to the material damage inflicted . . . It is necessary to win the air battle before embarking on the land battle . . . Experience in battle shows that the degree and effectiveness of the air support which a military formation receives is related in a striking manner to:

a) The interest it takes in air matters.
b) The knowledge and proficiency it possesses in air support
   procedure and the part the Army has to play . . .
Technical developments in the air weapon continue apace and their
possibilities are bounded only by the imagination. It follows that land
operations are likely to be influenced more and more by air action.[34]

During the war, land-based aeroplanes weakened the control of inshore
waters by warships, as when 85 Japanese bombers sank the *Prince of Wales*
and the *Repulse* off Malaya on 10 December 1941, thus ending British plans
to intervene against the Japanese invasion of Malaya. These were the first
battleships sunk at sea solely by air attack and their loss demonstrated the
vulnerability of capital ships without aircraft protection to enemy air attack.
Air attack was also effective in reducing the ability of armies to rely on sea
routes for reinforcement, supply and withdrawal, as with German operations
against Crete in 1941, and the Crimea in 1941–42, and Soviet operations
against the Crimea in 1944. More German submarines were destroyed by
Allied aircraft than by surface vessels.

Conversely, the Japanese failed to provide adequate air cover to assist their
merchant fleet by reducing American submarine attacks. Japanese air power
could not compete in the long term, not least because of coordination failures
in its aero-industry. The Japanese also lacked a heavy bomber, while their planes
were deficient in armour and self-sealing tanks.[35] Despite these deficiencies, the
Japanese were still more effective in the air than the Italians, who could not
wrest control from the RAF of air lanes on their doorstep to North Africa.

Air power was also used for airborne operations, both glider and parachute
attacks, as in the German attacks on Denmark, Norway, Belgium and the
Netherlands in 1940 and on Crete in 1941 (although in the last case German
losses were so great that Hitler ordered that no similar operation should be
repeated), the capture of the Sumatran oilfields by the Japanese in 1942, and
the Allied attacks on Normandy and at Arnhem in 1944 and on Rangoon in
1945. Many other such attacks were planned – for example, an American
parachute attack on Rome in 1943. These attacks represented a major
expansion of military capability, although only relatively small forces and,
certainly, only forces without equipment such as heavy armour could be
transported and they have rarely been used since World War Two.

Air power also created opportunities for the supply and reinforcement of
land and sea forces by air. This was particularly valuable where road links
were unreliable and where units were isolated. Thus, the British in Burma
benefited greatly from aerial resupply, and thus from command of the air, in
1944,[36] and the Americans advancing along the north coast of New Guinea
that year depended heavily on land-based air support.[37]

The use of air power to try to destroy the economic capability and civilian
morale of opponents was its most controversial aspect. German terror

bombing of undefended cities, such as Warsaw (1939), Rotterdam (1940) and Belgrade (1941), deliberately caused heavy civilian casualties, 17,000 people being killed in Belgrade. For Britain, the preservation of national independence had traditionally required a strong and successful fleet, but German air and, with the coming of the V1s in 1944, missile attack revealed that command of the sea could no longer protect Britain from bombardment, even if it could still thwart or inhibit invasion. The Germans also bombarded Dover with long-range guns from the other side of the English Channel. The defensive perimeter of the country was thus extended. Although the Germans did not develop a long-distance heavy bomber force, their bombers could still attack Britain from bases in north-western Europe, while the ground-to-ground V2 missiles, which could travel at up to 3,000 mph, could be fired from a considerable distance, although their explosive payload was small. In strategic terms, however, Britain, which was bombarded by V2s from German bases in the Netherlands in 1944-45, was no longer an island.

Long-distance American bombing had a similar effect on Japan. By early 1945 the systematic destruction of Japanese cities and infrastructure, and blockade, were seen as the alternative to a costly invasion and a much longer conflict. More generally, strategic bombing, made more feasible by four-engined bombers, such as the American B-29 "Super Fortress", and, against Germany, the British Lancaster, as well as by heavier bombs, developments in navigational aids and training, and the introduction of long-range fighter escorts, especially the American P-38s (twin-engine Lightnings), P-47s (which used drop fuel tanks) and P-51s (Mustangs, which also used drop fuel tanks), caused heavy civilian casualties in Germany and Japan. Over 30,000 people were killed in one British raid on Hamburg in 1943. The Mustangs were able to provide necessary escorts, but also, in 1944, to seek out German fighters and thus win the air war above Germany. This contrasted with the Luftwaffe's failed offensive on Britain in 1940-41.

The Mustang's superiority to German interceptors was demonstrated in late February and March 1944, when major American raids in clear weather on German sites producing aircraft and oil led to large-scale battles with German interceptors. Many American bombers were shot down, but the Luftwaffe also lost large numbers of planes and pilots. The latter were very difficult to replace, in large part because training programmes had not been increased in 1940-42 as was necessary given the scale of the war, and this helped to ensure that, irrespective of aircraft construction figures, the Germans would be far weaker. Towards the end, the Germans could not afford the fuel for training, while a lack of training time was also a consequence of the shortage of pilots. By the time of the Normandy landings, the Germans had lost the air war.

The effectiveness, as well as the morality, of bombing has been the subject of considerable debate. The latter was raised at the time, for example by Bishop Bell of Chichester,[38] but the general consensus was that the bombing campaign was a deserved return for earlier German air attacks, and also was likely to disrupt the German war effort and hit morale. As far as the latter was concerned, the hopes of inter-war air power enthusiasts were not fully realized. Few air power enthusiasts argued during the war that bombing alone could win. It was generally accepted that bombing should be part of an integrated strategy. This was certainly the case from 1942. In January 1944, a group of scholars, asked by the US Army Air Forces commander to determine whether strategic bombing could force Germany out of the war by that spring, reported:

> Although the blockade and bombing have deranged Germany's economic structure, [the] German military economy has not been crippled at any vital point . . . Although bombing has made a vital contribution to the ultimate defeat of Germany and although complete defeat cannot be achieved without an acceleration and intensification of bombing, it is improbable that bombing alone can bring about a German collapse by Spring of 1944.[39]

Despite the limited precision of bombing by high-flying aeroplanes dropping free-fall bombs, strategic bombing was crucial to the disruption of German and Japanese logistics and communications, largely because it was eventually on such a massive scale. It also acted as a brake on Germany's expanding production of weaponry, which had important consequences for operational strength. In addition, the Germans diverted massive resources to anti-aircraft defence forces, for example the 88 mm anti-aircraft gun, which was also very effective against Allied tanks, as well as much of the Luftwaffe itself. These might otherwise have made a major contribution on the Eastern and, later, the Western Front.

The British and Americans lost 21,900 bombers over Europe and suffered casualty rates among air crew that would have been considered unacceptable for infantry. Especially prior to the introduction of long-range fighters, bombers were very vulnerable, and cripplingly heavy casualty rates occurred in some raids, for example those of the American 8th Air Force against the ball-bearing factory at Schweinfurt in August and October 1943. Heavily armed bomber formations lacking fighter escorts proved far less effective both in defending themselves and in destroying targets than had been anticipated.

This helped lead to a major shift. In place of precision bombing came area bombing, with its attendant goals of destroying urban life and its concomitant heavy civilian casualties. The hope that this would inflict heavy damage on the German state was not fulfilled, but area bombing did disrupt the war economy. Worker morale and organizational effectiveness were hit, and the production of military supplies in 1944 was lower than projected.[40] The US Army Air Forces (USAAF) never officially switched to area bombing over

Europe. Their winter months campaigns often became area bombing operations in practice, but not as a deliberate policy, unlike the RAF's, which clearly were. The USAAF did have a plan for a final knockout terror bombing raid on a German city, hopefully to be Berlin, planned for the latter stages of the war. Over Japan they did switch emphatically to area bombing.

The German economy, especially the oil industry, aircraft production and communications, was savagely hit by air attack. Attacks on communications affected the rest of the economy, limiting the transfer of resources and the process of integration. In addition, by 1943, Anglo-American bombing had wrecked 60 per cent of Italy's industrial capacity and badly undermined Italian morale. Such bombing directly benefited the Allied war effort. For example, thanks to bombing, the construction of a new, faster class of U-boat – type XXIII – was delayed, so that it did not become operational until April 1945, too late to challenge Allied command of the sea. More generally, the air attack intensified economic disruption and speeded up defeat.

The availability of large numbers of bombers reflected Allied industrial capability. American production rose to 29,365 in 1943.[41] The Allies considerably out-built their opponents in the air. By late 1940, the British were producing more than twice as many fighters as the Germans, helping them to defeat German air attacks: the planes, especially the fast and manoeuvrable Hurricanes and Spitfires, were also effective. In 1942, even before the American economy had been put on a full war footing, the Allies produced 101,000 aeroplanes, the Axis only 26,000. Numbers alone, however, were not the sole issue. The Allies also developed the ability to organize production so that it could be retooled quickly for improved marks and to ensure the production of a range of planes with different capabilities.[42]

Bombing was linked to long-distance photo-reconnaissance missions, which provided information to identify targets and to assess success. Photo-reconnaissance also helped in planning land operations, as with the German attack on the Soviet Union in 1941 and the Soviet attack on Berlin in 1945, when aerial photography provided detailed plans of German defences for the Soviet artillery.

Aside from specific damage to particular targets, it was also claimed that area bombing would cause heavy casualties, which would terrorize the civilian population and put pressure on their governments. However, efforts to break civilian morale through bombing had only partial effect in Britain or Germany, or in Japan until nuclear bombs were used. British morale and industrial production were not badly damaged by aerial attack, and certainly less so than had been feared before the war, when large numbers of cardboard coffins had been prepared for the expected mass casualties and there was widespread preparation for airborne gas attacks. None, in fact, were mounted. In turn, British Bomber Command ignored intelligence reports that stressed the limited value of the area bombing of German cities. This obstinacy reduced the value of air attack and possibly led to a misuse of resources.

However, it is possible that the impact of bombing on civilians has been underestimated. A recent study of Nuremberg has suggested that bombing was responsible for a serious decline in civilian morale from 1943, a process of social dissolution, and a matching crisis of self-confidence in the Nazi party. The non-atomic bombing of Japan badly hit urban life and shook morale.[43]

Unable to mount an effective response to heavy American air raids (let alone have a deterrent capability to hit American targets), the Japanese government was put under great pressure during the closing stages of the war. Initially, the American raids, which in part were motivated by a desire to revenge Pearl Harbor, had been long-distance and unsupported by fighter cover. This led to attacks from a high altitude, which reduced their effectiveness. The precision raids that were launched were hindered by poor weather, especially strong tail winds, and difficulties with the B-29's reliability, as well as the general problems of precision bombing within the technology of the period.

From February 1945, however, there was a switch to low-altitude night-time area bombing of Japanese cities, which reflected the views of General Curtis LeMay, the commander of the 21st Bomber Group. The impact was devastating, not least because many Japanese dwellings were made of timber and paper and burned readily when bombarded with incendiaries, and the population density was high. The fighters based in Iwo Jima from April 1945 could provide cover for the B-29s that had been bombing from more distant Saipan since November 1944. Weaknesses in Japanese anti-aircraft defences, both planes and guns, eased the attacker's task and enabled LeMay to increase B-29 payloads by removing their guns. In 1944–45, American bombers destroyed over 30 per cent of the buildings in Japan. Over half of Tokyo and Kobe were destroyed, and on 10 March 1945, in the first major low-level raid on Tokyo, more people were killed than in the atomic bomb attack on Nagasaki. The deaths of 100,000 people in terrible circumstances was accompanied by another million becoming homeless.

Bombing culminated in the dropping of atomic bombs on Hiroshima and Nagasaki in August 1945, as a result of which over 280,000 people died, either at once or, eventually, through radiation poisoning. This transformed the situation, precipitating a Japanese surrender. The use of atomic bombs was to be very controversial, but seemed justified at the time given the likely heavy Allied casualties that would arise from an invasion. Such an invasion had appeared the only way to force Japan to accept quickly terms that would neutralize its threat to its neighbours. In addition, it was necessary to secure the surrender of the large Japanese forces in China and South-East Asia. The atom bombs showed that the Japanese armed forces could not protect the nation. They were thus a major blow to militarism.[44]

The Germans and Japanese had both been interested in developing an atomic bomb, but neither had made progress comparable to that of the Allies. The Germans had not pursued their research into the bomb because they thought it would take too long to develop. They felt that the war would or could be finished using conventional weapons long before the bomb would be ready, an instance of overconfidence affecting technological options, although one encouraged by their successes in 1939–41. Hostility to "Jewish physics" also affected the Germans.[45]

This underlines the crucial role of choices in war. Hitler's priorities were questionable. For example, he squandered the German lead in jet-powered aircraft, ordering that the Me262 should not be used as an interceptor, despite its effectiveness in the role. Rockets were another questionable policy. Although the V2 could travel 200 miles in five minutes, the technology was too limited to enable it to be aimed accurately. Neither could either the V1 or the V2 pack much of an explosive punch. The rocket programme was neither cost-effective, nor displayed much insight into the psychology of German's opponents.[46]

## After 1945

The use of the atom bomb in 1945 ensured that in the post-war world there was a new thrust to air power, one provided by the apparent ability of a small number of bombs to make a decisive difference. This played a major role in American strategy, and air power was seen as rectifying the weakness of Western forces on land compared to the numerical preponderance of their Communist rivals.[47] This was linked to the creation in 1947 of an independent air service in the USA, with the United States Air Force (USAF).[48] In order to fulfil its independent role, and to take the leading part in the Cold War with the Soviet Union, American air force thinking was dominated by strategic nuclear bombing. The ability to strike at Soviet centres was seen as both an effective deterrent and as the essential purpose of American air power. This emphasis was given force by the role of officers from Strategic Air Command in the senior ranks of the Air Staff, by a fascination with aerial self-sufficiency and big planes, and by the absence of a powerful drive for integrated warfare, which would have encouraged the development of doctrines for cooperation with the army and navy.[49] Strategic nuclear bombing also played a major role in British air planning.[50]

The USAF nonetheless argued that it still had a part to play in conventional warfare, for example in the Korean War of 1950–53, where it claimed that its conventional bombing inflicted much damage on North Korea and helped lead America's opponents to accept the armistice. Heavy damage was certainly inflicted, for example in 1952 to hydroelectric generating capacity, although it is not clear that the bombing campaign was as effective as was to be claimed.[51] Looking ahead to the Vietnam War, the bombing in the Korean War was also more limited than it had been in World War Two. Aside from the decision not to use atomic bombs, in 1950 air force suggestions of the firebombing of the major industrial cities in North Korea were not initially implemented, although once the Chinese had entered the war later in 1950, major incendiary attacks were launched on North Korea.

Air capability increased significantly after World War Two. The nature of aeroplanes changed as jet power was generally adopted. This greatly increased the options open to plane designers in terms of speed, range and weight, increasing aeroplane effectiveness and affecting aerial conflict. The firepower of planes was also enhanced by the development of guided missiles, especially the American heat-seeking Sidewinder, which went into service in 1956. After 1945, aerial conflict was far more significant than that between warships. In the Korean War, the Chinese were supported by the advanced MIG-15 fighters of the Manchurian-based Soviet "Group 64", and mastery of the air space over North Korea was contested. The war saw dogfights between jet aircraft with Mig-15s fighting American F-86 Sabres. Jet fighter-bombers, such as the American F-84 Thunderjet, made their first appearance, and they came to play a major role, replacing more vulnerable World War Two period planes. In the 1950s, the Americans also deployed long-range jet bombers (B-47s and B-52s) as well as jet tankers (KC-135s).

After 1945, leading air forces retained their World War Two functions of ground-support and strategic bombing, although smaller air forces lacked this range. Ground support played a major role in Israeli operations. Air power was crucial to the Israelis, given the small size of the state and the outnumbering of their ground forces by the Arab powers. They were able to gain air superiority at the outset of the Six-Day War in 1967, and then attack Arab forces.

Ground-support and strategic bombing were employed by the Americans in the Korean and Vietnam Wars. In 1966, the weekly number of American air sorties in Vietnam frequently exceeded 25,000. Frustration with the limited opportunities for, and success of, ground-support and interdiction bombing in Korea and Vietnam encouraged an emphasis on strategic bombing, which drew on the experience of World War Two and the force structure and doctrine of the USAF. The USAF dropped a greater weight of bombs on South-East Asia in the Vietnam War than on Europe in World War Two. This bombing was seen as likely to affect political will and to damage economic resources. In both cases, the results were disappointing. In Operation Rolling Thunder, 643,000 tons of bombs were dropped on North Vietnam, but this did not destroy the North Vietnamese war machine nor the will to fight. As a consequence of the long-term emphasis on strategic bombing, the USAF was perhaps not sufficiently flexible to try alternatives,[52] although, on a far smaller scale, Anglo-Australian bombing in the 1950s had achieved very little in counter-insurgency operations in Malaya.

The auxiliary functions of air power, supply and reinforcement became even more important after World War Two. For example, American-supported units in Laos in 1964–72 relied on the mobility provided by Central Intelligence Agency (CIA) aeroplanes. Airports became points of strategic importance: Soviet tanks were flown into Prague airport in 1968 when the Czech government was overthrown.

Although the logistical capability of air power is easily exaggerated, air power could be used to move large numbers of troops overseas more rapidly than ships. The first American troops to arrive in South Korea in 1950 did so by air. In response to disorder in the Dominican Republic in the spring of 1965, the USA airlifted 23,000 troops in less than two weeks. Considerable Soviet airlift capacity was demonstrated in Angola in 1975.

Improvements in the size, power and range of helicopters after World War Two has seen them play an increasing role in the movement of troops and in attacking ground positions. The French used them in Algeria in the 1950s, and the British made effective use of helicopters in support of Malaysia against Indonesia in 1964. In Vietnam, the Americans made extensive tactical use of helicopters in order to provide mobility and firepower. Helicopters played a major role as mobile artillery and troop transports, and enabled the Americans to extend greatly the range of their forces. However, their initial success led to somewhat inflexible tactics; and their relatively low speed made them vulnerable to attack from the ground; the Viet Cong shot down over 2,300.

More generally, air power became prey to improved anti-aircraft weaponry. In 1954, the French stronghold at Dien Bien Phu in North Vietnam lost air support due to both artillery bombardment of the airstrip and Chinese anti-aircraft weaponry. Soviet-supplied surface-to-air missiles inflicted heavy casualties on American bombers over North Vietnam in 1965–68. In the Arab–Israeli War of 1973, Israel's American aeroplanes proved vulnerable to Soviet ground-to-air (SAM 6) missiles: air losses were 5 per cent to other aircraft, 40 per cent to conventional anti-aircraft guns, and 55 per cent to missiles.

This was an instance of the degree to which leads in weaponry were countered with new weaponry or with the development of new tactics and/ or strategy. This was true of helicopters as well as aeroplanes. The extent to which aerial resupply and attack capabilities were affected by anti-aircraft weaponry, limiting the safety of low-level operations and thus affecting the vertical space of the aerial battlefield, greatly compromised one of the major aspects of air power. Similarly, the failure of American air power to coerce North Vietnam or to offer effective interdiction of Vietnamese supply routes underlined the folly of thinking that air power alone could ensure victory. Fuller wrote to an American correspondent in July 1965,

> Today your government and its military advisers would appear to have accepted the concept that the way to defeat Communism in Vietnam is by bombing when clearly the precepts garnered from World War Two should have told them that ideas cannot be dislodged by TNT.[53]

To end on this note is not to suggest that air power was of limited value, but rather to assert that its capability rested (and rests) on being part of an integrated fighting system with an operational doctrine that relies on cooperation between arms and seeks to implement realizable political goals.

The era from the mid-1930s to the early 1950s was a period when aero-technology was inexpensive enough, but potent enough to produce an age of mass industrial air power. Prior to the mid-1930s, the effectiveness of air power was very limited, while, by the early 1950s, the provision of a mass of air power resources was increasingly expensive. Furthermore, the nature of the Vietnam War limited the aerial effectiveness of the major air power.

CHAPTER EIGHT

# The Retreat from Empire: Singapore to Mozambique, 1942–75

The leading colonial powers, Britain and France, were among the victors in World War Two, but their empires largely disappeared within two decades. This was one of the most important shifts of power in global history and, for that reason, is placed before a discussion of the more conventional military history of the post-war period. The two cannot be readily separated, but, by continuing the distinct theme of the West's military interaction with the rest of the world, this chapter both testifies to its importance and acts as a counterpoint to Chapter 1. Equally, it would be mistaken to suggest that this shift can only be discussed in military terms or, indeed, that it should primarily be discussed in these terms. However, there is still a military dimension that has to be addressed.

World War Two massively weakened the imperial powers. Two, Italy and Japan, lost their empires, but neither was treated as the German and Turkish empires had been at the close of World War One. During World War Two, the British occupied both Italian Somaliland and Libya, and Churchill considered the annexation of the latter, but such views now seemed anachronistic. The dominant role in the victorious coalition had been taken by the USA and the Soviet Union, both of which, albeit from different perspectives, had anti-colonial ideologies and saw no reason to view the expansion of the European empires with any favour; in fact, they questioned their continued existence. In practice, both the USA and the Soviet Union were imperial, if not colonial, powers and the war strengthened both their systems. American territorial power in the Pacific increased, while the Soviet state not only maintained its grip on Siberia, Central Asia, the Caucasus and Mongolia, but now also controlled most of eastern Europe. In 1944, the ostensibly independent "people's republic" of Tannu Tuva, formerly a vassal state of Mongolia, was incorporated into the Soviet Union.

Italy and Japan had lost their empires because of defeat in the war, but other powers, on the winning side, found theirs gravely weakened by the strains of the war. In particular, the British, Dutch and French had suffered heavily at the hands of Japan in South-East Asia. The prestige of the British empire in the region was held to be fatally compromised by the humiliating surrender of Singapore in 1942 to the Japanese (a non-white Asian power). It was for this reason that British leaders were keen that their forces should regain Singapore. In September 1944, Admiral Sir Geoffrey Layton, Commander-in-Chief Ceylon, wrote of

> the vital importance of our recapturing those parts of the Empire as far as possible ourselves. I would specially mention that recapture of Burma and its culmination in the recovery of Singapore by force of arms and not by waiting for it to be surrendered as part of any peace treaty . . . the immense effect this will have on our prestige in the Far East in post-war years. This and only this in my opinion will restore us to our former level in the eyes of the native population in these parts.

Mountbatten strongly agreed.[1]

However, alongside the view that Japanese success helped ensure the redundancy of European imperial strategies in Asia, and, crucially, destroyed their prestige, it is also possible to focus on the political and resource costs of the European wars of 1914–45. As a result, Britain's decision to abandon its colonial presence in India can be seen as stemming in part from conflict within the Western system rather than as simply a response to the war with Japan or to growing indigenous pressure on Britain to "quit India", as the World War Two slogan put it. Shrewd observers at the end of the war might have seen that the end of overseas European empire was in sight, especially as the metropolitan powers were financially exhausted.

Nevertheless, there were still hopes among some in Europe of a recovery of imperial military greatness. Imperial authority was reimposed, and rebellions, for example against the French in Madagascar in 1947–48, were suppressed, or at least confronted, although opposition to the reimposition of French rule in Syria was successful in 1945. In May 1946, Sir Claude Auchinleck, then Commander-in-Chief India, had to explain to Sir Francis Tucker, Head of Eastern Command in India, that the latter's proposal for a British protectorate over what he termed Mongol territory from Nepal to Bhutan was not realistic. Tucker had wanted to prevent any threat to India from the north. Instead, there was talk of India only being given independence if it agreed to help in the defence of other imperial possessions, specifically Aden, Burma and Malaya, and an expectation that an independent India would accept a continued presence by British forces.[2]

These hopes were misplaced, and there was a major retreat from empire. The British renounced control over India (1947), which became India and

Pakistan, as well as over Burma, Ceylon and Palestine (1948), and Newfoundland (1949). In 1954, British troops were withdrawn from the Suez Canal Zone, after fighting two years earlier had indicated the cost of staying on.

## Decolonization struggles

Returning to Indonesia after the Japanese withdrawal, the Dutch were unable to suppress nationalist resistance in 1947, although, with the support of local allies, they did limit the extent of Java and Sumatra controlled by the nationalists, who had declared independence in 1945. American anti-colonial pressure, post-World War Two weakness, guerrilla warfare, and nationalist determination forced the Dutch to accept Indonesian independence in 1949, and the Indonesians then moved into Dutch Borneo, the Celebes, the Moluccas, the Lesser Sunda Islands and West Timor.

However, both Britain and France were determined to remain imperial powers and were ready to fight to that end. Independence for the Indian sub-continent was intended to provide the means for continued informal control. Indeed, the government sent troops to maintain the British presence in the economically crucial colony of Malaya, in the face of a Communist insurrection: in the Malayan Emergency of 1948–60, it took 300,000 men to defeat a Communist force that never exceeded 6,000. The British made effective use of helicopters; improved their intelligence system; carefully controlled the food supply, so that the Communists lost direct access; resettled much of the rural population, a crucial move; and used counter-insurgency forces skilled in jungle craft. They also did not allow the Emergency to deter them from their political course: moves towards independence. Their opponents lacked adequate Chinese and Russian support.[3]

Ernest Bevin, Foreign Secretary from 1945 until 1951, hoped to use imperial resources to make Britain a less unequal partner in the Anglo-American alliance. Nevertheless, India had been the most populous and important part of the British empire, and the area that most engaged the imaginative attention of the British. Once India had been granted independence, it was difficult to summon up much popular interest in the retention of the remainder of the empire. Although global commitments were reduced in some areas, elsewhere they were maintained, but the stress was now on informal influence through security pacts and economic links. In south-west Arabia, Britain pursued a forward policy involving a vigorous assertion of British interests. Aside from an attempt to create a federation in the Aden Protectorates, there were also ambitious plans for economic development, a drive into the interior in search of oil, and a determined attempt to exclude Yemeni and Saudi influence. However, these measures led to an increased political and military commitment to the region, which proved unsustainable against the local and external opposition that the new policies stimulated.

In 1956, the weakness of the imperial response and the limited domestic popularity of empire were exposed in the Suez crisis. Britain and France attacked Egypt, in an intervention publicly justified as a way of safeguarding the Suez Canal, which had been nationalized by the aggressive Egyptian leader Gamal Abdel Nasser. His Arab nationalism was also seen as a threat to the French position in Algeria and to Britain's Arab allies. The invasion was poorly planned, but it was abandoned, in large part, because of American opposition. Concerned about the impact of the invasion on attitudes in the Third World, the Americans, who were ambivalent about many aspects of British policy, refused to extend any credits to support sterling, blocked British access to the International Monetary Fund until it withdrew its troops from Suez and refused to provide oil to compensate for interrupted supplies from the Middle East. American opposition underlined the vulnerability of the British economy, was crucial in weakening British resolve and led to a humiliating withdrawal. It can be seen as the end of Britain's ability to act wholly independently; from then on, there was an implicit reliance on American acceptance.

The Suez crisis and the overthrow of the pro-British Iraqi government in 1958 revealed the limitations of British strength. This encouraged a new attitude towards empire, which led to rapid decolonization, especially in Africa, but also in the West Indies and Malaysia. Decolonization was hastened by a strong upsurge in colonial nationalist movements, particularly in West Africa, which policy-makers did not know how to confront, as they sought to rest imperial rule on consent, not force. Decolonization proceeded on the simple assumption that Britain would withdraw from those areas that it could no longer control (or, equally importantly, from those areas where the cost of maintaining a presence was prohibitive). Colonies also appeared less necessary in defence terms, not least because in 1957 Britain had added the hydrogen bomb to the atom bomb.[4] The American government encouraged decolonization and also sought to manage it as a means of increasing informal American control.[5]

The military dimension of decolonization included not only the containment of independence movements, but also a process of changing the character of locally raised forces. Prior to independence, these were developed in the hope that imperial influence, or at least an order beneficial to Western interests, would continue. In 1960, Mountbatten, then Chief of the Defence Staff, noted,

> The East African Governors are concerned at the slow rate of Africanisation of the King's African Rifles, and in particular with the problem of providing African officers quickly . . . With the example of the Congo disaster before them, African politicians are pressing

strongly for the early provision of African officers, and it would appear only sensible to support them by producing officers of known reliability.[6]

Although criticized by some right-wing Conservatives, decolonization was not a central issue in British politics. In part, this was because the British empire was seen as being transformed into the Commonwealth, rather than lost. The British view of empire was important. The logic of Britain's imperial mission, bringing civilization to backward areas of the globe, allowed Britain to present the granting of self-government as the inevitable terminus of empire. The contraction of empire was also relatively painless, because interest in much of it was limited. This was not the case with some traditional Conservative interests, such as the military, but was true of much of the party's middle-class support.

The Labour government of Harold Wilson, 1964–70, decided to abandon Britain's military position "east of Suez" and focus defence priorities on western Europe. British forces were withdrawn from Aden in 1967, the Persian Gulf in 1971 and Singapore in 1974 (they had been much scaled down in 1971). This reflected both serious British economic problems and a political decision for a more modest imperial reach and a different international stance.[7]

At the same time, the abandonment of empire entailed conflict with those dissatisfied with the pace, for example in Aden. The British were also involved in warfare in protecting the newly independent Commonwealth. In 1963–65, there was a confrontation in support of Malaysia against Indonesia. The Indonesians had good weapons, especially anti-personnel mines and rocket launchers, but the British and Commonwealth troops were well-led, well-trained and versatile, and benefited from complete command of sea and air, a good nearby base at Singapore, excellent intelligence and an absence of significant domestic opposition in Britain. Anglo-Malaysian firmness prevented the situation deteriorating until a change of government in Indonesia in 1965 led to negotiations.[8] In 1961, the British successfully deployed forces to dissuade the Iraqis from invading Kuwait.

For the French, the Suez crisis was a small part of a major and sustained effort to retain its colonies, involving bitter conflicts in Indo-China in 1946–54 and in Algeria in 1954–62.[9] In Indo-China, the Chinese-supplied Viet Minh pushed the French back from their border posts, but were defeated in mass attacks on French positions in the open areas of the Red River delta in North Vietnam in 1951 and 1952, for example at Vinh Yen and Mao Khé, and in the Day River campaign. Nevertheless, the Viet Minh succeeded in 1954 in defeating the French in position warfare at Dien Bien Phu. This was a forward base developed across Viet Minh supply lines by French parachutists, in order to lure the Viet Minh into a major battle. Thanks to their mass infantry attacks, the Viet Minh suffered more casualties, but the isolated

French stronghold, denied air support due to artillery bombardment of the airstrip, fell after a 55-day siege; the Viet Minh had American 105 mm cannon, captured by the Chinese Communists in the Chinese Civil War, and also Chinese anti-aircraft weapons.

Despite their superior weaponry, the poorly led French had finally proved unable to defeat their opponents in either guerrilla or conventional warfare, and they abandoned Indo-China in 1954. They were also unsuccessful in Algeria, despite committing considerable resources to its retention. French forces in Algeria rose from about 65,000 in late 1954 to 390,000 in 1956, after first reservists and then conscripts were sent. The dispatch of both these groups was unpopular, and greatly increased opposition to the conflict within France. In order to concentrate on Algeria, which had been declared an integral part of France (and thus not a colony) in 1848, the French granted Tunisia independence in 1956, although nationalist guerrilla activity there since 1952 had made only limited impact in the towns. The French protectorate in Morocco, where guerrilla activity had become widespread in 1955, also ended in 1956.

Algeria was different. It was dominated by a settler population (*colons*) of over a million, and the eight and a half million native Moslems had no real power and suffered discrimination. An insurrection by the Front de Libération Nationale (FLN) began in October 1954, but, at first, it was restricted to small-scale terror operations. These destabilized the French relationship with the indigenous Moslems: loyalists were killed, while the French found it difficult to identify their opponents and alienated Moslems by ruthless search and destroy operations; relations between *colons* and Moslems also deteriorated. In 1955, the scale of FLN operations increased, and the war hotted up with massacres, reprisals, and a commitment by the French to a more rigorous approach. This also led to more effective French tactics. Static garrisons were complemented by pursuit groups, often moved by helicopter. These helicopter assault forces were stepped up in 1959, in large part in response to the arrival of significant numbers of large helicopters: Boeing Vertol H-21 helicopters, called *bananes*, which could fly entire units as well as light artillery. Eventually, the French deployed 175 helicopters, as well as 940 aircraft. The designation of large free-fire zones in which aircraft could bomb and strafe freely increased the effectiveness of the aircraft. Unlike later insurgent forces under air attack, the FLN lacked anti-aircraft missiles.

Air reconnaissance and attack, and helicopter-borne units took part in a series of sweeps in north Algeria in 1959, killing large numbers of insurgents. *Harkis* – locally raised auxiliaries – served to consolidate control in swept areas. These sweeps gravely damaged the FLN within Algeria, although other FLN units remained outside, attacking French positions from the Tunisian frontier.

In some respects, the Algerian War prefigured that in Vietnam. The FLN was badly damaged in 1959, just as the Viet Cong was to be in 1968, but the continued existence of both created pressure for a political solution. This helped to set General de Gaulle, who had formed a government in 1958 and become President at the close of the year, against the *colons* and much of the military leadership in Algeria, who were against negotiations with the FLN. In 1960, the *colons* tried to seize power in Algiers, but were faced down by de Gaulle. In early 1961, de Gaulle ordered a truce, and an attempt by some of the army to seize power in Algeria was unsuccessful. The Organisation Armée Secrète (OAS) then began a terror campaign against both the Gaullists and Moslems. The resulting three-part struggle of the government, the OAS and the FLN, led to extensive slaughter in 1962 as independence neared. The agreement with the FLN provided for security for the *colons*, but most fled to France.

A summary of this conflict illustrates the general difficulty of mounting effective counter-insurgency operations. Tough anti-insurrectionary measures, including torture, which was seen as a justified response to FLN atrocities, gave the French control of Algiers in 1957. However, although undefeated in battle and making effective use of helicopter-borne units, the French were unable to end guerrilla action in what was a very costly struggle. And French moves were often counter-productive in winning the loyalty of the bulk of the population – "the battle for hearts and minds" as it was later called in Vietnam. Aside from the difficulty of operating active counter-insurgency policies, there was also a need to tie up large numbers of troops in protecting settlers and in trying to close the frontiers to guerrilla reinforcements.[10]

Although it is easy to see the failure of the French as a failure of colonialism, Algeria returned to civil conflict in 1992 as the FLN state proved unable to meet expectations and was perceived as corrupt and Westernized. The fundamentalist Islamic terrorists of the FIS destabilized the state by widespread, brutal terror and the government adopted the earlier techniques of the French, including helicopter-borne pursuit groups, large-scale sweep and search operations and the use of terror as a reprisal.

The intractable nature of this conflict, which is still continuing, suggests that it is misleading to see Western military and political structures and methods as at fault in the failures of counter-insurgency operations in the 1950s and 1960s. It is also appropriate to note successes, as with the British suppression of the Mau-Mau uprising in Kenya in 1952-56. In this, the British benefited from a wide-ranging social reform policy, including land reform, in which the government distanced itself from the white colonists, as well as from the successful use of loyal Africans, including former insurgents, and the success of air-supported forest patrols and larger-scale sweep operations. Britain conceded independence to Kenya in 1962.

Two years earlier, France had granted independence to most of its African possessions, although it maintained considerable political, economic and military influence. Defence and military cooperation agreements were the basis for a system of military advisers, and the French maintained their influence by intervention.[11]

Other empires also crumbled. Belgium abandoned the Belgian Congo in 1960, and the British conceded independence to most of the rest of their empire. The major effort to retain a colonial empire after the French withdrew from Algeria was made by Portugal. Guerrilla movements in Portugal's colonies began in Angola in 1961, Guinea-Bissau in 1963 and Mozambique in 1964. The Portuguese benefited from divisions among their opponents, especially between the Movimento Popular de Libertção de Angola (MPLA) and União National para a Independência Total de Angola (UNITA) in Angola, from the support of South Africa, and from their weaponry, including tactical air support and helicopters. Napalm and aggressive herbicides were also used. The Portuguese were able to retain control of the towns, for example crushing a rising in Luanda in 1961, but found it impossible to suppress rural opposition. Their opponents could operate from neighbouring states. Guerrillas moved from attacks on border villages to a more extensive guerrilla war, which sought to win popular support and to develop liberated rural areas. Nevertheless, the Portuguese were still able to control many key rural areas, especially the central highlands of Angola. Until 1974, the 70,000-strong army in Angola, supported by secret police, paramilitary forces, settler vigilantes and African informers, effectively restricted guerrilla operations there and, more generally, protected the 350,000 white settlers in the colony.[12] However, a left-wing revolution in Portugal in April 1974, which owed much to military dissatisfaction with the war and to hostility to military service,[13] led to the granting of independence to the colonies the following year. In 1975, Franco, the long-standing Spanish dictator, died. This was followed by withdrawal from the Spanish Sahara the following year. In 1977, when Djibouti became an independent state, France withdrew from its last African territory.

Opposition to imperial rule in Africa looked back to earlier resistance to the imposition of imperial rule,[14] but post-1945 mass nationalism was also affected by political movements current in the period, not least socialism. Indeed, it is possible to trace a development in post-war decolonization struggles, with a growing politicization in terms of more "modern" political ideologies, as well as their location in the Cold War. This was particularly the case in Africa from the mid-1960s. Some earlier uprisings, such as the Mau-Mau and that in northern Angola among the Bakongo, showed many facets of old-style peasant uprisings or militant tribal identity. Although these elements still played a part, the uprisings from the mid-1960s were more explicitly located in a different ideological context, that of revolutionary socialism. There was direct reference to the revolutionary war principles of Mao Tse Tung, leader of the successful Chinese Communist revolution, training by foreign advisers, especially from the Soviet Union and China, and a provision of more advanced weapons, although many did not arrive in any quantity until the early 1970s. Anti-personnel and anti-vehicle mines restricted the mobility of counter-insurgency forces on land, and Soviet SAM-7 missiles hit their low-flying aircraft and helicopters. In addition, the guerrillas benefited from Soviet manual rocket-propelled grenade launchers, and from the durable Kalashnikov AK-47 self-loading rifle, which became the guerrilla weapon of preference.

The impact of these shifts could be seen in Portuguese Africa. In Angola, the MPLA's military wing, the EPLA, received weaponry and training from Communist powers, including Cuba, and sought to follow Maoist principles, although the Portuguese were able to inflict heavy casualties on them. The sense of a wider struggle was captured in the name of two forward bases – Hanoi I and II. Also in Angola, the Frente Nacional de Libertaçao de Angola (FNLA) received Chinese weaponry. In Mozambique, the Frenta de Liberataçáo de Mozambique (FRELIMO), formed in 1962, were steadily able to widen the sphere of operations. A wider economic strategy was seen in operations from 1968 against the Cabora Bassa dam project on the Zambezi, a project that linked South Africa to Portugal. By 1972, FRELIMO was operating further south near Beira. Militarily, Soviet and Chinese rocket launchers, and from 1974 SAM-7 anti-aircraft missiles shifted the balance of military advantage, and it was clear that Portugal could not win. In Guinea-Bissau, PAIGC had SAM-7 missiles from 1973 and Cuban instructors. The missiles challenged Portuguese air superiority and powerfully contributed to a sense that the Portuguese had lost the initiative. Although the Portuguese were reasonably successful in Angola, failure elsewhere sapped support for the war in the army and in Portugal.[15]

## The Korean War

Aside from struggles focused on decolonization, there have also been others that can more explicitly be located in the Cold War and which followed a more traditional military pattern. There was no neat chronological divide prior to 1975 between these two kinds of struggle. The first serious conflict between Western and non-Western states that cannot be located primarily in terms of the process of decolonization (although it was an element) was the Korean War (1950–53). This indicated that the Cold War was not going to be confined to Europe. The Communists had won in the Chinese Civil War of 1945–49, but the Americans were determined that they should not be allowed further gains in East Asia.

In Korea, in 1950, what can be seen as a civil war between two ideologically contrasting authoritarian regimes was greatly affected by foreign intervention, sufficiently so for this conflict, like the later Vietnam War, to be generally seen in terms of this intervention. Communist North Korea began the war in June 1950 by invading South Korea. The war was not fought by the American-led United Nations coalition in order to create an American or United Nations colony; rather, the coalition forces were determined to maintain their policies of collective security and containment, and were concerned that a successful invasion of South Korea would be followed by Communist pressure elsewhere, possibly on Berlin or on Taiwan.

The Americans were better able than they would have been in the 1930s to fight the war because of their role in World War Two, but, since then, there had been a dramatic decline of available *matériel*, for example of amphibious ships from 610 in 1945 to 81 in 1950; and American fighting effectiveness had also declined, as was shown by the experience of some American units in the first year of the Korean War. Even when their fighting quality improved, the Americans were fought to a standstill by the determined North Korean and Chinese armies.

The naval dimension was an important element in the conflict. Concerned to limit the war, the Soviet Union did not attack American naval supply routes, and the small North Korean and Chinese navies were in no position to do so: in the recent Chinese Civil War, the Nationalists, not the Communists, had controlled Chinese naval power. Equally, there was no American or United Nations blockade of China.

After almost being driven into the sea at the end of the peninsula in the first Communist onslaught, the Americans managed to rescue the situation by the daring landing at Inchon in September 1950. Carried out far behind the front, about 83,000 troops were successfully landed and pressed on to capture Seoul, wrecking the coherence of North Korean forces and their supply system. This enabled the American forces in the Pusan area in the south to drive the North Koreans back into their own half of the peninsula and north towards the Chinese frontier. This was not welcome to the Chinese, who suddenly intervened in October 1950, exploiting American overconfidence.

No such intervention had been anticipated by General MacArthur, Supreme Commander of the United Nations forces in Korea, who had believed that by advancing to the frontier at the Yalu River he would end the war. Attacking in force against the overextended coalition forces, the Chinese drove them out of North Korea in late 1950, capturing Seoul in January 1951. They proved better able to take advantage of the terrain, and outmanoeuvred the coalition forces, who were more closely tied to their road links. The heroism of some retreating units limited the scale of the defeat, but, nevertheless, it was a serious one. Thanks to control of the sea, it was possible to evacuate some troops by sea, especially from Hungnam, thus limiting the losses.

The Chinese were fought to a standstill that February and May as American supply lines shortened, and as Chinese human-wave frontal attacks fell victim to American firepower. Heavy Chinese losses of men and equipment, and American reinforcements, led the Chinese commander, P'eng The-huai, to abandon the attack in late May. Thereafter, the war became far more static, with the front near the thirty-eighth parallel, operational intensity and casualties fell, and lengthy negotiations became more important.[16]

The war, and tension with the Soviets in Europe, provoked a massive increase in American military expenditure: as a percentage of total government expenditure, it rose from 30.4 per cent in 1950 to 65.7 per cent in 1954. The Korean War certainly increased American sensitivity to developments and threats in East Asia, with an extension of the containment policy towards the Communist powers, concentrated army, navy and air power in Japan, and a growing commitment to the Nationalist Chinese in Taiwan, where they had taken refuge in 1949. More generally, a sense that the situation might slip out of control through a "domino effect", as the fall of one country to Communism led to the fall of others, encouraged Americans to their fateful commitment to South Vietnam from 1954.

## The Vietnam War

Vietnam had been partitioned after the defeat of the French in 1954. The Communist Viet Minh were left in control of North Vietnam, and an American-supported government was established in South Vietnam, where, from 1957, it faced a Communist rebellion by the Viet Cong, which led to more overt and widespread American intervention. From 1964, units of the North Vietnamese army were infiltrated into South Vietnam. The commitment of American "advisers" to South Vietnam encouraged pressure for its protection and for increased support. Apparent attacks on American warships by the North Vietnamese in the Gulf of Tonkin off Vietnam, in 1964, led Congress to pass a resolution permitting the president "to take all necessary measures to repel any armed attack against the forces of the United States and to prevent further aggression", in short to wage war without proclaiming it. This was the preferred American option because President Johnson wanted to avoid an explicit choice between war and disengagement, and he could more easily apply the strategic concept of graduated pressure. In a general sense, the credibility of American power was at issue and there was a belief in Washington that the line against further Communist expansion had to be drawn somewhere, and that South Vietnam was the place.

By the end of 1964, American forces in South Vietnam had reached 23,000; they shot up to 181,000 in 1965, 385,000 in 1966, and a peak of 541,000 in January 1969. Massive American involvement was supplemented by troops from Australia, New Zealand, South Korea (48,000 troops), Thailand and the Philippines, although the war effort was less international than the Americans had wished and than had been the case in the Korean War.

The Communists were well led and organized, and their political system and culture enabled them to mobilize and direct resources and to maintain a persistent effort. American involvement enabled North Vietnam to promote the war as a national crusade against Western imperialism. Military struggle and political indoctrination were seen to act in symbiosis. The North

Vietnamese and Viet Cong were more willing to suffer losses than were the Americans. Limited war theory is a Western concept, and American strategy was wrongly based on the assumption that unacceptable losses could be inflicted on the North Vietnamese in the way that they could on the Americans:

> Early in the war, US policymakers opted for a war of attrition based in part on an imperfect understanding and unrealistic expectations of the ability of American firepower to send a persuasive message. The Communist forces never did crack, despite the ever-increasing levels of destruction. In the end it came down to a classic Clausewitzian test of wills and national resolve

and the Americans cracked first, after attrition had led to stalemate.[17]

Viet Cong morale was sustained despite heavy casualties. This extended to the soldiers who built the Ho Chi Minh trail; they were inferior troops in military terms, but believed that they could attain status by doing these menial tasks. They were also taught to believe that if they died – as most did – their descendants would be rewarded, for instance in the distribution of land. The political context also had a more direct impact on American grand strategy. Concern about the possible Chinese response, as in the Korean War, discouraged any American invasion of North Vietnam.

Direct, mass Viet Cong attacks on American positions were generally repulsed with heavy casualties, for example at Plei Me in 1965, and at The Sanh and in the A Shau Valley and, especially, in the Tet Offensive in 1968. This involved Viet Cong and North Vietnamese attacks on cities and other bases across South Vietnam. The most serious and longest battle was waged for control of the city of Hue, much of which fell on 31 January. The city was not regained until 25 February, after difficult house-to-house struggles within its walls and an eventually successful cutting-off of supply routes into the city. The Americans lost 216 dead, the South Vietnamese forces 384 dead and their opponents over 5,000. Part of the nature of the conflict, as well as its brutality, was shown by the slaughter or "disappearance" of about 5,000 South Vietnamese civilians by the Viet Cong during their occupation: their crime was that they came from social categories judged unacceptable in the Maoist society that the Communists were trying to create.

While the Americans could repel mass attacks on their strong-points and drop thousands of bombs from a great height without opposition, they could not deny control of the countryside to their opponents. The jungle nature of the terrain gave the Viet Cong ideal cover and gave superior American technology little to aim at. The military's search-and-destroy tactics, pursued until 1968 in order to build up a "body count" of dead Viet Cong, were of limited effectiveness, not least because it was difficult to "fix" the Viet Cong. Instead, they tended to control the tempo of much of the fighting. Creighton Abrams, who became American commander in 1968, preferred instead to rely on small-scale patrols and ambushes, which, he argued, provided less of a target to his opponents than large-scale sweeps. Abrams set out to contest the village-level support the Viet Cong enjoyed. The Americans also tried to lure the Communists on to killing grounds by establishing "fire bases": positions supported by artillery and infantry.

Conversely, in the 1970s the Communists came to rely more heavily on conventional operations mounted by the North Vietnamese. This was a consequence not only of the casualties that the Tet Offensive had inflicted on the Viet Cong, but also of the failure of Rolling Thunder, the bombing of North Vietnam, to destroy the war-supporting capability of North Vietnam, and, also, of the air offensives launched against the Ho Chi Minh trail.

Although American and South Vietnamese counter-insurgency policies worked in some parts of Vietnam, they were generally unsuccessful. The pacification programme entailed a "battle for hearts and minds" involving American-backed economic and political reforms, but these were difficult to implement, not only due to Viet Cong opposition and intimidation, and the effectiveness of their guerrilla and small-unit operations, but also because the South Vietnamese government was half-hearted and corrupt. The American army, lacking a reliable political base in South Vietnam, preferred to seek a military solution, and to emphasize big-unit operations, not pacification.[18]

In 1968, domestic financial and economic problems, as well as political opposition, led Johnson to reject a military request for an additional 205,000 men in Vietnam. Military difficulties combined with political pressures within the USA resulted in an attempt to shift more of the burden back on to the South Vietnamese army by improving its capability, and some success was achieved. Indeed, Vietnamese units fought better in response to the Tet Offensive than had been anticipated. Yet the context was very different to the use of large numbers of native troops in European imperial forces earlier in the century.

Domestic opposition in America to involvement in Vietnam rose because of the duration of the conflict and because the goals seemed ill defined. By denying the Americans victory in the field, the Viet Cong helped to create political pressures within America. The conscription necessary to sustain a large-scale American presence in an increasingly unpopular war played a major role in this process. Most of the Americans who went to Vietnam were volunteers, not draftees, but in 1965–73 about two million Americans were drafted and draftees accounted for a third of American deaths in Vietnam by 1969. The war led to a massive increase in anti-war sentiment. Opposition was widely voiced and "draft dodging" common. Johnson abandoned his re-election bid in 1968 because he had failed to end the war, and his successor, Nixon, pressed ahead with substituting Vietnamese for American troops so that he could bring the men back home.

At the same time, in 1970, Nixon widened the scope of the war by launching a ground invasion of Cambodia to weaken the Communist presence there.

This "incursion" succeeded in the short term, helping to strengthen the position of the South Vietnamese army in South Vietnam. However, the operation, of dubious legality, further lessened support for the war in America, and helped the Communists to seize power in Cambodia in 1975. In 1971, a comparable invasion of Laos by the South Vietnamese without American support failed with heavy losses. The following year, the North Vietnamese launched a Spring Offensive, a conventional invasion of South Vietnam across the Demilitarized Zone between the two states. This led to a heavy American air response, in the Linebacker I air campaign of May to October 1972, which hit the North Vietnamese supply system, cutting the movement of supplies to their forces. The conventional nature of the force that had invaded South Vietnam – 14 divisions, including tanks and trucks that required fuel – made the air attacks more devastating than those directed against the Viet Cong had been. This had a major impact on the conflict on the ground. After initial success in April and May, the invading force was held off by the South Vietnamese and land was regained.

Using the pressure of further heavy air attacks, Nixon was able to negotiate a peace settlement, which was signed in January 1973. The American withdrawal, however, left South Vietnam vulnerable and, in April 1975, it was overrun in the Ho Chi Minh Campaign by a renewed invasion from the north. Conventional North Vietnamese divisions achieved what the Viet Cong fighting in more adverse conditions in 1968, and the earlier conventional attack in 1972, had failed to do. The North Vietnamese made good use of tanks in 1975 and ably integrated them with infantry and artillery. In contrast, when used at An Loc in 1972, they had fallen victim to American helicopter-fired wire-guided missiles and anti-tank weapons. In 1976, the two halves of Vietnam were reunited as the Socialist Republic of Vietnam.[19]

The Vietnam War demonstrated that its being the foremost world power did not mean that a state could beat, say, the sixtieth power, because power existed in particular spheres and was conditioned by wider politial circumstances, especially, in this case, the danger of a confrontation with other Communist powers and growing opposition to the war in the USA. The wider point had been true throughout the period, but attitudes to the use of Western power, both within the West and elsewhere, were different to the earlier situation. The combination of nationalism and the mass mobilization of people and resources that had characterized industrializing nations in the nineteenth century spread to the non-European world and helped to undermine the logic and practice of colonial control. The "right to rule" colonial peoples could not be sustained in the political climate of the later twentieth century. There were examples of successful military counter-insurgency operations, but the political contest was lost. Imperialism became ideologically and politically bankrupt, and this factor was to be more important in the collapse of Western control over most of the world than changes in military capability.

# CHAPTER NINE

# Military Power in the West, 1946–1975

There was no major conflict in the Western world in these three decades, and yet there was a massive and dangerous confrontation of conventional forces between NATO and the Warsaw Pact in Europe, backed by intercontinental nuclear forces capable of destroying the planet. This was the Cold War, the great "super-power" stand-off that lasted 45 years until the collapse of the Soviet Union at the start of the 1990s.

## The Cold War

Wartime alliances frequently do not survive peace. This was particularly true of World War Two, because of the ideological division between the Soviet Union and the Western powers. Arguably, the alliance did not survive the war itself: by 1944 differences over the fate of eastern Europe were readily apparent. General Ismay complained, in March 1944, about disputes over the future borders of Poland: "If Stalin doesn't see eye to eye with us, how can we collaborate with him in the days to come? And if we don't collaborate with him, I can see little hope for the future of the world".[1]

The Cold War was not a formal or frontal conflict, but a period of sustained hostility involving a protracted arms race as well as numerous proxy conflicts in which the major powers intervened in other struggles. These conflicts sustained attitudes of animosity, exacerbated fears and contributed to a high level of military preparedness. Just as nineteenth-century theorists of international relations had concentrated on conflict, so their Cold War successors concentrated on confrontation rather than conciliation, affecting both the public, and political and military leaders. Military planning was affected. Strategic theory was given a formal role, including institutional continuity and a place in decision-making processes.

A feeling of uncertainty on both sides, of the fragility of military strength, international links, political orders and ideological convictions, encouraged a sense of threat and fuelled an arms race that was to be central to the Cold War. Indeed, in many respects the arms race *was* the Cold War. Both sides claimed to be strong but declared that they required an edge to be secure: this was the inherent instability of an arms race, where only the mutually assured destruction (MAD) threatened by massive nuclear stockpiles eventually brought a measure of stability. Aside from the competition between the USA and the Soviet Union to produce and deploy more and better weapons, there were also subsidiary arms races between the competing services of individual states.

The Soviet Union initially lacked the atom bomb, but its army was well placed to overrun western Europe, and could only have been stopped by the West's desperate use of nuclear weapons. Ideologically and culturally, in 1945 each side felt threatened by the other. The American offer of Marshall Aid to help recovery after World War Two was rejected by the Soviet Union as a form of economic imperialism, and this created a new boundary line between the areas that received such aid and those that did not. The Soviet abandonment of cooperation over occupied Germany and the imposition of one-party Communist governments in eastern Europe, which culminated with the Communist coup in Prague in 1948, led to pressure for a response. Soviet actions appeared to vindicate Churchill's claim in March 1946 that an "Iron Curtain" was descending from the Baltic to the Adriatic. Force played an important role in the imposition of Communist control. Thus, King Michael of Romania was forced to abdicate after the palace in Bucharest was surrounded at the close of 1947 by troops of the Romanian division raised in the Soviet Union.

The war had been followed by the creation of occupation zones in Germany and Austria. These involved the military of Britain, France, the USA and the Soviet Union in a number of tasks for which they were poorly prepared, including controlling large numbers of refugees and prisoners of war, seeking to run large areas and a devastated economy, and preventing rebellions. These tasks have been underrated, but they were very demanding. The *de facto* partition of Germany between the Soviets and the Western powers ensured that Germany played a central role in the Cold War.

Before the death of Hitler there had already been fighting in Greece. German evacuation in 1944 led to an accentuation of conflict between left- and right-wing guerrilla groups, and then, in order to thwart a left-wing take-over, to military intervention by the British on behalf of the right. Having arrived in October, the British were fighting the Communist National Popular Liberation Army (ELAS) on behalf of the returned exile government two months later. A fragile armistice was negotiated in February 1945. Attempts to reach a compromise failed, leading to a second stage of the war in 1946-49.[2]

The debacle of 1940, when France had fallen and Britain had been threatened with invasion, had revealed that guarantees by Britain and other European powers of each other's territorial integrity were of limited effectiveness. After the war, there was interest in the idea of a western European "Third Force", independent of the USA and the Soviet Union, and Britain and France signed the Treaty of Dunkirk in 1947, but, in response to fears about Soviet plans, an American alliance appeared essential. In February 1947, the British acknowledged that they could no longer provide the military and economic aid deemed necessary to keep Greece and Turkey out of Communist hands. Instead, the British successfully sought American intervention. Similarly, in 1949, the British encouraged the Americans to become involved in resisting Communist expansion in South-East Asia: the French were under pressure in Indo-China, the British in Malaya.

Concerned about Communism, the Americans did not intend to repeat their inter-war isolationism. The Berlin Crisis of 1948, in which the Soviets blockaded West Berlin, led to the stationing of American B-29 strategic bombers in Britain. In the event of war, they were intended to bomb the Soviet Union. The threat of the use of the atom bomb helped bring a solution to the crisis, but the bombers remained. East Anglian bases, especially Lakenheath and Mildenhall, became little Americas. The American economy had expanded greatly during the war, both in absolute and in relative terms, and it had the manufacturing capacity, organizational capability and financial resources to meet the costs of post-war military commitments.

In 1949, the foundation of NATO created a security framework for western Europe. The USA abandoned its tradition of isolationism, played a crucial role in the formation of the new alliance and was anchored to the defence of western Europe. An analysis of World War Two that attributed the war and Hitler's initial successes to appeasement led to a determination to contain the Soviet Union. The establishment of NATO was followed by the creation of a military structure, including a central command and, eventually, by German rearmament: Germany was admitted to NATO in 1955, when the Allied High Commission came to an end, laying the basis for German rearmament within an alliance system. This was seen as necessary given the problems of the other European NATO powers:

> By mid-1953 it was becoming increasingly evident that German forces were regarded as replacements for units which Britain and the other NATO countries could not provide to meet even the smaller force goals of the revised Alliance strategy.[3]

The western zones of Austria were also remilitarized with American support.

From 1950, substantial American forces were stationed in Europe, thus increasing US commitment to the region.[4] In December 1950, an American Supreme Allied Commander, General Eisenhower, was appointed for NATO.

Looked at differently, Western policy had been militarized, America had become a national security state, and the division of Europe had been cemented,[5] but such critical remarks pay insufficient attention to the destabilizing character of Stalin's policy.

The Korean War, in which the Western powers intervened under the authority of the United Nations, led to a major increase in Western military spending, most heavily in the USA, but also important among its allies. Thus, in Canada, which sent troops to Korea and played an active role in NATO, defence spending rose from $196 million in 1947 to $1.5 billion in 1951. Under American pressure, Britain embarked in 1950 on a costly rearmament programme, which undid recent economic gains and strengthened the military commitment that was to be such a heavy post-war economic burden.

By the early 1950s, the requirement and strategy for atomic defence and war in Europe were in place: the American forces there had to be protected. A clear front line was also in place across Europe. The fate of Greece had been settled, placing her in the Western camp, in large part as a result of the international context. Foreign intervention there was crucial, particularly the provision of American aid to the government, and the eventual cutting of aid to the Communists, especially after the Tito–Stalin breach of 1949. Thanks to its anti-Communism, Spain could be brought into the Western alliance.

Conversely, anti-Communist guerrillas in Albania, the Baltic republics, Bulgaria, the Ukraine and Yugoslavia, unsupported by the West, had all been suppressed. Some of these conflicts involved substantial forces and heavy casualties, although many are obscure. This is true, for example, of Soviet campaigns in the Baltic republics and the Ukraine in the late 1940s. It has been suggested that the Soviets lost 20,000 men in suppressing opposition in Lithuania alone.

NATO and the Soviet-led Warsaw Pact prepared and planned for conflict throughout the rest of the period. NATO, for example, developed airfields,[6] telecommunications, and an oil pipeline system. The premiss behind Western planning was the need to repel a Soviet attack. There were variations in the intensity of confrontation. The Soviets came close to attacking in the early 1950s, but Stalin's death in 1953 led to a relaxation of tension. This was marked by the withdrawal of Soviet forces from their occupation zone in Austria in 1955. Austria became a buffer zone, very different from Germany, where the forces of NATO and the Warsaw Pact continued to be in close and hostile proximity.

Even when international tensions eased, as with the *détente* that followed the death of Stalin, and the election in 1952 of Eisenhower, who favoured negotiations over nuclear arms, as President, and the second *détente* in the latter years of Khrushchev's primacy, there remained an uncertainty and a sense that the other bloc was seeking to take advantage. The Americans failed to appreciate the depth of Soviet economic problems. *Détente* was a matter not of the end of the Cold War, but of its conduct at a lower level of tension.

Furthermore, Soviet willingness to use force to maintain its interests within its own bloc, most prominently by invading Hungary in 1956 and Czechoslovakia in 1968, helped to maintain tension. In 1956, the determined use of Soviet armour in Operation Whirlwind crushed popular opposition in Hungary. The Soviets also used air attacks and helicopters. In response, the Hungarians attacked tanks with Molotov Cocktails (petrol bombs) and sniped at Soviet troops. Without Western support, and heavily outnumbered, the resistance was crushed, with about 20,000 killed, and 200,000 going into exile. Soviet forces lost 2,250 dead, missing and wounded.[7]

In 1968, about 250,000 Soviet troops, backed by Polish, Hungarian and Bulgarian forces, suppressed a more liberal Communist regime in Czecho-slovakia, although there was less fighting than in Hungary in 1956. The government decided not to offer armed resistance, as it feared the consequences for the civilian population and knew that there was no prospect of Western support. Demonstrators relied on non-violent protest, for example throwing paint against tanks. Even so, 96 Soviet soldiers were killed, as well as about 200 Czechs and Slovaks. The protests had a major impact on international opinion, but failed to dislodge the Soviets, and Czechoslovakia remained under firm Communist control until the fall of the Soviet bloc. More minor uprisings had been suppressed in East Germany in 1953 and in Poznan in Poland in 1956.

The military was not only used to enforce Soviet-supported orthodoxy in satellite states; it also played a role in internal politics. This was most clearly seen in 1953, when Marshal Zhukov played a key role in the power struggle that followed the death of Stalin. The chief of the secret police, Lavrenti Beria, had hoped to seize power and was already one of a triumvirate with Nikita Khrushchev and Georgii Malenkov. The latter two won the support of Zhukov, who, in 1947, had been dismissed as Supreme Commander of the Ground Forces when Beria had charged him with disloyalty. In 1953, Zhukov had Beria arrested and guarded until he was executed. Deputy Minister of Defence from 1953, and Minister from 1955, Zhukov was dismissed by Khrushchev in 1957 when he seemed too powerful.

The availability of paramilitary forces ensured that the Red Army did not have to play a major role in internal policing. In 1962, Soviet army commanders refused orders to fire on civilians rioting in protest against food shortages and wage cuts at Novocherkask. Instead, Ministry of Interior troops were used; they killed 24 civilians, including children, and restored "order". The border defences constructed in part to stop people leaving eastern Europe were manned by paramilitary units.

Despite the impact of what Eisenhower called the "military–industrial" complex, the political role of the military was limited in the USA. Eisenhower served two terms as US President because he was elected; there had been no coup. However, American activity in Latin America to a certain extent mirrored that of the Soviet Union in eastern Europe, and the military also absorbed a large part of government expenditure and technological and scientific expertise.

Force continued to play a role in Mediterranean Europe. Spain and Portugal remained right-wing dictatorships until 1975 and 1974 respectively, and post-war Republican attempts to challenge the Franco regime in Spain were defeated, as was an attempted coup in Portugal in 1946.[8] In 1967, the army seized power in Greece, holding it until 1974. The change in government in Portugal occurred as a result of a coup, while the fall of the military regime in Greece owed much to its role in the Cyprus crisis of that year: a coup there led to a government supporting union with Greece, but this provoked a Turkish invasion, which led to an effective partition of Cyprus between an independent Greek Cyprus and a Turkish-dominated North Cyprus. The military regimes of Europe were subsumed into the competing blocs of the Cold War; thus, in 1953, the USA and Spain signed an agreement giving the Americans rights to establish air bases in Spain.

A military coup by the French army in Algeria had failed in 1961, in large part because much of the army remained loyal, and in 1968 the French government under de Gaulle, a former general, was driven to seek military backing when confronted with serious student and worker demonstrations. The promise of such support helped stiffen the government and it was not necessary to move the army into the cities. The French government was not "militarized". In Britain, troops were used in labour disputes, for example in the docks in the late 1940s. They were also deployed during the firemen's strike of 1977–78, while in 1978–79, 46,000 troops were put on standby to maintain essential services during the threatened strikes of the "Winter of Discontent". From 1969, troops were deployed in Northern Ireland to maintain order.

The military continued to play a major role in Latin America. The military had seized power in Argentina and in Bolivia in 1943. There were also coups in Argentina in 1955, 1962 and 1966, the Dominican Republic in 1963, Guatemala in 1944, 1954 and 1963, Bolivia in 1951, Colombia in 1953 and 1957, Peru in 1948, 1962 and 1967, Venezuela in 1948 and 1958, Honduras in 1957, 1963 and 1972, Panama in 1968, and Chile and Uruguay in 1973. As in Europe, this process was in part linked to the Cold War. Thus, the American government supported the Chilean army under General Pinochet when it overthrew the Marxist Allende government in 1973. More generally, the perceived Communist threat led to close links between the USA and Latin American military and authoritarian rulers and, from the mid-1950s, to the Americanization of Latin American military establishments. They were restructured in accordance with American views, and many officers were trained in the USA. Whereas, until the 1940s, the Americans had been concerned about German influence in Latin America and, specifically, in their military, now the challenge was seen as more insidious, because Communism was feared, both as a geostrategic threat, directed by the Soviet Union, and as a diffuse social challenge to the coherence and stability of Latin American regimes.

The fall of Cuba to Castro in 1959 had been a major shock. It indicated not only the potential strength of guerrilla operations in the right military circumstances, but also the role of the political context. The army offensive against Castro in 1958 was poorly coordinated and lacked both adequate air power and foreign support. Once the campaign had failed, the government suffered a crucial loss of nerve, and lost the initiative with fatal consequences. However, the subsequent attempt to spread Communist insurgency to Bolivia was unsuccessful. Castro's lieutenant, Che Guevara, was captured there in 1967 and executed. Elsewhere, the military also played a major role in suppressing radical insurrectionary movement, for example in Uruguay, where the Tupamaros guerrillas were crushed in the mid-1970s.

## Nuclear weaponry

Overhanging all else was the nuclear deterrent. America's nuclear monopoly, which had not been used to coerce the Soviet Union, had lasted only until 1949, when the Soviet Union completed its development of an effective bomb. This had required a formidable effort, as the Soviet Union was devastated by the impact of World War Two, and it was pursued because Stalin believed that only a position of nuclear equivalence would permit the Soviet Union to protect and advance its interests. However, such a policy was ruinous financially, harmful to the economy, as it led to the distortion of research and investment choices, and militarily dangerous, as resources were used that might otherwise have developed conventional capability. Although the Communist regimes that followed Stalin, after he died in 1953, introduced changes in some aspects of policy, they did not break free of his legacy of nuclear competition.[9] Britain, France and China followed with their own atomic bombs in 1952, 1960 and 1964, respectively.

Conversely, neither West Germany nor Japan developed such technology. This reflected the absence of any policy of *revanche* on the part of the post-war leadership that gained control after Western occupation ceased, but also accorded with American-directed Western security policies: "by late 1963 a system had more or less taken shape . . . Germany would remain non-nuclear, and thus dependent on America for security; and American troops would remain on German soil indefinitely".[10]

Delivery systems for nuclear weapons had, in the meantime, changed radically. In the late 1940s and early 1950s, the Soviet Union had been within range of American bombers based in Britain, but the USA had been out of range of Soviet nuclear attack.[11] In 1954 the Americans advanced the theory of massive nuclear retaliation in response to any Soviet use of their larger non-nuclear forces, in Europe or elsewhere, although in 1954–55 there was fear of a "bomber gap", with Soviet planes able to drop atomic weapons on North America. This encouraged the construction of early warning radar systems in Canada (designed to warn of Soviet attacks over the North Pole): the Pinetree Network in 1957, and the Distant Early Warning and Mid-Canada Lines in 1957. The North American Air Defence Command was important to the development of joint air-defence systems involving the USA and Canada.

The deployment of B-52 heavy bombers in 1955 had upgraded American delivery capability. A small number of aircraft appeared able, and rapidly, to achieve more than the far larger Allied air force had achieved against Germany in 1942–45. Thus, deterrence appeared both realistic and afford-able.[12] It was hoped that it would serve to deter both conventional and atomic attack, although doubts were expressed about the former.

The situation changed in 1957, when the Soviet Union launched Sputnik I, the first satellite, into orbit. This revealed a capability for intercontinental rockets that brought the entire world within striking range, and thus made the USA vulnerable to Soviet attack, both from first-strike and counter-strike. The strategic possibilities offered by nuclear-tipped long-range ballistic missiles made investment in expensive rocket technology seem an essential course of action, since they could go so much faster and, unlike planes, could not be shot down.

From 1957 there was a twofold Western response to the enhanced Soviet capability. Notions of graduated nuclear retaliation through the use of "tacti-cal" (short-range) nuclear weapons in association with conventional forces, based in western Europe, were complemented by a policy of developing an effective intercontinental retaliatory second-strike capability. This entailed replacing vulnerable manned bombers with more inaccessible submarines equipped with Polaris missiles and with land rockets based in reinforced silos. The range and invulnerability of American nuclear weaponry were thus enhanced. The Americans fired their first intercontinental ballistic missile in 1958, and, in 1960, followed with the first successful underwater firing of a Polaris rocket. Submarines could be based near the coast of target states, and were highly mobile and hard to detect. They represented a major shift in force structure, away from the American air force and towards the navy, which argued that its invulnerable submarines could launch carefully controlled strikes, enabling a more sophisticated management of deterrence and retaliation. To the Soviets, this threatened to be a first-strike capability.

In 1965, Robert McNamara, the American Secretary of Defense, felt able to state that the USA could rely on the threat of "assured destruction" to deter a Soviet assault. That did not prevent further attempts by the nuclear powers to enhance their nuclear attack and defence capabilities. In 1970, the Ameri-cans deployed Minuteman III missiles equipped with multiple independently targeted re-entry vehicles (MIRVs), thus ensuring that the strike capacity of an individual rocket was greatly enhanced.[13] As a consequence, warhead numbers, and thus the potential destructiveness of a nuclear exchange, rose greatly.

The inhibiting effect of the destructive potential of intercontinental nuclear weaponry served as much to enhance the possibility of a nuclear war by increasing interest in defining a sphere for tactical nuclear weapons and in planning an effective strategic nuclear first strike, as it did to lessen the chance of a great power war, or to increase the probability that such a conflict would be essentially conventional. During the Cold War, the crucial strategic zone was defined as the North European Plain, and the Soviet Union had a great superiority in conventional forces there. This led to a series of responses in NATO planning, each of which focused on the degree to which nuclear weaponry would be involved and when. The essential stages were: an immediate nuclear response to a conventional Soviet assault; the massive nuclear retaliation outlined in 1954 by John Foster Dulles, the American Secretary of State; the flexible response announced by McNamara in 1962, a theory capable of many interpretations; and, eventually, American stress on an enhanced conventional response.[14]

President Kennedy's (1961–63) increase in defence spending in the early 1960s, apparent Soviet deficiencies revealed during the Cuban crisis of 1962, and the prospect of retaliation by American nuclear strength, both tactical (e.g. one-mile range atomic bazookas) and strategic, served to lessen the Soviet threat in Europe. However, the Soviet response threatened the American position in the 1970s. The Soviet Union was able to make major advances in comparative nuclear potency, producing a situation in which war was seen as likely to lead to MAD. As a consequence, MAD-based strategies of deterrence and of graduated response were developed, on the American side, although it was never clear whether the Soviets agreed with the "nuclear calculus" as it was called. The nuclear programme helped, if not to bankrupt the Soviet Union, at least seriously to exacerbate a very high level of military expenditure, which distorted the economy and created serious social strains.

The capacity to destroy the planet in a few seconds, and the changing means of destruction and of delivery, dramatically altered the potency of military technology. Nuclear weaponry provided a small number of powers with the capacity to inflict tremendous loss, but, since 1945, none has been willing to do so because of the fear of some equal, or worse, retaliation. This restraint also reflects the degree to which the utter destructiveness of atomic weaponry is widely viewed as an absolute deterrent, a moral as well as a prudential restraint on conflict. Without this, it is possible that the Cold War would have become hot, more specifically that the Soviet Union would have used its superiority in land forces to invade West Germany, thus propping up both its system and its defences. Indeed, it was feared that the Korean War might be the first stage of World War Three, and/or that western Europe might receive similar treatment to South Korea. As NATO countries were unable to match the build-up their military planners called for, there was a growing stress, especially from 1952, on the possibilities of nuclear weaponry both as a deterrent and, in the event of war, as a counterweight to Soviet conventional superiority.

This encouraged an interest in tactical nuclear weaponry, and in the atom bomb as a weapon of first resort. The last was pushed by Eisenhower, NATO's first Supreme Allied Commander from 1950 until 1952 and US President from 1953 until 1961. The cost of raising conventional capability was a factor, as were the manpower implications, and, more specifically, the particular vulnerability of Western forces to Soviet attack in western Europe. Thus, nuclear weaponry appeared less expensive and politically more acceptable, as well as militarily more effective either as a deterrent or, in the event of deterrence failing, as a decisive combat weapon. This policy led to what was termed the "New Look" strategy and, more particularly, to the enhancement of the American Strategic Air Command which resulted in the USAF receiving much more money in defence allocations than either the army or the navy. The number of divisions in the army fell from 18 on June 1956 to 14 by December 1956, and the number of naval vessels from 973 to 812.[15]

The decline in conventional capability both harmed the USA in the Vietnam War and further ensured a reliance on nuclear weaponry. America's allies were also faced with difficult policy choices. In 1958, Mountbatten observed, "there certainly isn't going to be enough money for a very large independent deterrent which can inflict unacceptable damage on Russia as well as having the 88 [ship] Navy and the all-Regular Army with adequate equipment".[16] The defence plans of America's allies, both in western Europe and in the Far East, came to rely on the American nuclear umbrella, although part of the rationale behind the Anglo-French independent nuclear deterrents were doubts that the Americans would use theirs if Europe alone were attacked.

In December 1955, the NATO Council authorized the use of atomic weaponry against the Warsaw Pact, even if the latter did not use such weaponry. This was reaffirmed by President Kennedy in 1961 during the Berlin Crisis, because West Berlin was particularly vulnerable to Soviet attack; although Kennedy sought to move from the idea of "massive retaliation" with nuclear weaponry to that of "flexible response".

The fact that atomic weaponry has not been used since 1945 is a product of a balance of deterrence, concern about domestic and foreign opinion and the degree to which the range of rocket-delivery systems has left no areas immune from attack. The latter, in turn, has increased tension about the military plans of often distant powers, while attention has also been focused on the deployment of rockets. More recently, the concern has arisen over the possible behaviour of so-called "rogue states", who might get their hands on nuclear or biological weaponry.

In the early 1960s, anxieties about the nuclear balance encouraged Kennedy to aim for a strategic superiority and Khrushchev to decide to deploy missiles in Cuba, thus bringing the world close to nuclear war. In 1962, the Americans considered an attack on Cuba, and imposed an air and naval quarantine to prevent the shipping of further supplies. Kennedy also threatened a full retaliatory nuclear strike. The Soviet Union agreed to remove the missiles, but the gap between decision, use and strike had been shown to be perilously small.

In Europe, where the armed forces of the two competing blocs were concentrated, the gap was even smaller. There, the military had to prepare for war and also had to play a major role in deterring war. In terms of "hot war", this led to a military stalemate that continued until the collapse of Soviet Europe and the unification of Germany in 1989. In terms of "cold war", this stalemate permitted a registration of shifts of political alignment and accommodation. As it was also unlikely that any conventional conflict between the two blocs would be anything less than devastating (and would rapidly become nuclear), the nuclear deterrent prevented the devastation of high-tech conventional warfare between well-resourced alliances.

The destructive power of nuclear weapons increased when the atomic bomb was followed by the hydrogen bomb. The USA first exploded the bomb in 1951, and was followed by the Soviet Union in 1953, Britain in 1957, China in 1967, and France in 1968. The hydrogen bomb employed a nuclear explosion to heat hydrogen isotopes sufficiently to fuse them into helium atoms, a transformation that released an enormous amount of destructive energy. The development of this technology by both Britain and France enabled them to present themselves as great powers.

Although atomic weaponry was not used, it played a major role in the post-war military history of the West, not least in strategic planning and force structures. For example, American possession of the bomb made it possible to demobilize Western forces after World War Two, and thus to reduce the political and military costs of commitment to western Europe and confrontation with the Soviet Union. However, the value of this strategy and weaponry was limited. Even before the Soviets, unexpectedly early, developed an atomic bomb in 1949, it was clear that the weaponry was not sufficiently flexible (in terms of military and political application or acceptance of its use) to meet challenges other than that of full-scale war. Thus, the Americans did not use the atom bomb (of which they then indeed had very few – only nine in 1946) to help their Nationalist Chinese allies against the Communists in the civil war of 1945–49.[17] President Truman was ambivalent about nuclear strategy. American possession of the bomb did not deter the Soviets from intimidating the West during the Berlin Crisis of 1948–49.

Similarly, the atom bomb was not employed against the North Koreans during the Korean War, despite pressure from General MacArthur that atomic weaponry was necessary to counteract Chinese numerical superiority. Instead, that war was fought with a strengthened conventional military, although, in the latter stage, the use of the atom bomb was threatened in order to secure an end to the conflict. This encouraged the view that nuclear strategy had a major role to play in future confrontations, as indeed did the cost of fighting the Korean War and the extent to which it had revealed deficiencies in the American military.

Soviet acquisition of atomic weaponry greatly lessened its potential value to the Americans, although the USA sought to leap ahead with the hydrogen bomb. This was seen as a way both to reconfirm nuclear superiority and to permit the development of conventional strength. However, the American advantage was swiftly thwarted by the Soviet Union's development of the same weapon.

Atomic weaponry posed a real problem of how best to assess total military capability. This is always difficult for military analysts, but far more so for weaponry that has not been put to the test of conflict. Thankfully, atomic weapons have only been used twice in war. There has been no conflict between nuclear powers, and no employment of the greater and improved, post-1945 atomic weaponry. This weaponry can be seen as framed by existing assumptions, and as treated as an extension of already powerful military organizations and doctrines. First, it was used in 1945 and thereafter envisaged as a form of strategic bombing, although, in 1945, General Marshall also considered using atom bombs in tactical support of a landing on Kyushu. Secondly, the tactical nuclear weapons developed in the 1950s were treated as a form of field artillery. In short, established assumptions, organizations and strategy moulded the use and planned application of atomic technology.

This was also more generally the case. Thus the reorganization of the American army in the 1950s owed much to the background of the dominant generals:

> the American paratroop generals were so deeply prejudiced toward irregularly organized air-transportable light infantry divisions reminiscent of their personal wartime experience that they ignored the answers arrived at by the major European armies.[18]

In contrast, tank generals were more influential in the 1960s.[19]

## Change and continuity

However, nuclear weaponry also led to a major shift in the share of resources from the army towards, first, the air force, and then to submarines and land-based intercontinental missiles, capable of delivering atomic warheads. This contributed greatly to the sense of volatility in military structures and doctrines that can be seen in the decades following World War Two. At one level, the weapons and weapons systems of 1945 were still dominant in 1975, suggesting a degree of continuity not apparent when contrasting, say, 1900 and 1930. Tanks, field artillery, aircraft carriers and other weapons all suggested considerable continuity.

Yet, there were also major developments in armaments, especially in the enhancement of existing weapons systems. The technology of warfare became more sophisticated, in part as weapons and techniques developed in the latter stages of World War Two – such as jet aircraft, rockets and the underwater recharging of submarine batteries – were refined. In submarines, there were major advances in design, construction techniques, propulsion, communications, weaponry and surveillance. Competition hastened the development and acquisition of weapons such as jet fighters in the late 1940s and 1950s.

More generally, weaponry in which machinery played a major role, including, for example, complex automatic systems for sighting, ensured that skill rather than physical strength became more important for soldiering. Computers transformed operational horizons and command and control options from the 1960s. The notion that "the navy mans equipment, while the army equips men", became an increasingly limited description of modern armies. The premium on skill led to greater military concern about the quality of both troops and training, and encouraged military support for a professional volunteer force rather than conscripts.

The dissemination of advanced weaponry to ordinary units was a major facet of post-war upgrading. In particular, armies became fully motorized and mechanized as the character of infantry changed. This permitted the development of infantry doctrine that focused on rapid mobility, rather than on advances on foot or essentially static position warfare. Thus, in the early 1960s, the Americans developed the M113 armoured personnel carrier while, in 1967, the Red Army introduced the high-speed Boevaya Mashina Pekhoty infantry vehicle capable of carrying eight men as well as a crew of three, protected by an air filtration system, and armed with a gun, a machine gun, an anti-tank guided missile and rifle ports. This was designed to give bite to the expansion in the number of Soviet motor vehicle divisions.[20]

The same process also characterized logistics. The horses of World War Two were replaced, but the role of rail was also minimized as the lorry came to dominate the supply system. Mobility was seen as necessary, as it was assumed, by both sides, that any war touched off by a Warsaw Pact invasion of western Europe would be rapid. A flexible defence was called for by Western strategists, not least with counter-attacks to take advantage of the use of nuclear weaponry.

Furthermore, only a flexible defence would allow the Western forces to regain and exploit the initiative. The skill of the Israelis against Arab defensive positions in the Six-Day War of 1967 and, eventually, after initial Arab successes, in the Yom Kippur War of 1973, appeared to show the vulnerability of forces with a low rate of activity. Conversely, but also putting an emphasis on mobility and tempo, the Soviets planned a rapid advance into NATO rear areas, which would compromise the use of Western nuclear weaponry. Essentially building on the operational policy of their advance in the latter stage of World War Two, with its penetration between German defensive hedgehogs, the Red Army put a premium on a rapid advance.

The range of weaponry increased. For example, weapons, such as defoliation chemicals and infrared viewing devices, were able to alter the physical environment of conflicts, the latter making effective night fighting more feasible. Sophisticated weaponry was expensive, in both nominal and real terms. Industrial advanced mass-production capacity and the ability to fund it were crucial. Metal-bashing processes remained important, but a greater role than hitherto was played by advanced electronic engineering. The high costs of the Cold War placed a crippling burden on the Soviet Union and helped limit the appeal of Communism to its citizens.

By 1990, or even, arguably, by the mid-1980s, when pressure for change became dominant in Soviet governmental circles, the Cold War had been clearly lost by the Soviet Union. This was less clear in the mid-1970s as the Western colonial empires finally crumbled and as the Vietnam conflict closed with the fall of Saigon to the Communists in 1975. At that time, the economic strength of the West seemed compromised by the economic strains following the oil price hike after the 1973 Arab–Israeli war. Simultaneously, the West appeared to be suffering from poor leadership. The Watergate Crisis in the USA had led not only to the fall of President Nixon in 1974, but also to a crisis of confidence in American leadership. Of the other Western powers, Britain was faced by a political crisis in 1974 linked to a miners' strike, and then by a more general crisis in the mid-1970s, as high inflation and trade union power contributed to an acute sense of malaise and weakness.

These problems were not registered in a major world conflict, although the Cold War heated up in Angola in 1975 with the USA supplying anti-Communist forces in the civil war there. Instead, the mid-1970s saw a number of treaties, especially the Helsinki Treaty of 1975, that, in recognizing the position and interests of the Eastern Bloc, appeared to consolidate its position. This *détente* was not the irritable harmony of allies, but a truce between rivals, and, in so far as it suggested that the Cold War was now less intense, it did not do so by marking any victory of the West. Whereas, in 1990, it became clear that a major struggle had ended with the victory of the West, this was not apparent in 1975. Instead, it seemed that both East and West still had all to play for in a world adapting to the end of the European colonial empires.

Furthermore, a process of revision in military thought, which was to put a premium on deep-space operations, was about to begin. Far from being wedded to particular force structures, strategies and tactics, military thinkers in both NATO and the Warsaw Pact were to devote the following 15 years to rethinking how to best fight war. The Soviets developed earlier concepts of deep battle under Marshal N. V. Ogarkov, who became Chief of the General Staff in 1977, while the Americans advanced the doctrine of Air Land Battle as their military reformulated its thinking and practice after the Vietnam War.[21] Although these forces did not wage war, had they done so, it would have been a different conflict to any conducted prior to the mid-1970s.

CHAPTER TEN

# Social and Political Contexts

Modern war is an affair of whole nations or groups of nations. The armed forces are merely the cutting edge of a mechanism which involves every single national activity.　　(General Ismay,　Progress Report as Secretary General of NATO, December 1952)[1]

Qualifications can (and should) be entered against any statement describing a long-term situation, but it is still helpful to view 1882–1975 as a period in which, in much of the West, it was accepted that universal male military service was a requirement the state could expect and enforce. Furthermore, in many states, this was made permanent by systems of peacetime conscription that provided both large numbers of troops and even larger numbers of trained reservists. In the last quarter of the twentieth century, this attitude collapsed in the face of social trends, especially rising individualism and a collapse in deference, as well as in response to altering military priorities. In some respects, this represented a new development, although it can also be seen as a return to the public cultures and force requirements of Britain and the USA in the early decades of our period, as neither had then sought conscription.

Nevertheless, Britain and the USA did not set the pattern for the major European Continental powers in the late nineteenth century. In Austria, France, Germany, Italy and Russia, the leading powers on the Continent, conscription played a major role in moulding society. Young men at an impressionistic age were exposed to state-directed military organization and discipline, and this state direction was centralized: the subcontracting of military functions to entrepreneurs and the autonomy of aristocratic officers were both ended or, at least, greatly eroded. Conscription was less expensive than hiring soldiers, at home or abroad, but it required a structure of training and authority that was under government control. Conscription also did not

197

guarantee a high degree of preparedness, a situation that helped to account for the frontal attack shock tactics of World War One.

Although the inclusive nature of conscription should not be exaggerated, especially in Russia, it helped in the militarization of society, so that the major social changes in nineteenth-century Europe did not lead to more pacific societies: competitive governing elites were able to draw on greater economic resources and patterns of organized and obedient social behaviour. At the same time, there was an opposition to conscription that undermines any stress on an unqualified militarist *zeitgeist* (spirit of the age). In 1889, Julius Verdy du Vernois, the German War Minister, proposed to extend military service to every fit man of military age, an increase of 115,000 men, in order to reduce dependence on reservists. The measure met widespread opposition, and the legislation passed in 1893 marked a compromise, including a cut in active duty to two years for most conscripts. In Barcelona in 1909, violent opposition greeted the call-up of 40,000 reserves to serve in Morocco. It was brutally crushed.

Conscripts served for about two or three years, and then entered the reserves, ensuring that substantial forces of trained men could be mobilized in the event of war, and that the state did not have to pay them in peacetime. Combined with demographic and economic growth, this cadre-reserve system increased the potential size of armies, but raised questions about their effectiveness.

Thanks to conscription, nationalism, and the increase in the scale of mobilization of resources in the nineteenth century, it became more apparent that war was a struggle between societies, rather than simply military forces. Conscription was seen as important to the ideological and political programme of modernization. Nationalism facilitated conscription without the social bondage of serfdom, because conscription was legitimized by new ideologies, stressing the duties of citizenship. It was intended to transform the old distinction between civilian and military into a common purpose.

The Nation in Arms was expressed in its armed forces. This had a number of manifestations. Troops were frequently stationed away from their localities. This practice, found for example in France and Italy, delayed mobilization, but it helped to break down the local identity of soldiers and to encourage an awareness of the nation. Moreover, the practice was greatly assisted by the spread of the rail network. Conscription and mass armies were more than just means to an end. They also reflected the values of society, more particularly of dominant male groups. The same was true of offensive doctrines. These were not simply a response to military circumstances, but also had an ideological value, reflecting an emphasis on courage, decisiveness and movement, all understood as contributing to glory.[2] The rulers of Wilhelmine Germany saw military service as a useful method for producing a disciplined and docile workforce.

It is also important to note the use of the military to police society, as well as other aspects of the political character of the armed forces. For example, in 1893–94, the Brazilian navy rebelled and blockaded Rio de Janeiro in an unsuccessful attempt to overthrow the government; in Greece, a group of officers seized power in 1909 before handing it to politicians willing to push through reform;[3] while in Portugal, army units played a key role in the successful coup of 1910 that led to the overthrow of the monarchy. Labour unrest was an important aspect of military activity. In the 1900s, the Canadian army was frequently used against strikes.[4] In 1910, sabotage by striking miners in South Wales led to the deployment of troops, while, in 1911, a general rail strike in Britain led to the deployment of troops, who killed two strikers in Liverpool.

A reminder of the political role of the military occurred in Ireland in March 1914, when, in the "Curragh Mutiny", Brigadier-General Hubert Gough and 59 other officers of the Third Cavalry Regiment stationed near Kildare at the Curragh Barracks resigned their commissions rather than impose Home Rule. No orders had as yet been given, so in fact there was no "mutiny". The crisis was defused when the War Office promised that they would not be ordered to do so and refused to accept the resignations. There was no Cabinet authorization for this assurance, given by the Secretary of War and the Chief of the Imperial General Staff, and they were both obliged to resign. The Prime Minister, Asquith, repudiated the assurance.

The crisis was a serious one, as many Ulster Protestants had been preparing to resist Home Rule by force. However, the outbreak of World War One shifted attention from Ireland, and Home Rule was shelved. The possible consequences of the Curragh Mutiny are thus unclear, but it suggested that the government would have encountered problems in using the army to impose an unwelcome solution on Ulster; this might have divided and politicized the armed forces. In contrast, the army was willing to act against strikers in 1910–11. The British situation serves as a reminder of the conditionality of military obedience. This was particularly true at the level of the officers, and was important in the relationship between army and state across Europe.

## World War One

The world wars saw a mobilization of societies for war, with large sections of their economies placed under governmental control and regulated in a fashion held to characterize military organization. For example, the Ministry of Munitions, created in Britain in 1915, was as much part of the military organization, and as vital, as the artillery it served. Other sections of society were not brought under formal direction, but can be seen as part of the informal organization of a militarized state.

The demands of war drove this process, as did the length of the conflict. Thus, for example, in 1916, the German Supreme Command responded to the Somme offensive by trying to increase greatly the production of munitions. The ability to mobilize resources, both men and munitions, was crucial. Thirty-seven million shells were fired by the French and Germans in their ten-month contest for Verdun in 1916. Such a use of artillery ensured that the cost of offensives soared. The availability of shells became a political issue in Britain in 1915, and a serious problem in France.

In order to meet such demand, governments extended their regulatory powers. These were designed to ensure that resources were devoted to war and to increase economic effectiveness. Even in the early stages of the war, governments felt it necessary to abandon pre-war practices in order to mobilize resources. The Germans passed war finance laws on 4 August 1914. Bread rationing began there in January 1915 as the British blockade took effect. The major German industries were taken under government control; although not publicly owned, the German economy was publicly controlled. In practice, this entailed an alliance between big business and the military. Rationing was widespread. Looking towards a policy that was followed far more systematically by the Germans in World War Two, Belgian workers were compelled to work in Germany, in order to compensate for the impact of German conscription. Large numbers of prisoners of war were also set to work.[5]

The Russian economy, in contrast, was poorly managed, with industrial production and transport both in grave difficulties by 1915. The War Industries Committees that had been set up were found wanting and in 1916 state monopolies took over coal and oil production. Russia was short of shells.[6] In France, the government controlled bread prices, and state-supervised consortia directed the allocation of supplies in crucial industries, although the production of munitions was left to entrepreneurs. A government-directed shoe industry was created, as was a chemical industry. State control was widely extended, but, unlike in Germany, there was an appropriate level of care for civilian needs, and thus morale.[7]

In Britain, new ministries included Munitions, Labour, Shipping and Information. A Food Production Department was created, and the food supply was regulated in order to cope with the impact on food imports of German submarine attacks. With the Food Production Act of 1917, the government imposed a policy of expanding tillage (land that was ploughed). It was more efficient to feed people a nutritious diet directly through cereal crops and vegetables, rather than indirectly via meat and milk. The price of grain was guaranteed and County Agricultural Executive Committees oversaw a 30 per cent rise in national cereal production. In part, however, the rise in output in 1917 and 1918 was a recovery after a major decline in food production in 1916, and, thanks also in part to a fall in meat and milk production, the calorific value of the food produced was similar to that in 1914. Furthermore, despite the attempts of the Board of Agriculture to claim the credit, the recovery owed much to favourable weather.

In Britain, instructions to the milling and baking industries led to a dilution of wheat flour, so that bread included more barley, beans and potatoes. The dirty-white colour of the resulting bread was a striking consequence of government regulation. The government also took over the control of the railways (in 1914), the coal mines (in 1917) and the flour mills (in 1918). Essential food prices were fixed in 1917, and coal and food were rationed from that year. Licensing hours were regulated. The government also increasingly intervened to fix wages.

Intervention was more successful in Britain and France than in Germany, where living standards fell, leading to a rise in death rates. This was in part due to the Allied blockade, but was also a consequence of less effective social administration in the fields of supplies, social welfare and medical services, although it is difficult to assess the balance between these two causes.[8]

There was also a major shift in attitudes towards the use of state power. The outbreak of war led in Britain to an initial period when the government proclaimed "business as usual", but also, in August 1914, to the passage of the Defence of the Realm Act, which brought both controls and the habit of control. The latter proved more insistent and lasting than had been intended. During the war, restrictions on state power across Europe declined and were not pressed.[9]

The same process could also be seen throughout the Western world. In Canada, food prices were controlled from 1916, and fuel prices from 1917. A Wheat Board operated from 1917, the year in which income tax was introduced. The Imperial Munitions Board organized the production of munitions and also established "national factories" to produce *matériel*.

Throughout Europe, war led to a more hostile attitude to aliens. In 1914, Hankey was concerned about aliens in London:

> They could do a tremendous lot of damage in an emergency by incendiarism (using petrol), destroying railways and telegraphs, and knocking on the head simultaneously most of the Cabinet ministers and principal government officials to say nothing of destroying power stations by short circuits, gas works, etc.

The price of total war was vigilance as well as mobilization.[10] In Germany, the military was given, under the Prussian Law of Siege, powers of arrest, search, censorship, opening mail, forbidding the sale of particular goods and closing businesses.[11] In Canada, the War Measures Act gave the government power over "enemy aliens" and radicals.

For all combatants, the mass management of resources, manufacturing and society became vital. War gave the states power and enabled them to circumvent many of the constraints and exigencies of pre-war politics. As such, it was a catalyst for modernization. This was certainly so in financial terms; governments were now able to tax and borrow as much as they thought necessary. Income tax in Britain doubled in the first year of the war.

Conscription systems were introduced in countries that lacked them, such as Britain (in 1916), New Zealand (in 1916), Canada (in 1917) and the USA (in 1917), or expanded, although conscription was rejected by Australia in two divisive referenda. Exclusions from conscription indicated limitations of the state: it was not introduced in Ireland or in all Maori areas in New Zealand, and was opposed and widely ignored in French-speaking areas of Canada. In Britain, conscription was seen as opposed to the liberal tradition of civil liberty, and there was powerful opposition to the proposal within the Liberal Party. A fudge, Lord Derby's semi-voluntary scheme, introduced in October 1915, failed to produce sufficient recruits, and political pressure led to the Military Service Act of January 1916, which introduced conscription for single men. In response to a sudden surge in weddings, the married followed in April. Very large percentages of the adult male population served in the war. Although far distant from the areas of combat, 40 per cent of all New Zealand men of military age (between 19 and 45) served overseas. Out of this 120,000, over 50,000 were injured and 18,000 died.

Millions of men served without resistance, although there were to be a number of conscientious objectors by the end of the war. Millions of men were needed. The war was far more labour intensive than conflict involving advanced industrial powers at the close of the twentieth century; not only were more men expected to serve, but also the industrial and transport support systems required far more labour. For example, over 13 million men served in the German armed forces during the war, which was a formidable organizational problem for the military and one that also posed major problems of adjustment for civilian society, the economy and cultural assumptions. Women replaced many of those who went to the front. Habits of mass mobilization acquired prior to the war, thanks to industrial labour, trade unions and the organization of democratic politics, contributed to this willingness to accept discipline and order, as also did passive acceptance of the social order. There had been a pre-war left-wing anti-militaristic tradition throughout Europe,[12] but it was always affected by the counter-appeal of patriotism, and in 1914 trade unions rallied to the state. In Germany, on 2 August 1914, unions signed an industrial truce that was designed to last for the entire war.

Many wanted to fight. The initial rush to enlist in Britain in August 1914, admittedly when the expectation was that the war would be "over by Christmas", was indicative of this. A sense of adventure was important, as was a presentation of the war as a struggle against evil.[13] Nevertheless, many who were given the choice to volunteer in Britain did not do so, while recent research on Germany has questioned the claims of a massive enthusiasm for war at its outset and has suggested that opponents outnumbered enthusiasts, and also that once war had begun the dominant theme was fatalistic acceptance, not enthusiasm. The middle class was more keen than the bulk of the population, and their voice was disproportionately strong. In addition, propaganda played a major role in moulding the popular response and how it was perceived.[14]

The creation and deployment of a mass volunteer army in Britain in 1914–15 was a testimony to the nature of public culture, as well as being a formidable administrative achievement. Furthermore, despite the strains of the war, there was no level of radicalism in the army comparable to the French and Russian armies in 1917. In 1916, Robert Blatchford, a patriotic ex-serviceman, attacked summary punishments in the army in articles in the *Sunday Chronicle* and the *Illustrated Sunday Herald*, but there was no widespread resonance within the armed forces.

Among all the combatants, the war effort was underpinned by government-directed or supported propaganda, which became more important in 1916 as war-weariness and demoralization increased and opposition to the conflict became more frequently voiced. In Britain, a Department of Information was founded, and in 1918 it became the Ministry of Information. Aside from printed propaganda,[15] there were efforts to use new media. Pressure to provide military facilities for film propaganda led, however, to a hostile response from military authorities.[16]

Alongside a stress on enthusiasm, comradeship and consent, it is necessary to note the extent to which coercion, and the threat of coercion, were employed to ensure military service. The shooting of deserters after summary judgements was a potent threat, and the nature of the campaigning, especially on the Western Front, made desertion difficult. However, widespread demoralization was particularly acute in the French and Russian armies in 1917 and in the German and Austrian forces the following year, in part as a result of massive casualties. The response among the French army (which passively mutinied) to the losses in the Nivelle offensive in 1917[17] ensured that, for the remainder of that year and in early 1918, the French army refrained from offensive operations. The refusal of the St Petersburg garrison to fire on strikers was instrumental in the fall of the Tsarist government in 1917. There were German and Austrian naval mutinies in late 1918, and the failure of the last Austrian offensive against Italy in June 1918 was followed by mutinies and mass desertion. Nevertheless, prior to 1917, there were few signs of widespread and sustained opposition to military service or the conduct of the war.

World War One was a major force for social change in Europe. Traditional assumptions were questioned, and social practices were affected by higher inflation, greater taxation, rationing, the absence of men and the spread of female employment and trade unionism. In Italy, inflation increased by over 300 per cent in 1915–18, and the national debt by 500 per cent. The British blockade hit German living standards, and privation contributed to the collapse of civilian morale in late 1918. More generally, the political, social and economic privileges and status of established elites and middle classes were qualified or challenged, and the stability of a number of countries was threatened.

Force also played a role in the internal politics of some of the combatants. In Ireland, a nationalist uprising was suppressed in 1916, and the same year agitation in Portugal led to the imposition of martial law. In December 1917, the Portuguese government was overthrown by a Revolutionary Committee under Major Sidonio Paes. The confused nature of the confrontation was captured by Major General Nathaniel Barnardiston, the Chief of the British Military Mission: "The fleet got to work . . . and the field pieces replied but were almost all short. I only saw one go over and none apparently anywhere near . . . There was intermittent rifle fire all night as rioters were looting shops etc."[18]

The situation in Britain shows how the war changed the position of women. New roles, many in industry, were performed by women. For example, large numbers of women workers were recruited by the Ministry of Munitions in 1915. The female percentage of trade unionists rose from 7.8 in 1900 to 17 in 1918. Women received higher wages than hitherto, although their wages remained lower than men's, and, in factories, women were controlled by male foremen. Whereas only 72 army sisters had been employed in British military hospitals in 1898, a total of 32,000 women served as military nurses in 1914–19, and women had a place in the command structure, and were able to give orders to male ward orderlies.

There was an important change in attitudes, such that, in 1918, it was possible to extend the vote to women of 30 and over, as long as they were householders, wives of householders, occupants of property worth £5 annually, or graduates of British universities; all men over 21 were given the vote, although younger men in the forces could also vote. Conscription appeared to require democracy; total war and universal participation walked hand-in-hand. It has been suggested that women's war work gained women the vote, but it has also been argued that (some) women got the vote because the politicians were terrified by the prospect of universal male suffrage. That, they knew, would have to come. Thus, enfranchising women in their maturity was seen as a defensive step to lessen the impact of the proletarian male vote. The women who did war work were predominantly propertyless and under 30.

In Britain, the impact of the war years on women was not simply restricted to work and the vote. New opportunities were related to increased mobility and independence. This included a decline in control and influence over young women by their elders, male and female. As a consequence, there was a new sexual climate. Chaperonage became less comprehensive and effective, and styles of courtship became freer; the number of illegitimate births rose to six per cent of the total in 1918.[19] Alongside the challenging of Victorian codes, however, class-based attitudes and practices nonetheless pervaded other areas. These were seen, for example, in recruitment and promotion within the armed forces and also in civilian war work. Furthermore, it has been suggested that the notion of a home front was an aspect of an affirmation of established gender concepts and roles, with women again seen as nurturers. Women who served near the front, for example nurses and telephonists with the American army, found that the military hierarchy expected them to fulfil traditional gender roles and made scant allowance for their contribution.[20] Notions of masculinity were also affected by the war, not least with an emphasis on conflict as fulfilling the gender role.[21]

Medical care benefited from war-driven modernization in coping with the massive casualties from the front. This was particularly true of orthopaedics, blood transfusion and psychiatry, although they did not necessarily translate quickly into civilian practice. In Britain, orthopaedics, like reconstructive surgery, struggled to survive as a medical speciality between the wars; blood transfusion was rarely used because there was only the most rudimentary supporting organization. It was not until World War Two that a comprehensive donor and storage organization was put in place. More generally, government action helped to improve public health. In Britain, in 1916, the government issued Regulation 406 of the Defence of the Realm Act, which banned, for the first time, possession of opium or cocaine by other than "authorized persons". The health of the population that remained in Britain improved, in part because of better conditions of work such as shorter hours and the introduction of industrial canteens. Government concern with the food supply was also important.

## Inter-war years

Rather than moving straight on to offer a comparable discussion of the impact of World War Two on society, it is worth considering the inter-war period. The profound crisis in military morale, especially, but not only, in the defeated countries, at the close of World War One, challenged the practices of military authority across much of Europe and played a major role in the political disorientation that immediately followed the war. At the same time, post-war demobilization altered the relationship between the military and civil society, and, in part, helped militarize the latter. Veterans were more likely than others to support the use of force. They were used in 1919 by right-wing groups in Germany and by the Hungarian Communists, and played a major role in the *squadre* that attacked Socialists in Italy from 1920. Although many veterans were not politically extreme, others proved active. Most who did so in the 1920s and 1930s deplored pacifism and attacked internationalists. Veterans proved important sources of recruitment to Mussolini, Hitler, Mosley, the Action Française and other far-right populist groups.

Veterans were not alone in rejecting a pacific civil society. In Germany, there was what has been termed a remilitarization of German public opinion from 1929, with the publication of militarist books, and criticism of pacifist or progressive works, for example films. The furore over the film *All Quiet on the Western Front,* which appeared in December 1930 and was soon banned in Germany, indicated the strength of the authoritarian, conservative, militaristic and nationalist set of assumptions and beliefs.[22]

In Britain and the USA, radical groups were not able to mount a serious challenge. Post-war demobilization and the absence of a Communist revolution ensured that the end of war was followed by an attempt to return to pre-war normality. In many respects this was successful, as is suggested by the avoidance of any breakdown in political order, although there was a tense situation at the end of the war.

The relative stability of inter-war Britain, all the more remarkable given the continuous existence of unemployment levels in excess of one million, owed much to the legacy of World War One. For those who survived and those who remained at home, the war acted as an integrating experience. Unlike in defeated Germany, the army became part of post-war society in Britain, as soldiers and civilians united in shared remembrance, a process eased by the very limited role of the army in dealing with labour unrest. The construction of the Cenotaph in Whitehall in 1920 bore eloquent testimony to the nation's desire to remember its own. The determination never to forget the sacrifice that the "lost generation" had made gave rise to a particular national outlook in the inter-war period. Those who had died were owed a Britain that would subdue conflict in the interests of community. Under these circumstances, it would be to betray the dead if matters were pushed to extremes. Nowhere was the link between conflict and betrayal seen more clearly than in the relative passivity surrounding the General Strike in May 1926. Similarly, war memorials could be found throughout the combatant countries.

The widespread horror at the casualties of World War One stimulated in some a commitment to pacifism, internationalism, and collective security through the League of Nations, created after the war to ensure the security of the post-war world. Explaining why a career in the army had lost its popularity, at a British Staff Conference in 1930, Colonel Ling stated baldly, "The use of war as a definite instrument of national policy is against the present state of public opinion".[23]

World War One had certainly challenged many cultural suppositions. It had a direct artistic impact, and it accentuated the already strong Modernist assault on traditional culture. War literature, both prose and poetry, is generally cited as evidence of the artistic impact, but it is also possible to look at paintings. Stanley Spencer, who had served as a medical orderly on the Salonica Front and then become an official war artist, was greatly affected by the war and, in 1927–32, recreated his own experiences in the murals he painted in the Sandham Memorial Chapel. Instead of a heroic view, there were hospital scenes, depicting the mundane but necessary care of the shattered, and images of everyday army life, such as *Reveille* and *Filling Water Bottles*. The scene of the front line, *Dug-out*, was one of grave-like trenches and a vegetation of barbed wire.

In some circles throughout the West the experience of war had brought pacificism, but a heroic account of the conflict was also actively propagated, for example in juvenile fiction.[24] There was a determination to honour the dead, and their sacrifice was presented as a national honour. The cult of fallen soldiers thus spoke to public celebration as well as private grief.[25]

There was also a Fascist glorification of war. Mussolini and Hitler believed that it was only through war that their regimes would fulfil their destiny, a belief, paradoxically, that helped to ensure they did not prepare adequately for a long war against societies that they despised and assumed would collapse rapidly. The Fascist glorification of war and the notion of rebirth through conflict came to have a major impact throughout Europe. These attitudes accentuated the consequences of an already extreme nationalism. This provided the context for the attention lavished on the military by the dictators in the 1930s, but also affected both force structures and operational doctrines.

The major conflicts of the inter-war period were civil wars, and this serves as a reminder of the danger of seeing the state mobilization of society as the key issue in the sociopolitical context of war. In civil wars, armed forces had to be rapidly formed, and then took part in a struggle in which military action was only part. Thus, in the Russian and the Spanish Civil Wars, both sides, in areas they controlled, slaughtered large numbers of people judged unacceptable because of their real or supposed affiliations, and saw this as part of the struggle and as preparing the way for an acceptably "cleansed" post-war society.[26] This was an attribute of total war that looked towards the widespread killing of civilians in areas occupied by the Germans in World War Two.

Another reminder of options is provided by force structure, not so much the issue of structure and doctrine within regular forces, but rather the question of the respective roles of these forces and of popular militias. This was an issue in a number of states, most particularly the Soviet Union in the 1920s and Spain during the Civil War. In the former case, Lev Trotsky was in favour of a workers' militia, which he presented as appropriate for a Communist state. However, this was resisted, not least by Mikhail Frunze, with the argument that a standing army was the only way to defeat the regular forces of other states. He was in favour of a career progression for officers, not elected officers, and for centralized, not local, control. With Stalin's support, Frunze's view prevailed, and he succeeded Trotsky as Commissar for Military and Naval Affairs in January 1925. Similarly, in the Spanish Civil War, there were on both sides proponents of militias, but Nationalist regular forces prevailed.

## World War Two

The coming of another world war, more global in its scope than the first, gave a renewed boost to the role of states and the machinery of governments. The mobilization of national resources led among the combatants to state direction of much of the economy, although the effectiveness of this varied. It was necessary to produce formidable amounts of equipment, to raise, train, clothe and equip large numbers of men, to fill their places in the workforce, and to increase the scale and flexibility of the economy. In the non-totalitarian societies, free trade and largely unregulated industrial production were both brought under direction. Economic regulation and conscription were introduced more rapidly and comprehensively than in World War One. The experience of state intervention in that conflict ensured that it was more effective in the second. Yet greater "effectiveness" was frequently unattractive, and is, anyway, difficult to assess. Whereas in World War One the Germans officially executed 48 of their soldiers, in World War Two nearly 20,000 were executed for desertion alone; in contrast, the British and Italians made less use of execution in World War Two. The experience of World War One encouraged British generals to be cautious about casualty levels and this led to an emphasis on somewhat slow-moving offensives in which there was a stress on firepower.

One aspect of effectiveness reflected the more widespread nature of World War Two. The entry of Japan into the war ensured that areas that had not had to fear invasion in World War One, especially Australia, India, New Zealand and the USA, had to take defensive precautions. Coastal defences were erected, for example on the coasts of Australia and New Zealand.

There were also changes between the two world wars that, in part, reflected developments in the intervening period, for example, developments in communications. World War Two was not only a "total war": the populations involved were also told it was a total war. State control or influence over the means of propaganda ensured that the greater access of the public to information, through mass literacy and ownership of radios, helped to create national views, or impressions of them, in accordance with the view of the state. In Britain, the British Broadcasting Corporation (BBC) played a major role in supporting the war effort, not least by successfully reaching outside the middle class and encouraging a sense of common experience and purpose. Radio comedy presented working-class life as in no way inferior, and wartime films were notable for their gritty realism and "bull-dog spirit". Cinema realism was also important in creating an image of a "people's war", as were films such as *Dawn Guard* and *Millions Like Us*.[27] In addition, nearly 1,900 official films were produced in Britain during the war, mostly by the Ministry of Information. Greatly influenced by the success of British propaganda in World War One, Hitler used propaganda effectively in Germany, although it helped mobilize people for only so long. Television did not play a role, but cinema newsreels were important.

For Hitler, peace and war were part of the same process, and the peacetime years saw an active moulding of society to further the same goals. Once war had begun, especially once the Soviet Union had been invaded in 1941, the conflict was seen as a people's struggle, and one that was presented in millenarian terms as a fight for racial mastery and a contest of wills. This helped ensure that Nazi ideology was at the centre of the military struggle and also influenced the way in which the war was waged, particularly the brutality shown to Russians and in occupied areas in eastern Europe. The major role of the SS in creating elite military units – the Waffen-SS – indicated the close relationship between ideology and the German war effort. Over 800,000 men served in the Waffen-SS, and it became an important part of Germany's fighting forces, serving under the operational command of the army, although it was a separate structure. It would be mistaken to imagine that Nazi influence was restricted to SS units. The genocidal treatment of the Jews from 1941 was not an exception, but rather the culmination of a totalizing ideological militarism. This had implications not only for the conduct of the war, but also for the home front; although conscription lessened the distinction between the two. The brutality shown to those judged unacceptable within Germany, and the harsh treatment of dissidents, were regarded not only as necessary but as part of the Nazi mission.[28]

Although it has received less attention, there was also great brutality on the part of the Soviet state. Those deemed unacceptable within the Soviet Union, including peoples such as the Crimean Tatars, who were seen as insufficiently anti-German, were harshly treated. Once the war was over, Soviet prisoners of war released from German camps were sent to Soviet forced labour camps, as they were judged suspect. There was similar harsh treatment of those who had fought for the resistance: after the war such independence was crime.

The impact of the war on a non-authoritarian society can be seen by considering Britain. The outbreak of war led to the passage of the Emergency Powers (Defence) Act of 1939, which extended the power of government. In 1939, conscription was introduced and new ministries were created for Economic Warfare, Food, Home Security, Information, Shipping and Supply, Power and Production. National wage-negotiating machinery was established in the coal industry, although it did not prevent a serious miners' strike in early 1944.

Farming provided a good example of the new interventionist character of government. Agriculture was subject to a hierarchy of control. Each county was administered by a separate War Agricultural Executive Committee, the members of which were appointed by the Ministry of Agriculture, and was in turn divided into districts controlled by district sub-committees. Unlike in World War One, the policy of encouraging tillage was imposed as soon as the war began. By 1945, tillage was 55 per cent more than the 1935–39 average. Information and labour direction were both part of the process. In June 1940, a farm survey was begun in order to assess productive capacity, and a more comprehensive survey followed from the spring of 1941. Farmers were provided with labour, especially young women from the Land Army, and machinery. The latter helped to ensure that World War Two established modern agriculture. Conversely, in Britain, the Soviet Union and elsewhere, the war also saw a major increase in urban allotments. These were very important as a source of potatoes, vegetables and meat (chicken and pigs), although animals were also kept in backyards. Aside from providing food, allotments indicated the way in which the war effort demanded full attention. Leisure was banished; workers farmed their allotments in the evening and on weekends.

In Britain, the war also transformed the state's relationship with society. Everything was brought under the scrutiny of government. Food rationing, for example, remoulded the nation's diet in accordance with nutritional science. It also allowed the state to rank citizens on need, a process also clearly seen in the Soviet Union, where dependents got the least. Rationing rested on a theory of equality. The war encouraged an inclusive notion of nationhood on the part of combatants. A language of inclusiveness and sharing, and a stress on the home "front", made social distinctions seem unacceptable, and this helped condition post-war politics.[29] The war affected all sections of society. In Britain, in response to the threat of German bombing, there were mass evacuations of children from the major cities (690,000 alone from London) at the outset of the war. This was the biggest state-directed move of civilians in British history, and the cause of much disruption.

The mobilization and inclusiveness so frequently stressed in discussion of the war were not always successful. Aside from the evidence of large numbers who sought to evade or profit from regulations, for example the extensive black market in Britain, there were also war economies that as a whole failed to meet the growth rates of other major combatants, most prominently Italy. There the government was unable to introduce an effective mobilization of resources. Taxes did not become realistic, there was only limited direction of the large industrial combines, and both weapons and weapons systems were delivered in insufficient quality and quantity.[30]

Bombing, evacuation, rationing and single parenting not only brought much hardship on the home fronts of the combatants, but also all contributed to a greater flexibility in social conventions. There was more freedom for women, because far more were employed, frequently away from home; because of an absence of partners; and, in part, because of different attitudes. In Britain, the last was indicated by wartime surveys, while films, such as *Waterloo Road* (1944) and *Brief Encounter* (1945), suggested that the war was offering new possibilities for relationships between the sexes, even at the cost of marriages. Divorce rates rose.[31] In America, also, the war led to a questioning of gender and racial roles and positions, and to pressure on established social mores; although there was also reluctance to embrace change. Thus, day-care centres operated at only a quarter capacity, as the vast majority of women with young children continued to be reluctant to work. In

Canada, the National Selective Service established in 1942 focused at first on single women. Married women were subsequently sought, not least through the Day Nurseries Agreement, but its day-care facilities were only introduced in Ontario and Québec. German occupation ensured that the war greatly increased pressure on French women. This raised their consciousness; many had to confront the experience of being single, as large numbers of men were prisoners or sent to work in Germany.[32]

Hitler was reluctant to conscript German women for the industrial workforce (although the Germans were quite happy to use the forced labour of non-German women). His conservative social politics led him to see German women as wives and mothers. This was but part of the more wide-ranging failure of the Axis powers to mobilize their resources, a failure that owed much to the social assumptions of their leaderships and to their mistaken expectation of a speedy victory. The Soviet Union was far readier to see women as a direct resource for the war effort, and one that should be controlled by the state. All able-bodied city women aged from 16 to 50 who were not students or looking after children under 8 were put under government direction in 1942, and thousands, uniquely, fought in the front line. All combatants were affected by these pressures. In New Zealand, by 1943, nearly one-third of factory workers were women. A Women's Land Service was created. Much of the female entry into the workforce was voluntary, but state direction was also used. As elsewhere, it was not only a case of more women working in New Zealand, but also of a change in the nature of the female workforce. Domestic service fell greatly, while factory work and white-collar work rose, and some women rose to positions of authority in the work place, rarely reached before.

Culture was also conscripted. German radio broadcast the German classics and presented the Third Reich as the bulwark of civilization. In Britain, the Ministry of Information used the Crown Film Unit to produce propagandist documentaries. The Ministry also established a War Artists' Scheme. Several thousand paintings and drawings were commissioned. Some showed bomb damage, including work by John Piper and Graham Sutherland's *Devastation in the City* (1941). Henry Moore and Feliks Topolski depicted people sheltering from German air raids in tube stations. Artists found less demand for landscapes and portraits. For many authors, also, the war provided the occasion for a shift to a new seriousness. Dorothy L. Sayers, best known for her earlier detective novels, produced a series of radio plays about the life of Christ, *The Man Born to be King* (1941–42).

This seriousness did not drown out other themes or styles. The war years saw the introduction into Britain of vigorous jive and jitterbug dances by American soldiers. Michael Tippett's oratorio *A Child of our Time* (1944) incorporated Negro spirituals. The Nazis, in contrast, banned jazz.

Thus World War Two put major pressures on society, even in totalitarian states. Combined with World War One, this helped ensure that the notion of normality as a re-creation of pre-1914 circumstances appeared increasingly tenuous. For political and military leaders, it was again clear that a rapid victory in a major war was unlikely, and that sustaining such a conflict would indeed have serious social implications. Confidence in popular responses varied, but was less pronounced than might be suggested by a focus on the wartime propaganda of togetherness. Instead, as in and after World War One, there was concern about the populace, specifically the working class. Whereas, however, a prime response in the 1920s had been the language of nationalism, after World War Two there was a greater attempt to raise general living standards and ensure social welfare; although these policies were mediated in terms of existing ideologies and state structures.

## Post-1945

The legacy of World War Two had a strong resonance in the late 1940s and 1950s. A sense of righteous struggle, an affirmed nationalism and a pride in military achievement can be found in the USA, the Soviet Union and Britain. Politicians from the war years continued to be influential, while most of their successors had seen military service in World War Two. In 1952 and 1956, the Americans elected General Eisenhower as President, followed, in 1960, by John F. Kennedy, who had served in the war. Veterans celebrated the military experience. These attitudes helped underpin willingness to serve in the Korean War and, at least initially, the Vietnam War, and, more generally, to bear the military and financial burden of the Cold War. Conscription continued. The draft was a collective experience of American manhood. By 1958, either as draftees or draft-induced volunteers, 70 per cent of eligible young American males had served under the colours. In Britain, conscription was seen as a just return for social welfare, and a measure necessary to show national resolve in the Cold War.[33]

The social and political context changed greatly in the late 1960s, heralding a new and very different age of Western warfare, one that was to be dominated by small regular forces and to lack the cultural attributes expressed in the notion of the Nation in Arms. The glorification of sacrifice in war that preceded and followed World War One ebbed rapidly in the 1960s. Anti-war attitudes came to dominate serious adult literature in the West, with war presented as callous disorder in popular works such as Joseph Heller's *Catch-22* (1961). "War" – i.e. now anti-war – poetry from the period of World War One (when it had very much expressed a minority viewpoint) became popular in the 1960s and 1970s. An anti-heroic ethos came to characterize much artistic work about war, for example the savage British theatrical indictment of World War One, Joan Littlewood's *Oh What a Lovely War!* (1963).

Many social currents were also at issue. These included individualism, hedonism and the atomization of society, none of which are conducive to militarism and bellicosity. The decline of fatalism in the West, combined with the wish to extirpate risk and to lesson personal exposure and responsibility, all counteracted bellicosity and also limited the courage or rashness without which battle is less likely. The military ceased to be a central symbol for state and society.

More generally, as wars became less frequent for Western states, they seemed less normal and normative. Instead, they were increasingly perceived as aberrations. It is also possible that feminism played a role. The rising influence of women interacted with changing notions of masculinity to challenge earlier definitions of the latter in terms of a willingness to fight.

The end of conscription ensured that far fewer men had any experience of the military as part of their normal course of life. Britain phased out conscription in 1957–63.[34] In France, where discontent with national service grew in the late 1960s, conscription was cut to a year in 1970.[35] In the Soviet Union, conscription was cut from three to two years in 1967, although more men were drafted, in place of a system in which many had not had to serve. The expansion of military service made it less popular, and led to an increase in desertion and in going absent without leave. In the USA in 1969, President Nixon decided to quieten popular anxieties about the Vietnam War and improve his prospects for re-election by eliminating the draft. This led, from 1973, to an all-volunteer force that reduced popular identification with the military. Opposition to militarism remained strong in post-war Germany and Japan even after the occupying powers had withdrawn their forces. In Portugal, the strain of conscription lessened support for the counter-insurgency wars in its colonies. In response to long tours of service in Africa, there was desertion and large-scale emigration by young men.

Regulars volunteered, but in most of Western society there was, by the early 1970s, a conditionality in attitudes towards the state and its demands that was very different to the situation a century earlier, and more specifically that in the early stages of World War One. In place of an automatic deference and, very often, an eagerness to serve, albeit often a critical response to the conditions of military life, there was now a sense that a positive reaction to the demands of the state arose from support for clearly expressed and correct policies. This more limited acceptance of government-conditioned popular responses to the use of military power as well as to aspects of military preparedness. The first was seen in hostility to the Vietnam War in the USA, the second in opposition to atomic weaponry, for example, the Campaign for Nuclear Disarmament (CND) launched in Britain in 1958.

This was part of a radically different social politics of war that transformed the context within which conflict was considered and prepared for. The military were increasingly seen as forces for national defence, not foreign intervention. There was a demilitarization of civil society that led to a decline in bellicose values. Furthermore, the nature of the state was reconceptualized. Imperial roles became redundant and were replaced by pressure for social welfare in order to secure a "better" society. Such pressure not only left fewer resources for the armed resources, but also created a dominant domestic political sphere in which military issues seemed irrelevant or of limited importance.

The suggestion that the West became less bellicose might seem ironic given its nuclear preponderance, the capacity of its weapons of mass destruction and the role of its industries in supplying weaponry to the rest of the world. In addition, other forms of Western "aggression" could be discerned, in the form of active economic and cultural imperialism. The latter certainly proved far more effective than war as a way to advance Western interests, as a consideration of the global situation of the USA in the early 1970s amply demonstrates.

The Soviet Union was to be affected by similar social and cultural forces to those seen in western Europe, but their impact was constrained and delayed by a more authoritarian political system that remained in control of the economy and was able to seek to direct society. A paranoid sense of vulnerability, which owed much to World War Two and something to Communist ideology, encouraged a major stress on military expenditure. Nearly a quarter of state expenditure went to military purposes in 1952, when the Soviet Union was not at war, and this figure increased as greater nuclear capability was added to the arsenal. Thus, the major economic gain of the 1950s and 1960s seen across most of the world brought only limited benefit in terms of Soviet living standards.

This had a serious long-term consequence for the stability of the Soviet system, for a lack of popularity made it difficult for the government to view change and reform with much confidence. As the turmoil of the 1990s was to show, the Soviet order sat increasingly uneasily on a society where individualism, consumerism and demands for change and freedom could not be accommodated by a command economy and Communist ideology. In 1989, an army officer was to complain that soldiers used "words in combination with 'I want' a lot".[36]

War and society, a major theme in books and courses over the past two decades, is a topic that can be addressed in a number of ways. One of the most important is that of discussing how changing cultural and social assumptions affected views on the use and goals of force, and thus military tasking. This was certainly true of the major shift that occurred at the close of our period, although it would be mistaken to underrate the importance within military history of autonomous developments in armed forces and in military capability, such as the increased sophistication of weaponry discussed in Chapter 9, with the attendant needs of a better trained and more professional military. The relationship between such developments, new political goals and shifts in the social context is complex; these factors were important to the new role of the Western military at the close of our period.

## CHAPTER ELEVEN

# *Conclusions*

Two points require stress at the close: variety and unpredictability. The first relates to the range of military tasks, and social and political contexts that can be seen throughout this period. For reasons of space, it is usual to underplay this variety and to focus on what appears to be the dominant trend, specifically to concentrate on paradigms and exemplars, but this is misleading for two reasons. First, it leads to an underrating of the variety of circumstances that pertained, and, secondly, it leads to an analytical model that is questionable. In particular, the notion that developments in a paradigmatic power explained what happened elsewhere, not least through a process of diffusion, is questionable. It underplays the variety and autonomy of military tasks and circumstances.

Unpredictability is also an important theme, as it challenges the explicit or implicit determinism of a stress on the quantity of resources and/or of gaps in technological capability. Unpredictability can be focused both by probing different outcomes for particular struggles and by looking at the more general lack of certainty about causal relationships in military development.

These general points can be fleshed out, for example, by looking at the war on the Eastern Front in 1941–45. In place of a past stress on how the enormity of the task (including distance, Soviet manpower and the winter), as well as how Hitler's foolish interventions thwarted Germany – i.e. on how blitzkrieg, understood as the leading edge of military modernity, could have prevailed, but was blunted – it is possible to point to Soviet fighting quality and the deficiencies of the German system in order to suggest that there was no clear hierarchy of military capability. This draws attention both to the difficulty of making academic judgements and to the contingent circumstances that played a role in success, for example, the absence of Japanese intervention against the Soviet Union in 1941, which allowed the Soviets to transfer forces to defend Moscow.

This book seeks to stress the deficiencies of a linear concept of military development. With more space, it would be easier to do so, for example, by focusing on Latin America, where the pursuit of domestic political objectives by force has played a far more important role than in North America. This has dominated the military culture of Latin American armed forces far more than the weaponry they employ.

A reminder of political contexts is necessary not only at the specific level, but also as a more general point about the writing of military history. Such contexts are generally probed by sociologists of military power, but their work has to be integrated into the mainstream of military history and to help shape its questions.

This is true not only of the organization and internal culture of the armed forces, but also of their interaction with the rest of society.[1] Thus, the conservatism of the military, especially of armies, is important, not least in their unwillingness to support radical domestic politics and general preference for order and stability. This was seen throughout the period. It led, for example, to action against peasant and worker discontent, as in the Romanian suppression of a major peasant uprising in 1907. Conservatism also led to the eventual disenchantment of much of the German military leadership with the radical populism of Hitler, and to the belated and unsuccessful attempt by some of them to remove him in the July Bomb Plot of 1944, although Hitler, in turn, was able to remould much of the army in accordance with Nazi ideology.[2]

It is also necessary to address such sociocultural parameters as different understandings of victory, loss and suffering. These different understandings of psychological considerations can be related to the varied cultural systems of the West, as can bellicosity, although there is no exact correlation. In particular, it is possible to discern four different types of state-culture: imperial-democratic (Britain, France), egalitarian (USA),[3] authoritarian left (Soviet Union), and authoritarian right (Wilhelmine and Nazi Germany, Fascist Italy),[4] although there were important variations within these categories. For example, the cultural politics of Britain and Germany in 1882 were both very different to those of 1939, as indeed were the collective experiences of their military and political leaderships. Contemporaries ascribed military characteristics to sociopolitical differences. Thus, Ian Hamilton, then General Officer Commanding Southern Command, suggested in 1906 that contrasts between the British and German armies reflected the preference for method and system in German society.[5]

It was crucial to Allied success in both world wars that the democracies were able to mobilize their resources and focus a national will in a way that totalitarian regimes thought only they could do. State types showed a contrasting ability to respond to the challenges of total war. It can be argued that the totalitarian systems were less adaptable (as well as being more bellicose) because command systems were inherently prone to impose inefficient direction, rather than to respond to advice and to interest groups. This conclusion would appear less significant if Germany had been the victor in 1918 or 1941, but that would not have vitiated the point that different societies had contrasting characteristics as war states. Furthermore, even if Germany had been the victor, it would still not have conquered Britain in 1918 or Britain and the USA in 1941. Possible success as a land power in the prime zone of operations would not have equated with greater overall effectiveness. However successful it had been against the Soviet Union, Germany would have been vulnerable to American atomic bombs.

Questions of the effectiveness of particular sociopolitical systems may seem far distant from such questions as why the Germans lost both world wars, but they are important to our understanding of military history, for they help provide us with the way to make wider sense of particular conflicts. Study of the latter, the operational dimension, and, even more, of individual battles, dominates military history. It is both approachable and valuable, but it cannot suffice if we want to probe the wider significance of the subject, as well as the dynamics of military development and capability that help explain the cause, course and consequences of particular wars.

# Notes

## Chapter 1: From Egypt to Ethiopia: Western Expansionism, 1882–1936

1. British Library (BL) Additional Manuscripts (Add.) 50300 fol. 176.
2. For a recent account stressing the role of economic interests, see A. Webster, "Business and Empire: A Reassessment of the British Conquest of Burma in 1885", *Historical Journal*, 43 (2000), pp. 1003–25.
3. BL Add. 49357 fol. 22.
4. Y. G. Paillard, "The French Expedition to Madagascar in 1895", in *Imperialism and War: Essays on Colonial Wars in Asia and Africa*, J. A. de Moor and H. L.Wesseling (eds) (Leiden, 1989), pp. 168–88.
5. R. M. Utley, *The Last Days of the Sioux Nation* (New Haven, CT, 1963) and *Frontier Regulars: The United States Army and the Indian, 1866–1891* (New York, 1973).
6. M. Kuitenbrouwer, *The Netherlands and the Rise of Modern Imperialism: Colonies and Foreign Policy, 1870–1902* (Oxford, 1991).
7. B. Vandervort, *Wars of Imperial Conquest in Africa 1830–1914* (1998), p. 126.
8. R. H. Rainero, "The Battle of Adowa: a Reappraisal", in Moor and Wesseling (eds), *Imperialism and War*, pp. 188–200.
9. S. Lone, *Japan's First Modern War: Army and Society in the Conflict with China 1894–1895* (1994).
10. Roberts to the Duke of Cambridge, 9 July 1885, Liddell Hart Centre for Military Archives, King's College London (LH) Hamilton papers 1/3/3, II, 265.
11. E. M. Spiers (ed.), *Sudan: The Reconquest* (1998).
12. R. Robinson (ed.), *Railway Imperialism* (Westport, CT, 1991); I. J. Kerr, *Building the Railways of the Raj 1850–1900* (Oxford, 1995).
13. J. Dunn, "'For God, Emperor, and Country!': The Evolution of Ethiopia's Nineteenth-Century Army", *War in History*, 1 (1994), p. 295.
14. Public Record Office (PRO) 30/40/14 fols 209–13; P. J. Hugill, *Global Communications since 1844: Geopolitics and Technology* (Baltimore, MD, 1999), pp. 29–46; D. R. Headrick, *The Invisible Weapon: Telecommunications and International Politics, 1851–1945* (New York, 1991).
15. P. D. Curtin, *Death by Migration: Europe's Encounter with the Tropical World in the Nineteenth Century* (Cambridge, 1989).

16. A. S. Kanya-Forstner, *The Conquest of the Western Sudan: A Study in French Military Imperialism* (Cambridge, 1969).
17. In the case of Somaliland in 1896, PRO 30/40/14 fol. 124.
18. BL Add. 50300 fol. 177.
19. W. A. Hoisington, *Lyautey and the French Conquest of Morocco* (New York, 1955).
20. D. Porch, *The Conquest of the Sahara* (1985).
21. M. C. Ricklefs, *A History of Modern Indonesia since c. 1300* (2nd edn, 1993), pp. 136–40.
22. BL Add. 49357 fols 5, 17–18, 21, 22–3.
23. B. M. Linn, *The US Army and Counterinsurgency in the Philippine War, 1899–1902* (Chapel Hill, NC, 1989), "Taking up 'The White Man's Burden': US Troop Conduct in the Philippine War, 1899–1902", in *1898: Enfoques y Perspectivas*, L. E. González Vales (ed.) (San Juan, Puerto Rico, 1997), pp. 111–42, and "The Pulahan Campaign: A Study in US Pacification", *War in History*, 6 (1999), pp. 45–71.
24. J. Bridgman, *The Revolt of the Hereros* (Berkeley, CA, 1981).
25. P. A. Cohen, *History in Three Keys: The Boxers as Event, Experience, and Myth* (New York, 1997); R. R. Thompson, "Military Dimensions of the 'Boxer Uprising' in Shanxi, 1898–1901", in *Warfare in Chinese History*, H. Van De Ven (ed.) (Leiden, 2000), p. 318.
26. D. G. Hermann, "The Paralysis of Italian Strategy in the Italian–Turkish War, 1911–1912", *English Historical Review*, 104 (1989), pp. 332–56.
27. Maxwell to Kitchener, 19, 23 May 1915, PRO 30/57/65, nos 906, 949.
28. Kitchener to Balfour, 6 Nov. 1915, PRO 30/57/66.
29. C. Badesi, "West African Influence on the French Army of World War One", in *Double Impact: France and Africa in the Age of Imperialism*, G. W. Johnson (ed.) (Westport, CT, 1985).
30. Greenhut, "The Imperial Reserve: The Indian Infantry on the Western Front 1914–15", *Journal of Imperial and Commonwealth History*, 12 (1983); D. Omissi, *The Sepoy and the Raj: The Indian Army, 1860–1940* (1994).
31. T. Tai-Yong, "An Imperial Home-Front: Punjab and the First World War", *Journal of Military History*, 64 (2000), pp. 371–410.
32. BL Add. 49699 fol. 85.
33. Lieutenant Colonel Sydney Muspratt to General Montgomery-Massingberd, then Deputy Chief of General Staff, India, 4 June 1921, LH Montgomery-Massingberd papers (MM) 8/22.
34. P. M. Holt and M. W. Daly, *A History of the Sudan* (5th edn, Harlow, 2000), p. 103.
35. PRO War Office (WO) 33/2764, p. 257.
36. General Rawlinson, Commander-in-Chief India, to Montgomery-Massingberd, 8 Nov. 1922, LH MM 8/27.
37. Rawlinson to Montgomery-Massingberd, 21 Sept. 1922, LH MM 8/27; J. Darwin, *Britain, Egypt and the Middle East: Imperial Policy in the Aftermath of War, 1918–1922* (1981); J. R. Ferris, *Men, Money and Diplomacy: The Evolution of British Strategic Policy, 1919–1926* (Ithaca, NY, 1989).
38. D. S. Woolman, *Rebels in the Rif: Abd el Krim and the Rif Rebellion* (Stanford, CA, 1968); J. Chandler, "Spain and her Moroccan Protectorate, 1898–1927", *Journal of Contemporary History* (1975), pp. 301–22, and "The Responsibilities for Annual", *Iberian Studies* (1977), pp. 68–75; C. R. Pennell, *A Country with a Government and a Flag: The Rif War in Morocco, 1921–1926* (Wisbech, 1986); S. E. Fleming, *Primo de Rivera and Abd-el-Krim: The Struggle in Spanish Morocco, 1923–1927* (New York, 1991).
39. J. E. Alvarez, "Tank Warfare During the Rif Rebellion", *Armor*, 106 (1997), pp. 26–8.
40. Alvarez, "Between Gallipoli and D-Day: Alhucemas, 1925", *Journal of Military History*, 63 (1999), pp. 75–98.
41. LH Ismay 3/1/1–83, quotes pp. 55, 58.
42. LH Ismay 3/1/20.
43. C. G. Segrè, *Fourth Shore: the Italian Colonization of Libya* (Chicago, IL, 1974).
44. M. Broxup, "The Last *Ghazawat*: The 1920–1921 Uprising", and A. Avtorkhanov, "The Chechens and Ingush during the Soviet Period", in M. Broxup (ed.), *The North Caucasus Barrier* (1992), pp. 112–45, 157–61, 183.

45. H. Schmidt, *The United States Occupation of Haiti, 1915–1934* (New Brunswick, NJ, 1971); B. J. Calder, *The Impact of Intervention: The Dominican Republic during the US Occupation of 1916–1924* (Austin, TX, 1984); D. Yerxa, *Admirals and Empire: The United States Navy and the Caribbean, 1898–1945* (Columbia, SC, 1991).
46. S. K. Fung, *The Diplomacy of Imperial Retreat: Britain's South China Policy, 1924–1931* (Oxford, 1991).
47. N. Shepherd, *Ploughing Sand: British Rule in Palestine, 1917–1948* (Piscataway, NJ, 2000).
48. F. Marwat, A. K. Khan and S. W. Krakakhel, "Faqir of Ipi", in *Afghanistan and the Frontier*, F. Marwat and S. W. Krakakhel (eds) (Peshawar, 1993), pp. 235–73.
49. Omissi, *Air Power and Colonial Control: The Royal Air Force 1919–1939* (Manchester, 1990).
50. M. Rosa de Madariaga, "The Intervention of Moroccan Troops in the Spanish Civil War: A Reconsideration", *European History Quarterly*, 22 (1992), pp. 67–97.
51. D. G. Boyce, "From Assaye to the *Assaye*: Reflections on British Government, Force and Moral Authority in India", *Journal of Military History*, 63 (1993), pp. 643–68.
52. Rawlinson to Montgomery-Massingberd, 21 Sept. 1922, LH MM 8/27.
53. Montgomery-Massingberd, Chief of the Imperial General Staff, reporting discussion with General Gamelin, to Viscount Halifax, Secretary of State for War, 17 Aug. 1935, LH MM 10/4/1.
54. A. Mockler, *Haile Selassie's War: the Italian-Ethiopian Campaign, 1935–1941* (New York, 1985).

# Chapter 2: The West, 1882–1913

1. BL Add. 50344 p. 131.
2. W. F. Sater and H. H. Herwig, *The Grand Illusion: The Prussianization of the Chilean Army* (Lincoln, NE, 1999).
3. BL Add. 50287 fol. 14. See, more generally, L. H. Addington, *The Blitzkrieg Era and the German General Staff, 1865–1941* (New Brunswick, NJ, 1971); S. Lackey, *The Rebirth of the Habsburg Army: Friedrich Beck and the Rise of the General Staff* (Westport, CT, 1995).
4. A. Mitchell, *Victors and Vanquished: The German Influence on Army and Church in France After 1870* (Chapel Hill, NC, 1984); T. K. Nenninger, *The Leavenworth Schools and the Old Army: Education, Professionalism, and the Officer Corps of the United States Army, 1881–1918* (Westport, CT, 1978).
5. C. Bassford, *Clausewitz in English: The Reception of Clausewitz in Britain and America, 1815–1945* (Oxford, 1994).
6. P. M. Kennedy (ed.), *The War Plans of the Great Powers 1880–1914* (1979); G. Rothenberg, "Moltke, Schlieffen and the Doctrine of Strategic Envelopment", in *Makers of Modern Strategy*, P. Paret (ed.) (Princeton, NJ, 1986), pp. 296–325; S. E. Miller, S. M. Lynn-Jones and S. Van Evera (eds), *Military Strategy and the Origins of the First World War* (2nd edn, Princeton, NJ, 1991); G. A. Tunstall, *Planning for War Against Russia and Serbia: Austro-Hungarian and German Military Strategies, 1871–1914* (Boulder, CO, 1993).
7. G. Ritter, *The Schlieffen Plan: Critique of a Myth* (1958); T. Zuber, "The Schlieffen Plan Reconsidered", *War in History*, 6 (1999), pp. 262–305; R. T. Foley (ed.), "Schlieffen's Last Kriegsspiel", *War Studies Journal*, 3 (1998), pp. 117–33 and 4 (1999), pp. 97–116. There is strong criticism of Schlieffen's legacy in A. Mombauer, *Helmuth von Moltke and the Origins of the First World War* (Cambridge, 2001).
8. Rothenberg, "The Austro-Hungarian Campaign Against Serbia in 1914", *Journal of Military History*, 53 (1989), p. 134.
9. H. L. Wesseling, *Soldier and Warrior: French Attitudes toward the Army and War on the Eve of the First World War* (Westport, CT, 2000).
10. A. Gat, *The Development of Military Thought: The Nineteenth Century* (Oxford, 1992), pp.

114–72; D. Porch, *The March to the Marne: The French Army, 1871–1914* (Cambridge, 1981); J. Snyder, *The Ideology of the Offensive: Military Decision Making and the Disasters of 1914* (Ithaca, NY, 1984); R. A. Prete, "The Preparation of the French Army Prior to World War I: An Historiographical Reappraisal", *Canadian Journal of History*, 26 (1991), pp. 241–66.

11. PRO WO 106/6187, p. 77.

12. PRO 30/40/13, p. 62; J. A. Grant, *Big Business in Russia: The Putilov Company in Late Imperial Russia, 1868–1917* (Pittsburgh, PA, 1999).

13. K. Neilson, "Russia", in *Decisions for War, 1914*, K. Wilson (ed.) (1995), p. 102.

14. N. Ferguson, "Germany and the Origins of the First World War: New Perspectives", *Historical Journal*, 35 (1992), p. 733.

15. K. D. Moll, *The Influence of History upon Seapower 1865–1914* (Stanford, CA, 1968), pp. 37–40.

16. W. H. McNeill, *The Pursuit of Power: Technology, Armed Force, and Society since AD 1000* (Oxford, 1982), pp. 237–8, 265–7.

17. I. McCallum, *Blood Brothers: Hiram and Hudson Maxim – Pioneers of Modern Warfare* (1999).

18. D. E. Showalter, "Marching in Step: Technology and *Mentalité* for Artillery, 1848–1914", in *Tooling for War: Military Transformation in the Industrial Age*, S. C. Chiabotti (ed.) (Chicago, IL, 1996), pp. 27–48.

19. S. Forster, "Facing 'People's' War: Moltke the Elder and Germany's Military Options after 1871", *Journal of Strategic Studies*, 10 (1978), pp. 209–30.

20. M. Howard, "Tools of War: Concepts and Technology", in *Tools of War: Instruments, Ideas, and Institutions of Warfare, 1445–1871*, J. A. Lynn (ed.) (Urbana, IL, 1990), p. 246.

21. BL Add. 50334 p. 131.

22. A. Echevarria, "A Crisis in Warfighting: German Tactical Discussions in the Late Nineteenth Century", *Militärgeschichtliche Mitteilungen*, 55 (1995), pp. 51–68; Hamilton, British Adjutant General, report on Saxon exercises, 1909, LH Hamilton papers 4/2/9, p. 60.

23. BL Add. 50101 fols 8, 16, 19–21.

24. PRO WO 33/2819 p. 26, 2816, p. 43.

25. PRO WO 33/2822 pp. 93, 10.

26. PRO 30/40/14, fol. 90.

27. J. Smith, *The Spanish–American War* (1994).

28. R. Schwartz, *Lawless Liberators: Political Banditry and Cuban Independence* (Durham, NC, 1989), p. 238.

29. N. Riall (ed.), *Boer War: The Letters, Diaries and Photographs of Malcolm Riall from the War in South Africa 1899–1902* (2000), p. 152.

30. For a good recent summary, W. Nasson, *The South African War, 1899–1902* (1999).

31. BL Add. 50344 pp. 131–3; S. P. MacKenzie, "Willpower or Firepower? The Unlearned Military Lessons of the Russo-Japanese War", in *The Russo-Japanese War in Cultural Perspective, 1904–05*, D. Wells and S. Wilson (eds) (1999), pp. 36–7.

32. G. C. Cox, "Of Aphorisms, Lessons, and Paradigms: Comparing the British and German Official Histories of the Russo-Japanese War", *Journal of Military History*, 66 (1992), pp. 389–401.

33. M. Howard, "Men Against Fire: The Doctrine of the Offensive in 1914", in *Makers of Modern Strategy from Machiavelli to the Nuclear Age*, P. Paret *et al.* (eds) (Princeton, NJ, 1986), pp. 510–26.

34. BL Add. 50344 p. 3.

35. BL Add. 52277B, fol. 164.

36. D. Herrmann, *The Arming of Europe and the Making of the First World War* (Princeton, NJ, 1996); D. Stevenson, *Armaments and the Coming of War: Europe, 1904–1914* (Oxford, 1996).

37. P. Gatrell, *Government, Industry and Rearmament in Russia, 1900–1914: The Last Argument of Tsarism* (Cambridge, 1994). For a more positive view, B. W. Menning, *Bayonets Before Bullets: The Imperial Russian Army, 1861–1914* (Bloomington, IN, 1993); J. M. B. Lyon, "'A Peasant Mob': The Serbian Army on the Eve of the Great War", *Journal of Military History*, 61 (1997), p. 493.

38. R. Hall, *The Balkan Wars 1912–1913: Prelude to the First World War* (2000).

NOTES

# Chapter 3: World War One, 1914–18

1. Thoughtful responses to the dominant interpretation include R. Prior and T. Wilson, "Paul Fussell at War", *War in History*, 1 (1994), pp. 63–80 and D. Englander, "Soldiering and Identity: Reflections on the Great War", *War in History*, 1 (1994), 300–18.
2. E. C. Helmreich, *The Diplomacy of the Balkan Wars, 1912–1913* (Cambridge, MA, 1938); A. Rossos, *Russia and the Balkans: Inter-Balkan Rivalries and Russian Foreign Policy, 1908–1914* (Toronto, 1981).
3. Among the large numbers of works on the subject, the following can be noted, F. Fischer, *War of Illusions: German Policies from 1911 to 1914* (1975); Z. Steiner, *Britain and the Origins of the First World War* (1977); S. R. Williamson, *The Origins of a Tragedy: July 1914* (Arlington Heights, IL, 1981); J. F. V. Keiger, *France and the Origins of the First World War* (1983); D. C. B. Lieven, *Russia and the Origins of the First World War* (1983); J. Joll, *The Origins of the First World War* (1984); Williamson, *Austria-Hungary and the Origins of the First World War* (1991); J. H. Maurer, *The Outbreak of the First World War: Strategic Planning, Crisis Decision Making, and Deterrence Failure* (Westport, CT, 1995); K. Wilson (ed.), *Decisions for War, 1914* (1995); H. Strachan, *The First World War. I: To Arms* (Oxford, 2001).
4. A. J. P. Taylor, *War by Timetable: How the First World War Began* (1969).
5. M. Trachtenberg, *History and Strategy* (Princeton, NJ, 1991), pp. 72, 96–8; J. Levy, "Preferences, Constraints, and Choices in July 1914", *International Security*, 15 (1990–91), pp. 151–86; D. Stevenson, "Militarization and Democracy in Europe before 1914", *International Security*, 22 (1997), pp. 147–8.
6. BL Add. 50287 fol. 71.
7. J. Horne and A. Kramer, *"German Atrocities" in 1914: Meanings and Memory of War* (2001).
8. For individual battles see, in particular, A. Horne, *The Price of Glory: Verdun 1916* (1962); A. H. Farrar-Hockley, *The Somme* (1964); R. Prior and T. Wilson, *Passchendaele, the Untold Story* (New Haven, CT, 1996); H. Strachan, "The Battle of the Somme and British Strategy", *Journal of Strategic Studies*, 31 (1998), pp. 79–95.
9. S. Badsey, "Cavalry and the Development of Breakthrough Doctrine", in *British Fighting Methods in the Great War*, P. Griffith (ed.) (1996), pp. 138–74.
10. T. Travers, "The Allied Victories, 1918", in *The Oxford Illustrated History of the First World War*, H. Strachan (ed.) (Oxford, 1998), p. 280.
11. BL Add. 49703 fol. 43.
12. BL Add. 49703 fol. 42.
13. P. R. Braim, *The Test of Battle: The American Expeditionary Forces in the Meuse–Argonne Campaign* (Newark, DE, 1987).
14. BL Add. 49703 fols 137–8.
15. BL Add. 49699 fol. 13.
16. R. B. Bruce, "To the Last Limits of Their Strength: The French Army and the Logistics of Attrition at the Battle of Verdun", *Army History*, 45 (1998), pp. 9–21.
17. P. Simkins, *Kitchener's New Armies* (Manchester, 1988).
18. D. Showalter, "From Deterrence to Doomsday Machine: The German Way of War, 1890–1914", *Journal of Military History*, 64 (2000), p. 709.
19. P. H. Liddle, *The British Soldier on the Somme 1916* (Camberley, 1996), pp. 31–2.
20. M. Middlebrook, *The First Day on the Somme* (1971).
21. M. Hardy, "'Be Cheerful in Adversity': Views from the Trenches, 1917–1918", Buckinghamshire Record Office, *Annual Report and List of Accessions, 1995*.
22. T. Ashworth, *Trench Warfare, 1914–1918: The Live and Let Live System* (1980); J. Ellis, *Eye-Deep in Hell: Trench Warfare in World War I* (New York, 1976); J. Keegan, *The Face of Battle: A Study of Agincourt, Waterloo and the Somme* (1976).
23. D. Showalter, *Tannenberg: Clash of Empires* (Hamden, CT, 1991).
24. N. Stone, *The Eastern Front 1914–1917* (1975); W. C. Fuller, "The Eastern Front", in *The Great*

223

*War and the Twentieth Century*, J. Winter, G. Parker and M. R. Habeck (eds) (New Haven, CT, 2000), pp. 30–68.

25. BL Add. 49699 fols 53–5.

26. G. E. Torrey, "Romania in the First World War: The Years of Engagement", *International History Review*, 14 (1992), pp. 462–79.

27. A. J. Barker, *The Neglected War: Mesopotamia, 1914–1918* (1967).

28. M. Hughes, "General Allenby and the Palestine Campaign, 1917–18", *Journal of Strategic Studies*, 19(4) (1996), pp. 59–88.

29. Kitchener to Prime Minister, 5 Nov. 1915, PRO 30/57/66. See also D. J. Dutton, "The Balkan Campaign and French War Aims in the Great War", *English Historical Review*, 94 (1979), pp. 97–113 and R. A. Prete, "*Imbroglio par excellence*: Mounting the Salonika Camaign, September–October 1915", *War and Society*, 19 (2001), esp. pp. 68–70.

30. Strachan, "The Battle of the Somme and British Strategy", *Journal of Strategic Studies*, 21 (1998), pp. 79–95; LH Benson A 3/7, pp. 1–2, 5.

31. C. Falls, *The Battle of Caporetto* (1966).

32. G. H. Cassar, *The Forgotten Front: The British Campaign in Italy 1917–1918* (1998).

33. T. Lupfer, *The Dynamics of Doctrine: the Changes in German Tactical Doctrine During the First World War* (Fort Leavenworth, KS, 1981); B. Gudmundsen, *Stormtroop Tactics: Innovation in the German Army 1914–1918* (New York, 1989); D. T. Zabecki, *Steel Wind: Colonel Georg Bruchmüller and the Birth of Modern Artillery* (Westport, CT, 1994); M. Samuels, *Command or Control? Command, Training and Tactics in the British and German Armies, 1888–1918* (1995).

34. Griffith, *Battle Tactics of the Western Front: The British Army's Art of Attack, 1916–1918* (New Haven, CT, 1994), p. 193.

35. G. Sheffield, "British High Command in the First World War: An Overview", in *Challenges of High Command in the Twentieth Century*, G. Sheffield and G. Till (eds) (Camberley, 1999), p. 23.

36. M. Middlebrook, *The Kaiser's Battle, 21st March 1918: The First Day of the German Spring Offensive* (1978).

37. J. Terraine, *To Win a War: 1918, the Year of Victory* (1978); R. Paschall, *The Defeat of Imperial Germany 1917–18* (Chapel Hill, NC, 1989); T. Travers, *How the War Was Won: Command and Technology in the British Army on the Western Front, 1917–1918* (1992); S. B. Schreiber, *Shock Army of the British Empire: The Canadian Corps in the Last 100 Days of the Great War* (Westport, CT, 1997); J. P. Harris, *Amiens to the Armistice: The BEF in the Hundred Days' Campaign, 8 August–11 November 1918* (1998).

38. BL Add. 49703 fols 128–9.

39. R. Prior and T. Wilson, "15 September 1916: The Dawn of the Tank", *Journal of the Royal United Services Institute*, 136(4) (Autumn 1991), pp. 61–5; D. J. Childs, *A Peripheral Weapon? The Production and Employment of British Tanks in the First World War* (Westport, CT, 1999); E. Greenhalgh, "Technology Development in Coalition: The Case of the First World War Tank", *International History Review*, 22 (2000), pp. 806–36.

40. J. Bailey, *The First World War and the Birth of the Modern Style of Warfare* (Camberley, 1996).

41. D. V. Johnson and R. L. Hillman, *Soissons 1918* (College Station, TX, 1999).

42. P. Griffith (ed.), *British Fighting Methods in the Great War* (1996).

43. M. Cornwall, *The Last Years of Austria-Hungary* (Exeter, 1996).

44. R. Chickering, *Imperial Germany and the Great War, 1914–1918* (Cambridge, 1998).

45. W. Deist, "The Military Collapse of the German Empire: The Reality Behind the Stab-in-the-Back Myth", *War in History*, 3 (1996), pp. 186–207; Strachan, "The Morale of the German Army, 1917–1918", in *Facing Armageddon: The First World War Experienced*, H. Cecil and P. Liddle (eds) (Barnsley, 1996), pp. 383–98.

46. B. Lowry, *Armistice 1918* (Kent, OH, 1996).

47. E. M. Coffman, *The War to End All Wars: The American Military Experience in World War I* (New York, 1968); D. F. Trask, *The AEF and Coalition Warmaking* (Lawrence, KS, 1993).

48. K. Burk, *Britain, America, and the Sinews of War, 1914–1918* (1984).

49. A. Palazzo, *Seeking Victory on the Western Front: The British Army and Chemical Warfare in World War One* (Lincoln, NE, 2000).

50. D. Showalter, "Mass Warfare and the Impact of Technology", in *Great War, Total War: Combat and Mobilization on The Western Front, 1914–1918*, R. Chickering and S. Förster (eds) (Cambridge, 2000), p. 83.

51. G. Hartcup, *The War of Invention* (1983); J. A. Johnson, *The Kaiser's Chemists: Science and Modernization in Imperial Germany* (Chapel Hill, NC, 1990).

52. BL Add. 49715 fol. 5, cf. fol. 6.

# Chapter 4: The Inter-war Years

1. PRO WO 106/6238, p. 19.

2. PRO Cabinet Office (CAB) 16/109, fol. 15.

3. M. F. Boemake *et al.* (eds), *The Treaty of Versailles: A Reassessment after 75 Years* (Cambridge, 1998).

4. G. Swain, *Russia's Civil War* (Stroud, 2000).

5. A. K. Wildman, *The End of the Russian Imperial Army: The Old Army and the Soldiers' Revolt* (Princeton, NJ, 1980), and *The End of the Russian Imperial Army: The Road to Soviet Power and Peace* (Princeton, NJ, 1987).

6. J. D. Smele, *Civil War in Siberia: The Anti-Bolshevik Government of Admiral Kolchak, 1918–1920* (Cambridge, 1998).

7. LH Kennedy 2/2.

8. D. Footman, *Civil War in Russia* (New York, 1960); P. Kenez, *Civil War in South Russia: The First Year of the Volunteer Army* (Berkeley, CA, 1971); E. Mawdsley, *The Russian Civil War* (1987); O. Figes, "The Red Army and Mass Mobilization during the Russian Civil War, 1918–1920", *Past and Present*, 129 (Nov. 1990).

9. V. G. Liulevicius, *War Land on the Eastern Front: Culture, National Identity and German Occupation in World War I* (Cambridge, 2000), pp. 228–32.

10. PRO WO 106/6238, pp. 19–23.

11. N. Davies, *White Eagle, Red Star: The Polish–Soviet War, 1919–1920* (1972).

12. Chetwode to General Sir Archibald Montgomery-Massingberd, 1 July 1921, LH MM 8/22; P. Hart, *The IRA and its Enemies: Violence and Community in Cork, 1916–1923* (Oxford, 1998); B. A. Follis, *A State under Siege: The Establishment of Northern Ireland, 1920–1925* (Oxford, 1995).

13. LH MM 9/5/7, memorandum by Colonel Lindsay, p. 2.

14. Montgomery-Massingberd, Chief of the Imperial General Staff 1933–6, to Lincolnshire Branches of the British Legion, 15 June 1940, LH MM 10/10.

15. B. H. Reid, *Studies in British Military Thought: Debates with Fuller and Liddell Hart* (Lincoln, NE, 1998); A. Gat, *British Armour Theory and the Rise of the Panzer Arm: Revisiting the Revisionists* (2000); H. R. Winton, *To Change an Army: General Sir John Burnett-Stuart and British Armoured Doctrine, 1927–1938* (Lawrence, KS, 1988); A. J. Smithers, *A New Excalibur: The Development of the Tank, 1909–1939* (1988); J. P. Harris, *Men, Ideas and Tanks: British Military Thought and Armoured Forces, 1903–1939* (Manchester, 1995). For a lively biography, A. Danchev, *Alchemist of War: The Life of Basil Liddell Hart* (1998). See, more generally, B. Bond, *British Military Policy Between the Two World Wars* (Oxford, 1980).

16. J. S. Corum, *The Roots of Blitzkrieg: Hans von Seeckt and German Military Reform* (Lawrence, KS, 1992); R. M. Citino, *The Path to Blitzkrieg: Doctrine and Training in the German Army, 1920–1939* (Boulder, CO, 1999).

17. A. R. Millett and W. Murray (eds), *Military Effectiveness II. The Interwar Period* (Cambridge, 1988); H. R. Winton and D. R. Mets (eds), *The Challenge of Change: Military Institutions and New Realities, 1918–1941* (Lincoln, NE, 2000).

18. Rawlinson to Montgomery-Massingberd, 16 July 1923, LH MM 8/28.
19. D. Massam, *British Maritime Strategy and Amphibious Capability, 1900–40* (D.Phil., Oxford, 1995).
20. W. O. Odom, *After the Trenches: The Transformation of US Army Doctrine, 1918–1939* (College Station, TX, 1999).
21. Montgomery-Massingberd to Chetwode, 3 Dec. 1928, LH MM 10/1.
22. PRO CAB 16/109, fol. 7.
23. PRO CAB 16/109, fol. 15.
24. B. M. Linn, *Guardians of Empire: The US Army and the Pacific, 1902–1940* (Chapel Hill, NC, 1997), pp. 251, xiv.
25. D. E. Johnson, *Fast Tanks and Heavy Bombers: Innovation in the US Army, 1917–1945* (Ithaca, NY, 1998).
26. W. Murray, "Does Military Culture Matter?", *Orbis*, 43 (1999), pp. 34–5.
27. LH Adam 2/1, p. 111, Milne Box 3, p. 2.
28. PRO WO 33/1512, p. 3. See, more generally, D. French, *Raising Churchill's Army: The British Army and the War Against Germany, 1919–1945* (Oxford, 2000).
29. A. Suchcitz, "Poland's Defence Preparations in 1939", in *Poland Between the Wars, 1918–1939*, P. D. Stachura (ed.) (Basingstoke, 1998), pp. 109–10.
30. P. D. Stachura, "The Battle of Warsaw, August 1920, and the Development of the Second Polish Republic", in Stachura (ed.), *Poland*, pp. 54–5.
31. Chetwode to Montgomery-Massingberd, 21 July 1921, LH MM 8/22.
32. D. R. Stone, *Hammer and Rifle: The Militarization of the Soviet Union, 1926–1933* (Lawrence, KS, 2000).
33. A. Gat, *Fascist and Liberal Visions of War: Fuller, Liddell Hart, Douhet, and Other Modernists* (Oxford, 1998).
34. B. R. Sullivan, "The Italian Armed Forces, 1918–40", in Millett and Murray (eds), *Military Effectiveness* II, 169–217.
35. J. Noakes, "The Nazi Revolution", in *Reinterpreting Revolution in Twentieth-Century Europe*, M. Donald and T. Rees (eds) (2001), pp. 109–10.
36. F. L. Carsten, *The Reichswehr and Politics* (Oxford, 1966); R. J. O'Neill, *The German Army and the Nazi Party 1933–1939* (1966); W. Deist, *The Wehrmacht and German Rearmament* (1981); A. Seaton, *The German Army 1933–45* (1982); I. Kershaw, *Hitler 1889–1936: Hubris* (1998), pp. 524–5 and *Hitler 1936–45: Nemesis* (2000), pp. 49–60.
37. R. Simpkin, *Deep Battle: The Brainchild of Marshal Tukhachevskii* (1987); L. Samuelson, "Mikhail Tukhachevsky and War-Economic Planning: Reconsiderations on the Pre-war Soviet Military Build-up", *Journal of Slavic Military Studies*, 9 (1996), pp. 804–47; S. W. Stoecker, *Forging Stalin's Army: Marshal Tukhachevsky and the Politics of Military Innovation* (Boulder, CO, 1998).
38. Report by Brigadier Molesworth, 19 Nov. 1938, PRO WO 106/1589, p. 5.
39. J. Erickson, *The Soviet High Command: A Military-Political History, 1918–1941* (1962).
40. A. Sella, "Khalklin-Gol: The Forgotten War", *Journal of Contemporary History*, 18 (1983), pp. 658–67; A. Coox, *Nomonhan: Japan against Russia 1939* (Stanford, CA, 1985).
41. R. R. Reese, *Stalin's Reluctant Soldiers: A Social History of the Red Army, 1925–1941* (Lawrence, KS, 1996); D. M. Glantz, *Stumbling Colossus: The Red Army on the Eve of World War* (Lawrence, KS, 1998).
42. M. S. Alexander, *The Republic in Danger: General Maurice Gamelin and the Politics of French Defence, 1933–1940* (Cambridge, 1992).
43. S. Ben-Ami, *Fascism from Above: the Dictatorship of Primo de Rivera in Spain, 1923–1930* (Oxford, 1983).
44. PRO WO 106/1578, pp. 1–7.
45. PRO WO 105/1588, pp. 2–7.
46. P. Preston and A. L. Mackenzie (eds), *The Republic Besieged: Civil War in Spain 1936–1939* (Edinburgh, 1996); M. Alpert, "The Clash of Spanish Armies: Contrasting Ways of War in Spain,

1936–1939", *War in History*, 6 (1999), pp. 331–51; C. Leitz and D. Dunthorn (eds), *Spain in an International Context, 1936–1959* (Oxford, 1999).

47. B. J. Fischer, *King Zog and the Struggle for Stability in Albania* (Boulder, CO, 1984) and "Albanian Highland Tribal Society and Family Structure in the Process of Twentieth Century Transformation", *East European Quarterly*, 33 (1999), pp. 287–91. I would like to thank Professor Fischer for his advice.

48. O. H. Radkey, *The Unknown Civil War in Soviet Russia* (Stanford, CA, 1976).

49. B. A. Shillony, *Revolt in Japan: The Young Officers and the February 26, 1936 Incident* (Princeton, 1973); L. Young, *Japan's Total Empire: Manchuria and the Culture of Western Imperialism* (Berkeley, 1998).

50. A. Grünberg, *The Chayanta Rebellion of 1927, Potosí, Bolivia* (D. Phil., Oxford, 1996), p. 137.

51. F. Katz, *The Life and Times of Pancho Villa* (Stanford, CA, 1998), p. 782.

52. B. Farcau, *The Chaco War: Bolivia and Paraguay, 1932–1935* (Westport, CT, 1996).

53. A. Kemp, *The Maginot Line: Myth and Reality* (1981).

54. R. A. Doughty, *The Seeds of Disaster: The Development of French Army Doctrine, 1919–1939* (Hamden, CT, 1985).

55. Montgomery-Massingberd to Viscount Halifax, Secretary of State for War, 17 Aug. 1935, LH MM 10/4/1.

56. N. Rich, *Hitler's War Aims* (New York, 1973–74); G. L. Weinberg, *The Foreign Policy of Hitler's Germany, 1937–39* (Chicago, IL, 1980); W. Murray, *The Change in the European Balance of Power, 1938–1939: The Path to Ruin* (Princeton, NJ, 1984); P. M. H. Bell, *The Origins of the Second World War in Europe* (2nd edn, Harlow, 1997); I. Lukes and E. Goldstein (eds), *The Munich Crisis, 1938: Prelude to World War II* (1999).

57. R. A. C. Parker, *Chamberlain and Appeasement: British Policy and the Coming of the Second World War* (1993); P. W. Doerr, *British Foreign Policy, 1919–1939* (Manchester, 1998).

58. W. K. Wark, *The Ultimate Enemy: British Intelligence and Nazi Germany, 1933–1939* (Ithaca, NY, 1985).

59. LH Adam 2/3, pp. 2–3.

60. M. Dockrill, *British Establishment Perspectives on France, 1936–40* (1999).

61. D. C. Watt, *How War Came* (1989); Parker, *Chamberlain and Appeasement*.

# Chapter 5: World War Two

1. M. Thomas, *The French Empire at War 1940–45* (Manchester, 1945).

2. C. Van Dyke, *The Soviet Invasion of Finland, 1939–40* (1997).

3. PRO PREM 3/328/5, pp. 24–6.

4. N. Jordan, "Strategy and Scapegoatism: Reflections on the French National Catastrophe, 1940", in *The French Defeat of 1940: Reassessments*, J. Blatt (ed.) (Oxford, 1998), pp. 13–38, esp. pp. 22–9; E. R. May, *Strange Victory: Hitler's Conquest of France* (New York, 2000), but see reviews in *English Historical Review* 116 (2001), 428–31 and *New York Review of Books*, 22 February 2001, pp. 37–40.

5. D. M. Glantz, *Stumbling Colossus: The Red Army on the Eve of World War* (Lawrence, KS, 1998).

6. Admiral Layton to First Sea Lord, 18 Dec. 1941, BL Add. 74796.

7. D. M. Glantz, *Kharkov 1942: Anatomy of a Military Disaster Through Soviet Eyes* (Rockville, NY, 1998).

8. For the fighting, A. Beevor, *Stalingrad* (1998).

9. Lieutenant-General Sir Henry Pownall to Ismay, 26 Ap. 1944, LH Ismay 4/26/2; I. L. Grant and K. Tamayama, *Burma 1942: The Japanese Invasion: Both Sides Tell the Story of a Savage Jungle War* (Chichester, 1999).

10. S. Weingartner (ed.), *The Greatest Thing We Have Ever Attempted: Historical Perspectives on the*

*Normandy Campaign* (Wheaton, IL, 1998). For a different recent perspective, M. Reynolds, *Steel Inferno: I SS Panzer Corps in Normandy* (New York, 1997).

11. LH Alanbrooke 6/2/35.

12. J. N. Rickard, *Patton at Bay: The Lorraine Campaign* (Westport, CT, 1999).

13. T. L. Tissier, *Zhukov at the Oder: The Decisive Battle for Berlin* (Westport, CT, 1996); C. F. Brower (ed.), *World War II in Europe: The Final Year* (1998).

14. H. Yahara, *The Battle for Okinawa* (New York, 1995).

15. J. R. Skates, *The Invasion of Japan: Alternative to the Bomb* (Columbia, SC, 1994), esp. pp. 254–7.

16. M. Cooper, *The German Army, 1933–1945: Its Political and Military Failure* (Lanham, MD, 1990) and J. P. Harris and E. H. Toase (eds), *Armoured Warfare* (1992).

17. J. A. Gunsburg, "The Battle of Gembloux, 14–15 May: the 'Blitzkrieg' Checked", *Journal of Military History*, **64** (2000), pp. 97–140.

18. Manchester, John Rylands Library, Special Collections GOW/1/2/2, pp. 33, 54, 1/2/1, p. 6. See also, S. W. Mitcham, *Rommel's Greatest Victory: The Desert Fox and the Fall of Tobruk, 1942* (Novato, CA, 1998).

19. LH Alanbrooke 6/2/37.

20. D. M. Glantz and J. M. House, *The Battle of Kursk* (Lawrence, KS, 1999).

21. W. S. Dunn, *Soviet Blitzkrieg: The Battle for White Russia, 1944* (Boulder, CO, 2000).

22. D. M. Glantz, *Zhukov's Greatest Disaster: The Red Army's Epic Disaster in Operation Mars, 1942* (Lawrence, KS, 1999).

23. M. D. Dobler, *Closing with the Enemy: How GIs Fought the War in Europe, 1944–1945* (Lawrence, KS, 1994) offers a different view from M. Van Creveld, *Fighting Power: German and US Army Performance, 1939–1945* (Westport, CT, 1982).

24. U. Herbert, *Hitler's Foreign Workers: Enforced Labor in Germany under the Third Reich* (Cambridge, 1997).

25. M. Knox, *Hitler's Italian Allies: Royal Armed Forces, Fascist Regime, and the War of 1940–1943* (Cambridge, 2000), p. 176.

26. E. E. Ericson, *Feeding the German Eagle* (New York, 1999).

27. D. M. Kennedy, *Freedom From Fear: The American People in Depression and War, 1929–1945* (Oxford, 1999), pp. 747–93.

28. K. E. Eiler, *Mobilizing America: Robert P. Patterson and the War Effort, 1940–1945* (Ithaca, NY, 1997).

29. K. Smith, *Conflict over Convoys: Anglo-American Logistics Diplomacy in the Second World War* (Cambridge, 1996).

30. C. P. Stacey, *Arms, Men and Government: The War Policies of Canada 1939–1945* (Ottawa, 1970).

31. M. Harrison (ed.), *The Economics of World War II: Six Great Powers in International Comparison* (Cambridge, 1998).

32. LH Alanbrooke 6/2/37.

33. D. Zimmerman, *Top Secret Exchange: The Tizard Mission and the Scientific War* (Montreal, 1996).

34. G. Hartcup, *The Effect of Science on the Second World War* (2000).

35. H. Deutsch and D. Showalter (eds), *What If? Strategic Alternatives of World War II* (Chicago, IL, 1997).

36. B. Fischer, "Resistance in Albania during the Second World War: Partisans, Nationalists and the SOE", *East European Diplomacy*, **25** (1991), pp. 21–47, and *Albania at War 1939–1945* (West Lafayette, IN, 1999).

37. H. Heer and K. Naumann (eds), *War of Extermination: The German Military in World War II, 1941–1944* (Oxford, 2000), quote p. 93.

38. P. Biddiscombe, *Werewolf! The History of the National Socialist Guerrilla Movement, 1944–1946* (Cardiff, 1998).

39. S. Hart, "Montgomery, Morale, Casualty Conservation and 'Colossal Cracks': 21st Army

Group's Operational Technique in North-West Europe, 1944–45", *Journal of Strategic Studies*, 19 (1996), pp. 132–53 and *Montgomery and Colossal Cracks: 21st Army Group in North-West Europe, 1944–5* (Westport, CT, 2000).

40. See, for example, R. Hart, *Clash of Arms: How the Allies Won in Normandy* (Boulder, CO, 2001), esp. pp. 409–19.

## Chapter 6: Naval Power and Warfare

1. BL Add. 49710 fol. 140.
2. BL Add. 48993 fol. 86.
3. J. F. Beeler, *British Naval Policy in the Gladstone–Disraeli Era 1866–1880* (Stanford, CA, 1997), p. 258.
4. T. Ropp, *The Development of a Modern Navy: French Naval Policy, 1871–1904* (Annapolis, MD, 1987).
5. L. Sondhaus, *Preparing for Weltpolitik: German Sea Power before the Tirpitz Era* (Annapolis, MD, 1997).
6. J. T. Sumida, *In Defence of Naval Supremacy: Finance, Technology, and British Naval Policy, 1889–1914* (Boston, MA, 1989) and "Sir John Fisher and the Dreadnought: The Sources of Naval Mythology", *Journal of Military History*, 59 (1995), pp. 619–38; N. A. Lambert, *Sir John Fisher's Naval Revolution* (1999).
7. C. H. Fairbanks, "The Origins of the *Dreadnought* Revolution: A Historiographical Essay", *International History Review*, 13 (1991), pp. 246–72.
8. W. E. Livezey, *Mahan on Sea Power* (Norman, OK, 1981); J. T. Sumida, *Inventing Grand Strategy and the Teaching Command: The Classic Works of Alfred Thayer Mahan Revisited* (Baltimore, MD, 1997).
9. W. R. Braisted, *The United States Navy in the Pacific, 1897–1909* (Austin, TX, 1958); W. R. Herrick, *The American Naval Revolution* (Baton Rouge, LA, 1966); B. F. Cooley, *Gray Steel and Blue Water Navy: The Formative Years of America's Military–Industrial Complex, 1881–1917* (Hamden, CT, 1979); M. R. Shulman, *Navalism and the Emergence of American Sea Power, 1882–1893* (Annapolis, MD, 1995).
10. A. B. Feuer, *The Spanish–American War at Sea: Naval Action in the Atlantic* (Westport, CT, 1995).
11. R. Mough, *The Fleet that Had to Die* (1958); D. C. Evans and M. R. Peattie, *Kaigun: Strategy, Tactics, and Technology in the Imperial Japanese Navy, 1887–1941* (Annapolis, MD, 1997).
12. L. Sondhaus, *Naval Warfare 1815–1914* (2001), p. 215.
13. For naval power down to 1914 see, in particular, Sondhaus, *Naval Warfare* and D. M. Schurman, *The Education of a Navy: the Development of British Naval Strategic Thought, 1867–1914* (Malbar, 1984); R. Walser, *France's Search for a Battle Fleet: Naval Policy and Naval Power, 1889–1914* (New York, 1992); Sondhaus, *The Naval Policy of Austria-Hungary, 1867–1918: Navalism, Industrial Development, and the Politics of Dualism* (West Lafayette, IN, 1994); S. A. Knight, "The Evolution and Processes involved in the Manufacture of Armour Plate up to the Great War", *Journal of the Ordnance Society*, 5 (1993), pp. 58–61.
14. C. P. Vincent, *The Politics of Hunger: The Allied Blockade of Germany, 1915–1919* (Athens, GA, 1985).
15. N. J. M. Campbell, *Jutland: An Analysis of the Fighting* (1986).
16. A. Gordon, *The Rules of the Game: Jutland and British Naval Command* (1996), pp. 514–15.
17. Kitchener to Balfour, 6 Nov. 1915, PRO 30/57/66.
18. BL Add. 50294 fol. 6, 49710 fol. 2.
19. M. Wilson, "Early Submarines", in *Steam, Steel and Shellfire: The Steam Warship 1815–1905*, R. Gardiner (ed.) (1992), pp. 147–57; N. Lambert (ed.), *The Submarine Service, 1900–1918*

(Aldershot, 2001).

20. H. H. Herwig, "Total Rhetoric, Limited War: Germany's U-Boat Campaign, 1917–1918", in *Great War, Total War: Combat and Mobilization on the Western Front, 1914–1918*, R. Chickering and S. Förster (eds) (Cambridge, 2000), p. 205.
21. BL Add. 49714 fol. 29.
22. BL Add. 49714 fol. 145.
23. BL Add. 49715 fol. 210.
24. J. Winton, *Convoy: The Defence of Sea Trade, 1890–1990* (1983); J. Terraine, *Business in Great Waters: the U-Boat Wars 1916–45* (1989).
25. G. Penn, *Fisher, Churchill and the Dardanelles* (1999).
26. P. G. Halpern, *The Naval War in the Mediterranean 1914–1918* (1987).
27. G. Nekrasov, *North of Gallipoli: The Black Sea Fleet at War, 1914–1917* (Boulder, CO, 1992).
28. P. G. Halpern, *A Naval History of World War I* (Annapolis, MD, 1994).
29. C. G. Reynolds, *The Fast Carriers: The Forging of an Air Navy* (New York, 1968); G. Till, "Adopting the Aircraft Carrier: The British, American, and Japanese Case Studies", in *Military Innovation in the Interwar Period*, W. Murray and A. R. Millett (eds) (Cambridge, 1996), pp. 191–226.
30. G. Till, *Air Power and the Royal Navy, 1914–1945* (1989).
31. T. C. Hone, N. Friedman, and M. D. Mandeles, *American and British Aircraft Carrier Development, 1919–1941* (Annapolis, MD, 1999); T. Wildenberg, *Destined for Glory: Dive Bombing, Midway, and the Evolution of Carrier Airpower* (Annapolis, MD, 1998).
32. Sumida, "'The Best Laid Plans': the Development of British Battle-Fleet Tactics, 1919–1942", *International History Review*, 14 (1992), pp. 682–700.
33. BL Add. 49699 fol. 84.
34. BL Add. 49045 fols 1–2.
35. E. S. Miller, *War Plan Orange: The US Strategy to Defeat Japan, 1897–1945* (Annapolis, MD, 1991).
36. S. Roskill, *Naval Policy between the Wars: I, The Period of Anglo-American Antagonism, 1919–1929* (1968); E. O. Goldman, *Sunken Treaties: Naval Arms Control Between the Wars* (University Park, PA, 1994); P. P. O'Brien, *British and American Naval Power: Politics and Policy, 1900–1936* (Westport, CT, 1998); E. Goldstein and J. H. Maurer, *The Washington Naval Conference: Naval Rivalry, East Asian Stability, and the Road to Pearl Harbor* (Ilford, 1994).
37. PRO CAB. 29/117 fols 78, 19; R. W. Fanning, *Peace and Disarmament: Naval Rivalry and Arms Control, 1922–1933* (Lexington, KY, 1995).
38. O. C. Chung, *Operation Matador: Britain's War Plans against the Japanese 1918–1941* (Singapore, 1997).
39. S. E. Pelz, *Race to Pearl Harbor: The Failure of the Second London Naval Conference and the Onset of World War II* (Cambridge, MA, 1974); R. G. Kaufman, *Arms Control During the Pre-Nuclear Era: The United States and Naval Limitation Between the Two World Wars* (New York, 1990).
40. T. R. Philbin, *The Lure of Neptune: German–Soviet Naval Collaboration and Ambitions, 1919–1941* (Columbia, SC, 1994), p. xiv.
41. H. H. Herwig, "Innovation Ignored: The Submarine Problem – Germany, Britain, and the United States, 1919–1939", in Murray and Millett (eds), *Military Innovation*, pp. 227–64.
42. R. Mallett, *The Italian Navy and Fascist Expansionism, 1935–1940* (1998).
43. PRO CAB. 16/109, fol. 9.
44. Sir Dudley Pound to Admiral Layton, 15 Sept. 1941, BL Add. 74796.
45. G. Rhys-Jones, *The Loss of the Bismarck: An Avoidable Disaster* (1999).
46. J. Buckley, *The RAF and Trade Defence 1919–1945: Constant Endeavour* (Keele, 1995); C. Goulter, "Sir Arthur Harris: Different Perspectives", in *Challenges of High Command in the Twentieth Century*, G. Sheffield and G. Till (eds) (Camberley, 1999), pp. 78–80.
47. Terraine, *Business in Great Waters*.
48. C. Blair, *Silent Victory: The US Submarine War Against Japan* (New York, 1963); M. Parillo, *The Japanese Merchant Marine in World War Two* (Annapolis, MD, 1993).

49. D. M. Goldstein and K. V. Dillon (eds), *The Pearl Harbor Papers: Inside the Japanese Plans* (Washington DC, 1993).

50. T. B. Buell, *The Quiet Warrior: A Biography of Admiral Raymond A. Spruance* (Boston, MA, 1974); E. B. Potter, *Nimitz* (Annapolis, MD, 1976); H. P. Willmott, *The Barrier and the Javelin: Japanese and Allied Pacific Strategies, February to June 1942* (Annapolis, MD, 1983); D. C. James, *The Years of MacArthur, 1941–1945* (New York, 1985); R. Spector, *Eagle Against the Sun: The American War with Japan* (New York, 1985); G. Bischof and R. L. Dupont (eds), *The Pacific War Revisited* (Baton Rouge, LA, 1997).

51. J. J. Sadkovich, *The Italian Navy in World War II* (Westport, CT, 1994); J. Greene and A. Massignani, *The Naval War in the Mediterranean, 1940–1943* (Rockville Centre, NY, 1999).

52. A. J. Levine, *The War Against Rommel's Supply Lines, 1942–1943* (Westport, CT, 1999).

53. M. A. Palmer, *Origins of the Maritime Strategy: The Development of American Naval Strategy, 1945–1955* (Annapolis, MD, 1990).

54. R. Spector, *At War. At Sea: Sailors and Naval Warfare in the Twentieth Century* (2001), pp. 358–65.

55. G. W. Baer, *One Hundred Years of Sea Power: The US Navy, 1890–1990* (Stanford, CA, 1993), p. 383.

56. Southampton, University Library MB1/I149.

57. P. Vial, "National Rearmament and American Assistance: The Case of the French Navy during the 1950s", in *New Interpretations in Naval History*, W. M. McBride (ed.) (Annapolis, MD, 1998), pp. 260–88.

58. M. Milner, *Canada's Navy: The First Century* (Toronto, 1999).

59. E. J. Marolda and O. P. Fitzgerald, *The United States Navy and the Vietnam Conflict, II: From Military Assistance to Combat, 1959–1965* (Washington DC, 1986); J. B. Nichols and B. Tillman, *On Yankee Station: The Naval Air War over Vietnam* (Annapolis, MD, 1987); R. J. Francillon, *Tonkin Gulf Yacht Club: US Carrier Operations off Vietnam* (Annapolis, MD, 1988).

60. G. E. Hudson, "Soviet Naval Doctrine and Soviet Politics, 1953–1975", *World Politics*, **29** (1976), pp. 90–113.

61. E. Rhodes, "'From the Sea' and Back Again: Naval Power in the Second American Century", *Naval War College Review*, **52**(2) (1999), pp. 22–3.

62. E. Rhodes, "Constructing Peace and War: An Analysis of the Power of Ideas to Shape American Military Power", *Millennium: Journal of International Studies*, 24 (1995), p. 84. For an earlier example, E. Rhodes, "Sea Change: Interest-Based vs. Cultural-Cognitive Accounts of Strategic Choice in the 1890s", *Security Studies*, 5(4) (1996), esp. pp. 121–2.

# Chapter 7: Air Power and Warfare

1. PRO WO 106/6/87, p. 185.

2. PRO PREM 3/328/5, pp. 23–6.

3. M. Paris, "The First Air Wars – North Africa and the Balkans, 1911–13", *Journal of Contemporary History*, 26 (1991), pp. 97–109.

4. Hamilton to Sir William Nicholson, 2 Jan. 1909, LH Hamilton Papers 4/2/7.

5. P. E. Coletta, *Admiral Bradley A. Fiske and the American Navy* (Lawrence, KS, 1980).

6. A. Gollin, *No Longer an Island: Britain and the Wright Brothers, 1902–1909* (1984) and *The Impact of Air Power on the British People and their Government 1909–14* (1989); J. H. Morrow, *Building German Airpower, 1909–1914* (Knoxville, TN, 1976).

7. BL Add. 49714 fol. 28.

8. M. Cooper, *The Birth of Independent Air Power* (1986).

9. L. Kennett, *The First Air War, 1914–1918* (New York, 1991); Morrow, *The Great War in the Air: Military Aviation from 1909 to 1921* (Washington DC, 1993).

10. H. Driver, *The Birth of Military Aviation: Britain, 1903–1914* (Woodbridge, 1997), pp. 273–4.
11. BL Add. 49703 fols 184–9.
12. G. K. Williams, *Biplanes and Bombsights: British Bombing in World War I* (Maxwell Air Force Base, AL, 1999).
13. J. J. Born, *Winged Gospel: America's Romance with Aviation, 1900–1950* (New York, 1983); M. Paris, *Winged Warfare: The Literature and Theory of Aerial Warfare in Britain, 1859–1917* (Manchester, 1992) and "The Rise of the Airmen: The Origins of Air Force Elitism, *c.* 1890–1918", *Journal of Contemporary History*, 28 (1993), pp. 123–41; R. Wohl, *A Passion for Wings: Aviation and the Western Imagination* (New Haven, CT, 1994); P. Fritzsche, "Machine Dreams: Airmindedness and the Reinvention of Germany", *American Historical Review*, 98 (1993), pp. 685–709.
14. C. Segrè, "Giulio Douhet: Strategist, Theorist, Prophet?", *Journal of Strategic Studies*, 15 (1992), pp. 69–80.
15. M. Smith, "'A Matter of Faith': British Strategic Air Doctrine Between the Wars", *Journal of Contemporary History*, 15 (1980), pp. 423–42.
16. A. F. Hurley, *Billy Mitchell: Crusader for Air Power* (New York, 1964).
17. B. D. Watts, *The Foundations of US Air Doctrine: The Problem of Friction in War* (Maxwell Air Force Base, AL, 1984); S. L. McFarland, *America's Pursuit of Precision Bombing 1910–1945* (Washington DC, 1995).
18. J. Ferris, "Fighter Defence Before Fighter Command: The Rise of Strategic Air Defence in Great Britain, 1917–1934", *Journal of Military History*, 63 (1999), pp. 845–84.
19. U. Bialer, *The Shadow of the Bomber: The Fear of Air Attack and British Politics, 1932–1939* (1980).
20. S. Ritchie, *Industry and Air Power: The Expansion of British Aircraft Production, 1935–1941* (1997); J. Buckley, *Air Power in the Age of Total War* (1999), pp. 109–10.
21. General Sir Philip Chetwode, Deputy Chief of the Imperial General Staff, to Montgomery-Massingberd, 20 July 1921, LH MM 8/22.
22. M. Smith, *British Air Strategy Between the Wars* (Oxford, 1984), pp. 83–4.
23. D. Omissi, *Air Power and Colonial Control: The Royal Air Force 1919–1939* (Manchester, 1990).
24. E. L. Homze, *Arming the Luftwaffe: the Reich Air Ministry and the German Aircraft Industry 1919–39* (Lincoln, NE, 1976); K. A. Maier, "Total War and Operational Air Warfare", in K. A. Maier *et al.*, *Germany and the Second World War* II (Oxford, 1991), pp. 31–59; J. L. Corum, *The Luftwaffe: Creating the Operational Air War, 1918–1940* (Lawrence, KS, 1997); J. L. Corum and R. R. Muller, *The Luftwaffe's Way of War: German Air Force Doctrine, 1911–1945* (Baltimore, MD, 1998).
25. S. Robertson, *The Development of RAF Bombing Doctrine, 1919–1929* (Westport, CT, 1995); P. S. Meilinger, "Trenchard and 'Morale Bombing': The Evolution of Royal Air Force Doctrine Before World War II", *Journal of Military History*, 60 (1996), pp. 243–70.
26. J. L. Corum, "The Spanish Civil War: Lessons Learned and Not Learned by the Great Powers", *Journal of Military History*, 62 (1998), pp. 313–34.
27. C. C. Crane, *Bombs, Cities and Civilians: American Airpower Strategy in World War Two* (Lawrence, KS, 1993).
28. V. Hardesty, *Red-Phoenix: The Rise of Soviet Air Power 1941–45* (Washington DC, 1982); P. Deichmann, *Spearhead for Blitzkrieg: Luftwaffe Operations Support of the Army 1939–45* (1996); R. R. Muller, *The German Air War in Russia* (Baltimore, MD, 1992); J. Hayward, *Stopped at Stalingrad: The Luftwaffe and Hitler's Defeat in the East, 1942–1943* (Lawrence, KS, 1998).
29. Hayward, "A Case Study in Early Joint Warfare: An Analysis of the *Wehrmacht*'s Crimean Campaign of 1942", *Journal of Strategic Studies*, 22 (1999), pp. 113–21.
30. P. Addison and J. A. Crang (eds), *The Burning Blue: A New History of the Battle of Britain* (2000); R. J. Overy, *The Battle* (2002).
31. P. S. Meilinger, "John C. Slessor and the Genesis of Air Interdiction", *Royal United Services Institute Journal*, 140 (August 1995), pp. 43–8.

32. Montgomery to Brooke, 17, 18 Feb. 1945, LH Alanbrooke 6/2/37.
33. I. Gooderson, *Air Power at the Battlefront: Allied Close Air Support in Europe 1943–45* (1998).
34. LH Alanbrooke 6/2/35, pp. 1, 5, 9, 29.
35. A. D. Harvey, "Army Air Force and Navy Air Force: Japanese Aviation and the Opening Phase of the War in the Far East", *War in History*, 6 (1999), pp. 174–204, esp. pp. 177–80.
36. H. Probert, *The Forgotten Air Force: The Royal Air Force in the War against Japan 1941–45* (1995).
37. S. R. Taaffe, *MacArthur's Jungle War: The 1944 New Guinea Campaign* (Lawrence, KS, 1998).
38. S. Garrett, *Ethics and Airpower in World War Two* (New York, 1993).
39. G. P. Gentile, "General Arnold and the Historians", *Journal of Military History*, 64 (2000), p. 179.
40. W. Murray, *Luftwaffe* (Baltimore, 1985); S. L. McFarland and W. P. Newton, *To Command the Sky: The Battle for Air Superiority – 1942–4* (Washington DC, 1991).
41. J. B. Rae, *Climb to Greatness: the American Aircraft Industry 1920–60* (1968).
42. A. Furse, *Wilfrid Freeman: The Genius Behind Allied Survival and Air Supremacy 1939 to 1945* (Staplehurst, 2000), pp. 281, 289.
43. R. J. Overy, *The Air War 1939–1945* (1987); H. Boog (ed.), *The Conduct of the Air War in the Second World War: An International Comparison* (New York, 1992); Sir Arthur Harris, *Despatch on War Operations*, S. Cox (ed.) (1995); A. Calder, *The Myth of the Blitz* (1991); N. Gregor, "A *Schicksalsgemeinschaft?* Allied Bombing, Civilian Morale, and Social Dissolution in Nuremberg, 1942–1945", *Historical Journal*, 43 (2000), pp. 1051–70.
44. R. B. Frank, *Downfall: The End of the Imperial Japanese Empire* (New York, 1999).
45. M. Walker, *German National Socialism and the Quest for Nuclear Power, 1939–1945* (New York, 1989).
46. M. J. Neufeld, *The Rocket and the Reich: Peenemünde and the Coming of the Ballistic Missile Era* (Washington, DC, 1995).
47. J. Slessor, *Strategy for the West* (1954); S. T. Ross, *American War Plans, 1945–1950* (New York, 1988).
48. R. E. McClendon, *Autonomy for the Air Arm* (Washington DC, 1996); H. S. Wolk, *Towards Independence: The Emergence of the US Air Force, 1945–1947* (Washington DC, 1996).
49. W. S. Borgiasz, *The Strategic Air Command: Evolution and Consolidation of Nuclear Forces 1945–55* (New York, 1996).
50. S. J. Ball, *The Bomber in British Strategy: Doctrine, Strategy and Britain's World Role 1945–60* (Boulder, CO, 1995).
51. C. C. Crane, "Raiding the Beggar's Pantry: The Search for Airpower Strategy in the Korean War", *Journal of Military History*, 63 (1999), pp. 885–920, and *American Air Power Strategy in Korea, 1950–1953* (Lawrence, KS, 2000).
52. D. J. Mrozek, *Air Power and the Ground War in Vietnam: Ideas and Actions* (Maxwell Air Force Base, AL, 1988); M. Clodfetter, *The Limits of Airpower: The American Bombing of North Vietnam* (New York, 1989); D. J. Dean, *The Air Force Role in Low-Intensity Conflict* (Maxwell Air Force Base, AL, 1986); C. H. Builder, *The Icarus Syndrome: The Role of Air Power Theory in the Evolution and Fate of the US Air Force* (New Brunswick, NJ, 1994).
53. Fuller to William Sloane, 2 July 1965, LH Fuller IV/6/42/1.

## Chapter 8: The Retreat from Empire: Singapore to Mozambique, 1942–75

1. Layton to First Sea Lord, 13 Sept., Mountbatten to Layton, 15 Sept. 1944, BL Add. 74796.
2. Manchester, John Rylands Library, Auchinleck Papers, nos. 1155, 1143, 1136.
3. E. O'Balance, *Malaya: the Communist Insurgent War, 1948–60* (1966).

4. D. R. Devereux, *The Formulation of British Defence Policy towards the Middle East, 1948–56* (1990); P. Darby, *British Defence Policy East of Suez 1947–1968* (Oxford, 1973); K. Pieragostini, *Britain, Aden and South Arabia: Abandoning Empire* (1991).
5. C. Fraser, "The 'New Frontier' of Empire in the Caribbean: The Transfer of Power in British Guiana, 1961–1964", *International History Review*, 22 (2000), pp. 583–610.
6. Southampton University Library, MB1/J79.
7. J. Pickering, *Britain's Withdrawal from East of Suez: The Politics of Retrenchment* (1998).
8. J. and D. S. Small, *The Undeclared War: The Story of the Indonesian Confrontation 1962–1966* (1971); P. Dennis and J. Grey, *Emergency and Confrontation: Australian Military Operations in Malaya and Borneo 1950–1966* (St Leonards, New South Wales, 1990).
9. A. Clayton, *The Wars of French Decolonization* (1994).
10. C. R. Shrader, *The First Helicopter War: Logistics and Mobility in Algeria, 1954–1962* (Westport, CT, 1999).
11. Clayton, *France, Soldiers and Africa* (1988); J. Chipman, *French Power in Africa* (Oxford, 1989).
12. L. Heywood, *Contested Power in Angola: 1840s to the Present* (Rochester, NY, 2000), p. 175.
13. R. M. Fields, *The Portuguese Revolution and the Armed Forces Movement* (New York, 1976).
14. T. Ranger, *Revolt in Southern Rhodesia, 1896–1897* (1967).
15. A. Clayton, *Frontiersmen: Warfare in Africa since 1950* (1999); M. Dhada, "The Liberation War in Guineau-Bissau Reconsidered", *Journal of Military History*, 62 (1998), p. 592.
16. C. Blair, *The Forgotten War: America in Korea, 1950–1953* (New York, 1987); P. Lowe, *The Korean War* (2000).
17. D. T. Zabecki, "Artillery Fire Doctrine", in *Encyclopedia of the Vietnam War*, S.C. Tucker (ed.) (3 vols, Santa Barbara, CA, 1998), vol. I, p. 49.
18. R. A. Hunt, *Pacification: The American Struggle for Vietnam's Hearts and Minds* (Boulder, CO, 1995).
19. Among the numerous works on the war, A. Krepinevich, *The Army in Vietnam* (Baltimore, MD, 1986); E. M. Bergerud, *The Dynamics of Defeat: The Vietnam War in Hau Nghia Province* (Boulder, CO, 1990); D. R. Palmer, *The Summons of the Trumpet: A History of the Vietnam War from a Military Man's Viewpoint* (New York, 1984); W. J. Duiker, *Sacred War: Nationalism and Revolution in a Divided Vietnam* (New York, 1995); R. E. Ford, *Tet 1968: Understanding the Surprise* (1995); J. Prados, *The Hidden History of the Vietnam War* (Chicago, IL, 1995). For the Army Chief of Staff in 1964–8, L. Sorley, *Honorable Warrior: General Harold K. Johnson and the Ethics of Command* (Lawrence, KS, 1998).

## Chapter 9: Military Power in the West, 1946–1975

1. Ismay to General Sir Henry Pownall, 14 Mar. 1944, LH Ismay 4/26/1.
2. J. S. Koliopoulos, *Plundered Loyalties: World War II and Civil War in Greek West Macedonia* (New York, 1999).
3. S. Mawby, *Containing Germany: Britain and the Arming of the Federal Republic* (1999), p. 118; J. M. Diefendorf, A. Frohn and H. J. Rupieper (eds), *American Policy and the Reconstruction of West Germany, 1945–1955* (Cambridge, 1993); N. Wiggerhaus and R. G. Foerster (eds), *The Western Security Community: Common Problems and Conflicting National Interests during the Foundation Phase of the North Atlantic Alliance* (Oxford, 1993).
4. S. W. Duke and W. Krieger (eds), *US Military Forces in Europe: The Early Years, 1945–1970* (Boulder, CO, 1993).
5. E. T. Smith, *Opposition Beyond the Water's Edge: Liberal Internationalists, Pacifists, and Containment, 1945–1953* (Westport, CT, 1999).
6. LH Ismay, progress reports as Secretary General of NATO, Dec. 1953, Dec. 1954, 3/21/3 p. 7, 3/21/5 p. 9.

7. J. Györkei and M. Harváth (eds), *1956: Soviet Intervention in Hungary* (Budapest, 1999).
8. D. L. Raby, "Controlled, Limited and Manipulated: Opposition under a Dictatorial Regime: Portugal, 1945–9", *European History Quarterly*, 19 (1989), pp. 74–6.
9. G. H. Quester, *Nuclear Monopoly* (New Brunswick, NJ, 2000); D. Holloway, *Stalin and the Bomb* (Oxford, 1994).
10. M. Trachtenberg, "The Making of a Political System: The German Question in International Politics, 1945–1963", in *From War to Peace: Altered Strategic Landscapes in the Twentieth Century*, P. Kennedy and W. I. Hitchcock (eds) (New Haven, CT, 2000), pp. 118–19.
11. W. S. Borgiasz, *The Strategic Air Command: Evolution and Consolidation of Nuclear Forces 1945–55* (New York, 1996).
12. B. Brodie, *Strategy in the Nuclear Age* (Princeton, NJ, 1965).
13. T. Greenwood, *Making the MIRV: A Study in Defence Decision Making* (Cambridge, MA, 1975).
14. B. Heuser, *NATO, Britain, France and the FRG: Nuclear Strategies and Forces for Europe, 1949–2000* (1997).
15. A. J. Bacevich, *The Pentomic Era: The US Army between Korea and Vietnam* (Washington DC, 1986).
16. Southampton University Library, MB1/I149.
17. H. R. Borowski, *A Hollow Threat: Strategic Air Power and Containment before Korea* (Westport, CT, 1982).
18. K. I. Sepp, "The Pentomic Puzzle. The Influence of Personality and Nuclear Weapons on US Army Organization 1952–1958", *Army History* 51 (Winter 2001), p. 10.
19. L. Sorley, *Thunderbolt: General Creighton Abrams and the Army of His Times* (New York, 1992).
20. W. B. Haworth, *The Bradley and How It Got That Way: Technology, Institutions, and the Problem of Mechanized Infantry in the United States Army* (Westport, CT, 1999); D. M. Glantz, *Soviet Military Operational Art: In Pursuit of Deep Battle* (Totowa, NJ, 1991); J. A. English, *Marching Through Chaos: The Descent of Armies in Theory and Practice* (Westport, CT, 1996), p. 154.
21. J. L. Romjue, "The Evolution of American Army Doctrine", in *The Origins of Contemporary Doctrine*, J. Gooch (ed.) (Camberley, 1997), pp. 70–3.

## Chapter 10: Social and Political Contexts

1. LH Ismay 3/21/1.
2. J. Snyder, *The Ideology of the Offensive: Military Decision-Making and the Disasters of 1914* (Ithaca, NY, 1914).
3. J. Smith, "Brazilian Diplomacy and Foreign Intervention in the Brazilian Naval Revolt, 1893–94", *Revista Complutense de Historia de América*, 26 (2000), pp. 117–34; T. Veremis, *The Military in Greek Politics: From Independence to Democracy* (1997).
4. D. Kerr and D. W. Holdsworth (eds), *Historical Atlas of Canada* III (Toronto, 1990), plate 39.
5. G. Feldman, *Army, Industry, and Labor in Germany, 1914–1918* (Princeton, NJ, 1966).
6. L. H. Siegelbaum, *The Politics of Industrial Mobilization in Russia, 1915–1917: A Study of the War-Industries Committees* (New York, 1984); N. Stone, "Organizing an Economy for War: The Russian Shell Shortage, 1914–1917", in *War, Economy, and the Military Mind*, G. Best and A. Wheatcroft (eds) (1976).
7. J. F. Godfrey, *Capitalism at War: Industrial Policy and Bureaucracy in France, 1914–1918* (Oxford, 1987).
8. J. Winter and J.-L. Robert (eds), *Capital Cities at War: London, Paris, Berlin 1914–1919* (Cambridge, 1997).
9. R. J. Q. Adams, *Arms and the Wizard: Lloyd George and the Ministry of Munitions* (1978); G. J. De Groot, *Blighty: British Society in the Era of the Great War* (1996).

10. BL Add. 49703 fol. 109.
11. R. Bessel, "Mobilizing German Society for War", in Chickering and Förster (eds), *Great War, Total War*, p. 444, fn. 32.
12. N. Stargardt, *The German Idea of Militarism: Radical and Socialist Critics 1866–1914* (Cambridge, 1914).
13. A. Marrin, *The Last Crusade: The Church of England and the First World War* (Durham, NC, 1985).
14. K. Grieves, *The Politics of Manpower, 1914–18* (Manchester, 1988); W. G. Natter, *Literature at War, 1914–1940: Representing the "Time of Greatness" in Germany* (New Haven, CT, 1999); J. Verhey, *The Spirit of 1914: Militarism, Myth and Mobilization in Germany* (Cambridge, 2000).
15. J. L. Thompson, *Politicians, the Press, and Propaganda: Lord Northcliffe and the Great War, 1914–1919* (Kent, OH, 1999); J. F. Williams, *Anzacs, the Media, and the Great War* (Sydney, 1999).
16. BL Add. 49714 fols 48–55.
17. L. V. Smith, *Between Mutiny and Obedience: The Case of the Fifth Infantry Division during World War I* (Princeton, NJ, 1994).
18. LH Barnardiston 3/4, 7–8 Dec. 1917.
19. D. Thom, *Nice Girls and Rude Girls: Women Workers in World War One* (1999).
20. S. R. Grayzel, *Women's Identities at War: Gender, Motherhood, and Politics in Britain and France during the First World War* (Chapel Hill, NC, 1999); S. Zeiger, *In Uncle Sam's Service: Women Workers with the American Expeditionary Force, 1917–1919* (Ithaca, NY, 1999).
21. T. Tate, *Modernism, History, and the First World War* (Manchester, 1998).
22. W. Wette, "From Kellogg to Hitler (1928–1933): German Public Opinion Concerning the Rejection or Glorification of War", in *The German Military in the Age of Total War*, W. Deist (ed.) (Leamington Spa, 1985), pp. 88–93; D. T. Murphy, *The Heroic Earth: Geopolitical Thought in Weimar Germany, 1918–1933* (Kent, OH, 1997).
23. LH Adam 2/1, p. 23.
24. M. Paris, "A Different View of the Trenches: Juvenile Fiction and Popular Perceptions of the First World War, 1914–1939", *War Studies Journal*, 3 (1997), pp. 32–45.
25. G. L. Mosse, *Fallen Soldiers: Reshaping the Memory of the World Wars* (Oxford, 1990).
26. M. Richards, *A Time of Silence: Civil War and the Culture of Repression in Franco's Spain, 1936–1945* (Cambridge, 1998).
27. S. Nicholas, *The Echo of War: Home Front Propaganda and the Wartime BBC, 1939–45* (Manchester, 1996); P. M. Taylor (ed.), *Britain and the Cinema in the Second World War* (1988).
28. O. Bartov, *The Eastern Front, 1941–1945: German Troops and the Barbarisation of Warfare* (1985) and *Hitler's Army: Soldiers, Nazis and War in the Third Reich* (Oxford, 1991); G. Hirschfeld (ed.), *The Policies of Genocide: Jews and Soviet Prisoners of War in Nazi Germany* (1986); T. Schulte, *The German Army and Nazi Policies in Occupied Russia* (Oxford, 1989); H. Herr and K. Naumann (eds), *War of Extermination: The German Military in World War II 1941–1944* (2000).
29. I. Zweiniger-Bargielowska, *Austerity in Britain: Rationing, Controls and Consumption, 1939–1955* (Oxford, 2000).
30. M. Knox, *Hitler's Italian Allies: Royal Armed Forces, Fascist Regime, and the War of 1940–1943* (Cambridge, 2000), esp. pp. 39–42.
31. G. Braybon and P. Summerfield, *Out of the Cage: Women's Experiences in Two World Wars* (1987); J. Harris, "War and Social History: Britain and the Home Front during the Second World War", *Contemporary European History*, 1 (1992), pp. 17–35; H. L. Smith (ed.), *Britain in the Second World War: A Social History* (Manchester, 1996).
32. R. Pierson, *"They're Still Women After All": The Second World War and Canadian Womanhood* (Toronto, 1986); H. Diamond, *Women and the Second World War in France, 1939–1949: Choices and Constraints* (1999).
33. G. Q. Flynn, *The Draft, 1940–1973* (Lawrence, KS, 1993); L. V. Scott, *Conscription and the Attlee Governments: The Politics and Policy of National Service, 1945–1951* (Oxford, 1993).

34. B. Bond, "The British Experience of National Service, 1947–1963", in *Die Wehrpflicht: Eintstehung, Erscheinungsfomen und politisch-militärische Wirkung*, R. G. Foerster (ed.) (Munich, 1994), pp. 207–15.
35. A. Horne, *The French Army and Politics 1870–1970* (1984), p. 89.
36. R. R. Reese, *The Soviet Military Experience* (2000), p. 153.

## Chapter 11: Conclusions

1. D. Avant, *Political Institutions and Military Change* (Ithaca, NY, 1994).
2. M. Knox, "1 October 1942: Adolf Hitler, Wehrmacht Officer Policy, and Social Revolution", *Historical Journal*, **43** (2000), pp. 801–25. For the navy's eager support, C. S. Thomas, *The German Navy in the Nazi Era* (1990).
3. M. D. Pearlman, *Warmaking and American Democracy: The Struggle over Military Strategy, 1700 to the Present* (Lawrence, KS, 1999).
4. For a searching analysis of differences between these regimes, M. Knox, *Common Destiny: Dictatorship, Foreign Policy, and War in Fascist Italy and Nazi Germany* (Cambridge, 2000).
5. LH Hamilton papers, 4/2/3, p. 24.

# Selected Further Reading

For reasons of space only a brief list is provided. It is best to follow recent work in the articles and reviews of specialist journals, particularly the *Journal of Military History* and *War in History*. The following offer valuable guides, and also include notes and bibliographies that offer guidelines to other literature.

P. Addison and A. Calder (eds), *Time to Kill: The Soldier's Experience of War in the West 1939–1945* (1997).

O. Bartov, *Hitler's Army: Soldiers, Nazis, and War in the Third Reich* (Oxford, 1991).

C. Bellamy, *The Evolution of Modern Land Warfare: Theory and Practice* (1987).

J. Bourke, *An Intimate History of Killing: Face-to-Face Killing in Twentieth-Century Warfare* (1999).

J. Buckley, *Air Power in the Age of Total War* (1999).

R. Chickering and S. Förster (eds), *Great War, Total War: Combat and Mobilization on the Western Front, 1914–1918* (Cambridge, 2000).

A. Clayton, *Frontiersmen: Warfare in Africa since 1950* (1999).

N. Ferguson, *The Pity of War* (1999).

M. Hastings, *Bomber Command* (1979).

H. Herwig, *The "Luxury" Fleet: The Imperial German Navy 1888–1918* (1980).

A. Horne, *The Price of Glory: Verdun, 1916* (New York, 1962).

A. Horne, *A Savage War of Peace: Algeria, 1954–1962* (1977).

P. Kennedy (ed.), *The War Plans of the Great Powers, 1880–1914* (1979).

M. Knox, *Common Destiny: Dictatorship, Foreign Policy, and War in Fascist Italy and Nazi Germany* (Cambridge, 2000).

W. Murray and A. R. Millett (eds), *Military Innovation in the Interwar Period* (Cambridge, 1996).

E. B. Potter, *Nimitz* (Annapolis, MD, 1976).

R. R. Reese, *The Soviet Military Experience* (2000).

N. A. M. Rodger (ed.), *Naval Power in the Twentieth Century* (1996).

L. Sondhaus, *Naval Warfare 1815–1914* (2001).

R. H. Spector, *The Eagle Against the Sun: The American War with Japan* (New York, 1984).

R. H. Spector, *After Tet: The Bloodiest Year in Vietnam* (New York, 1993).

R. H. Spector, *At War. At Sea: Sailors and Naval Warfare in the Twentieth Century* (2001).

H. Strachan (ed.), *The Oxford Illustrated History of the First World War* (Oxford, 1998).

H. Strachan, *The First World War. I: To Arms* (Oxford, 2001).

B. Vandervort, *Wars of Imperial Conquest in Africa 1830–1914* (1998).

J. Winter, G. Parker and M. R. Habeck (eds), *The Great War and the Twentieth Century* (New Haven, 2000).

R. F. Weigley, *The American Way of War: A History of United States Military Strategy and Policy* (Bloomington, IN, 1973).

G. Weinberg, *A World at Arms: A Global History of World War II* (Cambridge, 1994).

# Index

241

CPSIA information can be obtained
at www.ICGtesting.com
Printed in the USA
LVOW13s2304211216
518358LV00006B/163/P